Arguments for Protected Areas

Arguments for Protected Areas

Multiple Benefits for Conservation and Use

Edited by Sue Stolton and Nigel Dudley

publishing for a sustainable future

London • Washington, DC

First published in 2010 by Earthscan

Earthscan Ltd, Dunstan House, 14a St Cross Street, London EC1N 8XA, UK
Earthscan LLC, 1616 P Street, NW, Washington, DC 20036, USA

Earthscan publishes in association with the International Institute for Environment and Development

For more information on Earthscan publications, see www.earthscan.co.uk or write to earthinfo@earthscan.co.uk

ISBN: 978-1-84407-880-6 hardback
       978-1-84407-881-3 paperback

Typeset by Safehouse Creative
Cover design by Susanne Harris

A catalogue record for this book is available from the British Library

Library of Congress Cataloging-in-Publication Data

Arguments for protected areas : multiple benefits for conservation and use / edited by Sue Stolton and Nigel Dudley.
     p. cm.
  Includes bibliographical references and index.
   ISBN 978-1-84407-880-6 (hardback) -- ISBN 978-1-84407-881-3 (pbk.)   1. Protected areas--Management. 2. Ecosystem management. 3. Nature conservation . I. Stolton, Sue. II. Dudley, Nigel.
  S944.5.P78A76 2010
  333.95'16--dc22

                          2010007952

At Earthscan we strive to minimize our environmental impacts and carbon footprint through reducing waste, recycling and offsetting our CO_2 emissions, including those created through publication of this book. For more details of our environmental policy, see www.earthscan.co.uk.

This book was printed in the UK by TJ International, an ISO 14001 accredited company. The paper used is FSC certified and the inks are vegetable based.

Mixed Sources
Product group from well-managed forests and other controlled sources
www.fsc.org Cert no. SGS-COC-2482
© 1996 Forest Stewardship Council

FSC

Contents

Contributors

Alexander Belokurov has worked for WWF International for nine years adding to previous experience with the Ramsar Convention Secretariat and his work in Russia. His expertise is in environmental science and management, protected areas and landscape approaches. His current position is Manager, Landscape Conservation at WWF International.

Charles Besançon is the head of the Protected Areas Programme at the United Nations Environment Programme's World Conservation Monitoring Centre in Cambridge in the UK. His professional interests include connectivity conservation, transboundary cooperation and wilderness. Outside of work he enjoys photography, exploring mountains and reading.

Christine Bratrich studied biology at the University of Konstanz, Germany and has a PhD from the Swiss Federal Institute of Technology, Zurich. Between 2004 and 2008 she was Head of Freshwater at the Danube-Carpathian Programme of WWF International. She is currently executive director of ETHsustainability in Zurich.

José Courrau has a Ph.D. in Natural Resources. He is an independent consultant in biodiversity conservation, with emphasis on protected areas. Dr. Courrau initiated his 23 year career in the Costa Rican National Park Service. Since then he has worked as employee and consultant for governments, international NGOs and universities.

Glenn Dolcemascolo works with UNEP's Post Conflict and Disaster Management Branch as Technical Advisor on Disaster Risk Reduction with a focus on environmental management for disaster reduction. He facilitates a Thematic Platform on Environmental and Disaster Reduction through the International Strategy for Disaster Reduction (ISDR). He has a Ph.D. in environmental anthropology.

Nigel Dudley is an ecologist and runs Equilibrium Research with Sue Stolton. He has worked in over 50 countries, latterly mainly on issues related to protected area establishment and management. He is a member of WCPA and is an Industry Fellow at the University of Queensland, Australia, and is based in the UK.

Marivel P. Dygico is Project Manager for the Tubbataha Conservation Project of WWF-Philippines. She is currently specializing in marine protected areas and participatory coastal resource management and has previous experience in catchment and watershed management.

Dr. Britaldo Soares-Filho is an associate professor of the Department of Cartography at the Federal University of Minas Gerais (UFMG), Brazil. His interests focus on landscape dynamics modeling, especially the development of DINAMICA software and land-use change simulation models applied to environmental assessment and regional planning in the Amazon.

Dr. Brian Ford-Lloyd is Director of the University Graduate School at the University of Birmingham. He has worked on the conservation and genetic diversity of plant genetic resources for the last 40 years, publishing books and scientific papers, and teaching at University level. The advent of 'omics' technologies and the wealth of plant genetic resources offers new challenges to future research programmes.

Lawrence Hamilton is currently Emeritus Professor of Forest Conservation at Cornell University, New York and Senior Advisor (Mountains) for WCPA. He was the Senior Fellow at the East West Center (Hawaii) for 14 years, Professor at Cornell University for 29 years and a Zone Forester for the Ontario Government in Canada for 3 years.

Liza Higgins-Zogib is Manager, People and Conservation at WWF International. She leads Social Development for the Conservation Team, tasked with integrating social issues into WWF's conservation programme. Liza is completing a doctoral degree in Yoga Philosophy and Meditation with the International Vedic Hindu University, and is a practitioner and teacher of Raja Yoga.

Associate Professor Marc Hockings coordinates conservation and environmental management programmes in the Faculty of Natural Resources, Agriculture and Veterinary Science at the University of Queensland, Australia. Marc leads the programme within WCPA on Science and Management of Protected Areas and is a member of the Commission's Executive Committee.

Cara Dougherty Honzak, Senior Programme Officer, Population, Health and Environment, WWF US, has ten years of professional experience in a wide array of international environment and development projects, including five years as the population, health and environment technical advisor to WWF-US.

Orieta Hulea is the Head of Danube/Freshwater Programme at WWF Danube-Carpathian Programme. She holds a PhD in Biology and she has over ten years experience of working in nature conservation and water related policy in the Lower Danube region, including the Danube Delta.

Shelagh Kell MSc Dip Hort (Kew) is a Research Fellow at the University of Birmingham, where she specializes in the conservation of crop wild relatives. She is also Tutor, Research Supervisor and Associate Examiner for the Centre for Environment, Development and Policy, School of African and Oriental Studies, University of London.

Hyun Kim has dedicated 13 years of his professional career to environmental issues. He joined the Korea National Park Service as a programme officer in 1997 and in 2007 moved to the IUCN Asia Regional Office in Bangkok. In both organisations he has played a conduit role in developing joint activities and programmes in Asia.

Ashish Kothari, founder-member of Indian environmental group Kalpavriksh. Taught at the Indian Institute of Public Administration, coordinated India's National Biodiversity Strategy and Action Plan process, served on Greenpeace International's Board, currently chairs Greenpeace India's Board. Served as co-chair of TILCEPA, the IUCN Strategic Direction on Governance, Equity, Communities, and Livelihoods. Author or editor of over 25 books.

Zoltan Kun is executive director of the PanParks Foundation. He is a member of WCPA and represents PanParks in its European Steering Committee and is an advisory board member of Klagenfurt University's Msc programme on protected area management. He was a member of the international advisory board of the wild9 conference.

James P. Leape has been Director General of WWF International since 2005. A graduate of Harvard College and Harvard Law School, he began his career as an environmental lawyer. Leape first joined WWF in the US in 1989, and for ten years led their conservation programmes around the world, serving as Executive Vice President.

Yildiray Lise completed his B.Sc. and M.Sc. in Biological Sciences at the Middle East Technical University in Ankara, Turkey. He has worked for WWF-Turkey and BirdLife Turkey and is currently deputy manager of a UNDP/GEF project on enhancing coverage and management effectiveness of forest protected areas in Turkey.

Nik Lopoukhine has a BSc. in forestry and MSc. in plant ecology. He joined Parks Canada in 1981 and was employed as a science advisor in ecology before becoming the first Executive Director for Ecological Integrity in 2000. In 2001 he was appointed DG of the National Parks Directorate. He retired in 2005 and was elected as Chair of WCPA in 2004.

Dr. Kathy MacKinnon is the World Bank's Lead Biodiversity Specialist. She has extensive field experience, especially in Asia, on tropical ecology research, conservation and protected area planning and management. Kathy has worked extensively with international NGOs, especially IUCN and WWF, and government agencies in developing countries.

Josep-Maria Mallarach, independent environmental consultant, since 1980 has been working in planning, management and evaluation of protected areas. He is the joint coordinator of The Delos Initiative and member of the Steering Committee of the WCPA Specialist Group on Cultural and Spiritual Values of Protected Areas.

Stephanie Mansourian is an environmental consultant and has undertaken work for various UN agencies, IUCN, WWF and the international business school, IMD, with whom she co-wrote a book on sustainability partnerships. Prior to that she worked at WWF International where she built up and managed a programme on forest landscape restoration.

Dr. Vinod B Mathur is the Dean, Faculty of Wildlife Sciences at Wildlife Institute of India. He is Deputy Regional Vice-Chair of WCPA (Asia) and member of IUCN Commission on Ecosystem Management as well as IAIA. His areas of special interest include wildlife management, natural heritage conservation and impact assessment.

Nigel Maxted (BSc, MPhil, PhD, FLS) is a senior lecturer at the University of Birmingham. He focuses on *in situ* and *ex situ* plant genetic conservation, has published over 230 scientific paper and 12 books. He is Co-Chair IUCN SSC Crop Wild Relative Specialist Group and is a Senior Scientific Advisor for the GEF/World Bank on PGR Conservation.

Ali Mwachui manages the WWF Kiunga Marine National Reserve Project, he has seven years marine conservation experience and is trained in environmental management from Kenyatta University. He is currently pursuing his post graduate study at the University of Nairobi. Main areas of interest include integrated community-based natural resource management with a strong bias in the sustainable collaborative marine fisheries management.

Judy Oglethorpe is Managing Director of the People and Conservation programme in WWF-US; her work includes climate change adaptation, health, population, livelihoods and conflict. Previously she was Executive Director of the Biodiversity Support programme. Judy also has 14 years of conservation experience in East and Southern Africa.

Emilio Rodriguez is a biologist from the National University of Colombia, with 15 years experience in the National Parks. He worked as Amazon Regional Director and several times Director General in charge. He has worked with WWF since June 2009 as Coordinator of the Trinational Putumayo Project, a transboundary area between Colombia, Ecuador and Peru.

Manuel Ramírez is Senior Director of Conservation International's Southern MesoAmerica (Costa Rica, Panama, Nicaragua), Mexico and Central America Field Division. He has over 20 years of experience working in natural-resource management projects throughout Latin America. He has a degree in forestry engineering from the Institute Tecnológico de Costa Rica and a Masters from Yale University.

Jonathan Randall is a Senior Programme Officer with WWF-US and has worked on conservation, disaster risk reduction and water resources for the past ten years. He has consulted on emergency responses to cyclones, tsunamis, earthquakes and wildfires throughout Southeast Asia, Micronesia, the United States and Mozambique.

Jorge Alejandro Rickards-Guevara, Conservation Director, WWF Mexico. Jorge has more than 15 years experience designing and managing conservation programmes. He has established and worked in conservation organisations including the Mexico Nature Conservation Fund. He worked for the US Agency for International Development (USAID) and serves on several boards and technical committees related to natural resources and conservation.

Judy Rowell has a masters in environmental studies and has spent the last two decades working as a negotiator and environmental advisor for the Labrador Inuit Association. Following the completion of the land claims agreement she joined Parks Canada where she is now superintendent of the Torngat Mountains National Park.

Trevor Sandwith is Director of Biodiversity and Protected Areas Policy at The Nature Conservancy, and Deputy Chair of WCPA. He co-led the Transboundary Conservation Task Force for WCPA, while coordinating South Africa's Cape Action for People and the Environment Programme, focused on mainstreaming biodiversity conservation into social and economic development at scale.

John Senior is Manager of Strategic Partnerships at Parks Victoria (Australia). John manages alliances with other park authorities nationally and internationally. He has been involved in the 'Healthy Parks Healthy People' approach from original research to current adoption. John is a member of the WCPA Cities and Protected Areas and new Healthy Parks Healthy People Taskforces.

Wonwoo Shin has dedicated 30 years of his professional career on Environment and Natural Resources to South Korean Ministry of Environment (MKE) and Korea National Park Service (KNPS). Today, as the Executive Director of Park Conservation in KNPS, he provides strategic leadership for better management of protected areas across the country and in Asia.

Surin Suksuwan is Chief Technical Officer for Peninsular Malaysia Programme for WWF-Malaysia. He has been with WWF-Malaysia for about ten years and served a short stint at WWF International, during which he helped to coordinate the Arguments for Protection series. He is actively involved in the establishment of new protected areas and management effectiveness assessments

Sue Stolton (BA hons) established Equilibrium Research in partnership with Nigel Dudley in 1991. Her work focuses mainly on protected areas, in particular, issues relating to management and the wider values and benefits that protected areas can provide. Sue is a member of WCPA and the Commission on Environmental, Economic and Social Policy.

Edgardo Tongson has more than a decade of work experience in conservation and natural resources management. He joined WWF-Philippines in 1998 as a programme officer, was appointed Director in 2001 and Vice-President for Programmes in 2003. He now serves as senior consultant on Water Resources Management.

Anita van Breda is the Director of WWF-US's Humanitarian Partnerships programme based in Washington, DC. Anita has over 20 years experience in the field of conservation and natural resource management. She developed the Humanitarian Partnership programme to provide environmental sustainability guidance relative to disaster recovery and reconstruction.

Sam Weru is Conservation Director for WWF-Kenya. He is professionally trained and experienced in conservation and natural resource management, with 19 years experience in both government and WWF. Sam holds a B.Sc. in Wildlife Management, M.Sc in Biology of Conservation as well as several professional certificates/diplomas in the field of conservation management.

Acknowledgements

The editors would like to thank all those who have commented on the contents of this book and, in particular, WWF for supporting the Arguments for Protection project and the development of this volume.

List of Figures, Tables and Boxes

Figures

xvi   *Arguments for Protected Areas*

Tables

Boxes

List of Acronyms and Abbreviations

ARPA	Amazon Region Protected Areas
BMU	beach management unit
CBD	United Nations Convention on Biological Diversity
CHW	community health worker
CONANP	National Commission for Protected Areas, Mexico
CTP	Phoenix Futures Conservation Therapy Programme
CWR	crop wild relative
DFID	Department for International Development, UK
FAO	United Nations Food and Agriculture Organization
GSTC	Global Sustainable Tourism Criteria
HWC	Human Wildlife Conflict
ICCA	Indigenous and Community Conserved Area
INBio	National Institute of Biodiversity of Costa Rica
IPCC	Intergovernmental Panel on Climate Change
ISDR	International Strategy for Disaster Reduction
IUCN	International Union for Conservation of Nature
KNPS	Korea National Park Service
LDGC	Lower Danube Green Corridor
MOU	memorandum of understanding
MPA	marine protected area
NGO	non-governmental organization
NTFP	non-timber forest product
OECD	Organisation for Economic Co-operation and Development
PA-BAT	Protected Area Benefit Assessment Tool
PES	payment for environmental services
PHE	population-health-environment
PoWPA	Programme of Work on Protected Areas
REDD	reduced emissions from deforestation and forest degradation
TBPA	transboundary protected area

TNC	The Nature Conservancy
UMIYAC	Union of Traditional Yagé Healers of the Colombian Amazon
UNEP	United Nations Environment Programme
UNFCCC	United Nations Framework Convention on Climate Change
WCPA	World Commission on Protected Areas
WDPA	World Database on Protected Areas
WHO	World Health Organization
WWF	World Wide Fund for Nature (formerly World Wildlife Fund)

Foreword

Jim Leape, Nik Lopoukhine and Kathy Mackinnon

Protected areas occupy an almost unique role in the early 21st century, simultaneously celebrated and criticized by different social movements, both claiming to occupy the moral high ground. At the same time, in many parts of the world they are the only places not wholly dominated by human aspirations and influence, and the only hope for the survival of many of the world's plant and animal species.

This book is the result of many years spent trying to make sense of these paradoxes and to work out exactly how and where protected areas fit into efforts to produce a saner and more equitable world. Its genesis stretches back to 2000 and a conference organized in Thailand by the World Wildlife Fund (WWF) and the International Union for Conservation of Nature (IUCN) World Commission on Protected Areas (WCPA), looking at protected area management effectiveness. In their summing up statement Claude Martin and Adrian Phillips, then respectively the director of WWF International and the chair of WCPA, pointed out that biodiversity alone was no longer a sufficient reason for governments to maintain large areas in national parks, nature reserves and wilderness areas; if such places were to have long-term futures they needed to show how they deliver on a wider range of benefits to a bigger group of people. WWF's 'Arguments for Protection' series, to look at some of these broader benefits of protected areas, was sketched out the same evening over a meal in downtown Bangkok. The project was quickly supported by the World Bank and the first report, *Running Pure: The Importance of Forest Protected Areas to Drinking Water*, broke the record of the most downloaded report from the WWF website.

What was conceived as a reasonably quick review of protected area benefits has stretched to something more substantial and more complex: it has looked at both advantages and disadvantages of protected areas; developed new assessment tools for working out benefits and costs; and covered a far wider range of disciplines than first imagined. This book therefore draws on a decade of challenging and often very exciting research, which has frequently gone well beyond traditional conservation concerns – such as the significance of sacredness in nature, as well as a host of ecosystem services and other human benefits including hydrological, medical and agricultural issues. The project has, we believe, assembled the largest body of information about the benefits of protected natural ecosystems in the world and offers compelling evidence that such protection is a justified, cost effective and efficient way of delivering many social, cultural and biological services.

Ten years on, the arguments are more relevant than ever. Over the decade, we have seen both great gains and huge challenges for the concept of protecting wild nature. Governments are more committed to conservation and protected areas than they have ever been before, with 191 parties supporting a 'Programme of Work on Protected Areas' from the United Nations Convention on Biological Diversity (CBD) which provides a global framework for making progress. The potential for natural ecosystems to help mitigate and adapt to climate change is adding urgent new reasons for protecting natural habitats. The role of protected areas in health, water supply, recreation, food security, disaster mitigation and climate stabilization is bringing them to the attention of many actors far away from those interested in natural history and wilderness protection.

However, at the same time there continues to be a degree of resistance. Where protected areas have been set up by expropriating land and water from indigenous peoples and local communities a strong reaction has resulted. Despite fine words and principles from governments and non-governmental organizations (NGOs), the problems continue. There is also a backlash against protection from those whose motives are less altruistic. Agribusiness, large-scale fisheries, extractive industries, transport companies and the booming biofuel industry often look upon protected areas as an impediment to their business concerns and lobby, either openly or clandestinely, against the concept of maintaining areas in a natural or near natural state.

Protected areas need to balance a complicated range of practical and ethical issues; the most complicated of all being to balance ethical concerns for the survival of what we might call 'wild nature' with ethical concerns for people who live in rich and highly diverse natural habitats.

We believe that a proper understanding of the full range of values available from natural ecosystems, coupled with strong and varied governance structures and rule of law that ensure, at the very least, local participation in decision-making, can result in protected areas that are good for both people and nature. This book is one small contribution to attaining this ideal.

1

Protected Areas:
Linking Environment and Well-being

Sue Stolton

Just offshore from Hiroshima, the island of Itsukushima in the Seto Inland Sea is one of the holiest places in Japan, a shrine to Shintoism since the 6th century. Today it is also recognized as a World Heritage site. Its huge, red-painted temple gate uniquely stands offshore in the shallow waters of the bay, making a famous backdrop to wedding photographs and, on the day we visit, a home for a couple of kites whose forked tails are clearly visible as they fly leisurely around the pillars. Magnificent though the temple is, we are actually as interested in the forests that cover the rest of the island. Virtually all of Japan's lowland forests disappeared centuries ago under villages and rice paddies and today the only really old trees are found on land owned by the Buddhist and Shinto authorities. Being wooden, Japan's temples need periodic renewal and so the sacred forests have been protected, sometimes for millennia, partly to provide the occasional piece of high quality timber. In the process, the authorities have created one of the earliest forms of protected area in the world, providing irreplaceable habitats for plants and animals that have disappeared elsewhere.

Sue Stolton

Linking People and Their Environment

Individual countries or communities have consciously managed the natural environment for millennia, but it was only after the 1972 Stockholm Conference on the Human Environment recognized that 'The protection and improvement of the human environment is a major issue which affects the well-being of peoples and economic development throughout the world' that substantial global policies emerged linking natural assets to human existence (UN, 1972). Since then, the relationship between conservation and well-being has been a cause of much discussion and research, sparking a debate which intensified following the 1992 Rio Earth Summit.

In the last 50 years humans have transformed the planet more radically than at any other point in our history. Extinction rates are thought to be a thousand times higher than expected under natural conditions (CBD, 2006). As we destroy and degrade entire ecosystems we also lose the benefits that these ecosystems provide. Vital goods and services like pure drinking water, fertile agricultural soils and medicinal plants all come from a healthy environment. The Millennium Ecosystem Assessment estimates that around 60 per cent of the world's ecosystem services (including 70 per cent of regulating and cultural services) are being degraded or used unsustainably (MEA, 2005).

The Role of Protected Areas

Protected areas aim to maintain the benefits provided by natural ecosystems, or in some cases long-established manipulated ecosystems, which cannot be replicated in intensively managed landscapes. Human societies have protected land and water from long before the start of recorded history – to protect grazing pasture, maintain timber supplies, stop avalanches, provide game for hunting or allow secure places for fish to breed. People have also protected places for less tangible reasons: because they were considered sacred or simply because they were recognized as aesthetically beautiful.

The modern concept of a 'protected area' – known variously as national park, wilderness area, game reserve, etc. – developed in the late 19th century as a response to rapid changes brought to lands in former European colonies and concern at the loss of 'wilderness'. Protection was sometimes driven by a desire to stop species disappearing, as is the case with some of the colonially established parks in India, but also because colonizers were trying to retain remnants of the landscape that existed when they arrived. They often incorrectly assumed this to be in an untouched state, although in most cases ecology had been influenced by human activity for millennia. A handful of national parks in Africa, Asia and North America heralded a flood of protection that spread to Europe and Latin America and gathered momentum throughout the 20th century, and the number of protected areas continues to increase today. Most protected areas have been officially gazetted in the last 50 years – many even more recently – and the science and practice of management are both still at a relatively early stage.

The term 'protected area' embraces a wealth of variety, ranging from huge areas that show few signs of human influence to tiny culturally defined patches; and from areas so fragile that no visitation is allowed to living landscapes containing settled human communities. Although there are a growing number of protected areas near or within towns and cities, most are in rural areas. Early efforts often centred on preserving impressive landscapes, such as Yosemite National Park or the Grand Canyon in the US. More recently, recognition of extinction risk has switched the emphasis towards maintenance of species and ecosystems, and increasing efforts are made to identify new protected areas to fill 'gaps' in national conservation policies (Dudley and Parrish, 2006). The ecological repercussions of climate change are adding urgency to attempts to conserve what we can of the planet's diversity.

The earliest protected areas were generally imposed on the original inhabitants by the colonial powers, in much the same way that the rest of the land and water was divided up, and communities were often forcibly relocated from land that had in some cases been their traditional homelands for centuries. The practice of 'top-down' decision-making about protection carried on in many newly independent states in the tropics. Today, efforts by human-rights lobbyists and leadership from the Convention on Biological Diversity (CBD), set up following the 1992 Rio Earth Summit, are gradually resulting in greater democratic controls on the selection and agreement of protected areas, although the net costs and benefits are often still not evenly distributed.

Costs and Benefits of Protected Areas

Protected areas are the cornerstones of national and international conservation strategies. They act as refuges for species and ecological processes and provide space for natural evolution and future ecological restoration, for example, by maintaining species until management elsewhere is modified to allow their existence in the wider landscape or seascape.

Today protected areas are increasingly also expected to deliver a wide range of social and economic benefits. Assurances that protected areas will provide such benefits are often crucial to attracting the support needed for their creation, but delivering on these promises is seldom easy. In some cases it may mean broadening the scope of benefits delivered without undermining what protected areas were set up for in the first place, which is no simple task. However, if we do not understand and publicize the full range of benefits from protected areas we risk not only reducing the chances of new protected areas being established but even of seeing some existing protected areas being degazetted and their values lost.

It has been estimated that the cost of buying all of the world's biodiversity hotspots (i.e. the parts of the world with the highest diversity of plants and animals) outright is around US$100 billion – the equivalent of less than five years' expenditure on soft drinks in the US (Buckley, 2009). We are not suggesting this strategy but such comparisons help put conservation in context. In parallel with the problem that much important biodiversity remains unprotected, many areas that are protected are underfunded, poorly managed and, as a result, losing values. It has been estimated that the world spends around US$6.5 billion (2000 values) each year on the management of the existing protected area network; an amount considered to be woefully inadequate. To manage the existing terrestrial protected areas effectively, about 11 per cent of total land area, and expand the network to about 15 per cent of land area (bearing in mind the expanded network required by the CBD) has been estimated to require between US$20 and US$28 billion annually. In addition adequately protected marine reserves, covering some 30 per cent of total area, would cost at most around US$23 billion per year in recurrent costs, plus some US$6 billion per year (over 30 years) in start-up costs (Balmford et al., 2002).

Although these figures seem immense at first sight, the role protected areas play in providing us with multiple benefits should be an argument that this type of

Table 1.1 *Protected area economic values*

Site/system	Value	Source
Hypothetical: complete and effective global protected area network	Total goods and services with an annual value (net of benefits from conversion) of between US$4400 and US$5200 billion, depending on the level of resource use permitted within protected areas	Balmford et al., 2002
Protected area systems or groups of reserves		
USA: National Wildlife Refuges	All services: US$27 billion annually	Ingraham and Foster, 2008
Peru: protected area system	The current and potential benefits of Peru's protected areas contribute over US$1 billion per year to the national economy	SCBD, 2008
Individual protected areas		
Australia: Namadgi National Park	The economic value of providing water to Canberra's population is estimated to be at least AUS$100 million (over US$80 million) per year	Parks Forum, 2008
Cambodia: Ream National Park	Value to local residents of US$1.2 million a year, particularly from fishing resources	Emerton, 2005
Costa Rica: Tapantí National Park	Water supply for hydro-electricity US$1.7 million per year; recreation US$0.6 million per year; drinking water US$0.2 million per year	Bernard et al., 2009
Brazil: Brasilia National Park	Research estimated the total economic value at US$22 million per year	Adams et al., 2008
Indonesia: Lore Lindu National Park	Water-related benefits are valued at US$9 million	SCBD, 2008
Paraguay: Mbaracayu Biosphere Reserve	Average per-hectare value: carbon storage US$378/ha; timber harvest US$27.60/ha; existence value US$25/ha; bushmeat harvest US$15.59/ha; bioprospecting US$2.21/ha	Naidoo and Ricketts, 2006
UK: five protected areas in northeast England	Total value added is estimated to be £323 million (over US$500 million) of which £165 million (roughly US$275 million) was related to tourism expenditure	SQW Limited, 2004

Figure 1.1 *Three Khmer boys reading a book on fish conservation on the banks of the Tonle Sap River, Cambodia*

Source: © WWF-Canon/Zeb Hogan

investment is necessary. As shown in Table 1.1, there are beginning to be attempts to work out the economic value of protected areas. Although different methodologies are used and different benefits valued in the table (the complexities of valuation are noted, but not discussed here), the indication is that the benefits of protection are likely to far outweigh the costs.

Making the Case for Protected Areas

This book is based on the premise that ethical or emotional arguments about saving biodiversity are not enough to persuade governments or communities of the necessity to set aside large areas – or large enough areas – of land and water from development in perpetuity. To maintain and, where necessary, expand the protected area network we need to demonstrate its wider uses and appeal. Further, it is generally not enough to simply show that these values exist; they need to stack up economically and socially as well.

We take this approach with some caution. Sceptics argue that too much emphasis on ecosystem services and market-based conservation is a risky strategy, because if these do not prove to be as important as we hope, then we have lost the justification for protection (e.g. McCauley, 2006). We recognize these risks, but at the same time we believe that the risks of pinning all the hopes of conservation's most powerful tool on a fashion for saving wild species are even greater.

Conservation organizations tend to celebrate the creation of a protected area as a permanent victory for 'nature'. Over the past few years, between the two of us we have spoken to senior officials in eight different countries who have said openly that they regard their protected area designations as temporary and the list of degazetted protected areas continues to grow. The stimulus for the book, and the associated WWF Arguments for Protection project, is a conviction that we have a relatively brief window of opportunity to persuade governments and the public that commitments to protected areas, often made hurriedly to satisfy donors or even cynically to tie-up land that can be exploited later, have real value and are worth committing to and supporting over time.

This book thus aims to demonstrate that protected areas have a wide range of values, not always only economic, which provide a string of practical, cultural and spiritual benefits that cannot easily be met through other means. We are convinced that to identify, manage and promote these benefits is vital for the continued survival of protected areas.

We should mention an important caveat; not all protected areas will provide every kind of value. Failure to provide multiple benefits is not a sign that the protected area is a failure and, for example, an overemphasis on social values may detract from the primary reason that society sets aside protected areas. However, the underlying concept of multiple values remains extremely powerful.

Defining Protected Areas

IUCN defines a protected area as: 'A clearly defined geographical space, recognised, dedicated and managed, through legal or other effective means, to achieve the long-term conservation of nature with associated ecosystem services and cultural values.' (Dudley, 2008) The primary aim is to achieve the long-term conservation of nature, but achievement of this goal brings with it many associated ecosystem services and cultural values.

Protected areas exist under literally dozens of names and management models. To provide some structure, IUCN has agreed a set of six categories for protected areas, based on management objectives (Dudley, 2008). Like all artificial definitions these are imprecise and the distinction between them sometimes blurred, but they provide a succinct overview of the multiplicity of protected area types:

- Category I: strict protection (Ia Strict Nature Reserve and Ib Wilderness Area);
- Category II: ecosystem conservation and recreation (National Park);
- Category III: conservation of natural features (Natural Monument or Feature);
- Category IV: conservation of habitats and species (Habitat/Species Management Area);
- Category V: landscape/seascape conservation and recreation (Protected Landscape/Seascape);
- Category VI: sustainable use of natural resources (Protected Area with Sustainable Use of Natural Resources).

It would be fair to say that the precise boundaries of what is permitted inside a protected area are still being debated. Many older protected areas, which originally excluded people, have relaxed their rules in the face of protests or because managers recognized that the restrictions were unnecessary: Nyika National Park in Malawi, for example, once again permits local communities access to four traditional sacred sites for raindance ceremonies. The balance between use and protection, various trade-offs and the long-term maintenance of a protected area's values are seldom fixed at the time of the first management plan but rather evolve over years. It is a sensitive subject, with some NGOs reacting strongly against attempts to 'open up' protected areas and others arguing conversely against strict protection on human-rights grounds.

At present, many protected areas are owned and managed by national governments, but this is far from inevitable and a number of different governance types are recognized by IUCN (Dudley, 2008), covering a variety of private and community ownership patterns, as outlined in Table 1.2 below.

Table 1.2 *Different governance types in protected areas*

Government-managed protected areas	Federal or national ministry or agency in charge
	Local/municipal ministry or agency in charge
	Government-delegated management (e.g. to an NGO)
Co-managed protected areas	Transboundary management
	Collaborative management (various forms of pluralist influence)
	Joint management (pluralist management board)
Indigenous and community conserved areas	Declared and run by indigenous peoples
	Declared and run by local communities
Private protected areas	Declared and run by individual landowner/s
	Declared and run by non-profit organization (e.g. NGO, university or cooperative)
	Declared and run by for-profit organization (e.g. individual or corporate landowners)

Figure 1.2 *Huachipaeri Indian explaining the properties of Matico colorado leaves, which are used to treat rheumatism, Manu National Park, Peru*

Source: © WWF-Canon/André Bärtschi

The Continuing Need for New Protected Areas

From the information held by the United Nations Environment Programme (UNEP) World Conservation Monitoring Centre on its World Database on Protected Areas (WDPA) terrestrial protected areas now cover over 13 per cent of the world's land surface. Their establishment represents what is almost certainly the largest and fastest conscious change of management objectives in history. In addition over 12 per cent of marine coastal (intertidal) areas are protected, but only 4 per cent of the marine shelf (i.e. areas of over 200m depth) is protected (Coad et al., 2009).

Setting aside over a tenth of the planet's land surface for the protection of natural biological diversity already represents an extraordinary global recognition of the importance of wild nature. However, these statistics give a false impression of the strength of the world's protected area network. Many existing protected areas are remote, inaccessible or on land that is of little economic value – ice caps, deserts and mountains – and not in places with the highest levels of biodiversity. There are notable gaps remaining in terms of species that have not been protected (Rodrigues et al., 2004). More generally, freshwater and marine systems are poorly protected; for instance, less than 1 per cent of lake systems are in protected areas. Furthermore, many protected areas exist in name only or are poorly managed so that their values continue to decline. Isolated protected areas are at risk of losing species to inbreeding or accident even if they remain intact, unless they are extremely large (Bennett,

1999). Many remaining 'gaps' in national protected area networks are likely to be in the most difficult places to protect: valuable lowland forest, grasslands and heavily modified cultural ecosystems. Setting aside land in these places is not a simple matter; much will be in private ownership and powerful economic forces will be asking why they should be expected to forgo benefits in the name of conservation. Protected areas here are often required to provide a suite of benefits that extend well beyond traditional conservation.

In response to continuing concern about the rate of biodiversity loss, in February 2004 188 signatories to the CBD committed to expanding the world's protected area network, aiming to develop and maintain, 'comprehensive, effectively managed and ecologically representative systems of protected areas' by 2010 on land and by 2012 in marine areas (CBD, 2004). The accompanying Programme of Work on Protected Areas contains over 90 specific, time-limited actions for governments. Although these lay stress on the biological importance of protected areas they also recognize socio-cultural values and the importance of involving local communities in selection, designation and management of sites for protection. The CBD programme requires prior informed consent from local communities before future protected areas are established.

Trading Off between Protection and Development

In a crowded world with competing needs, protected areas always have to compete with other demands on land or water; indeed, if there were no other competing demands then probably a protected area would be hardly needed. Currently, the rapid rate of land-use and resource-change taking place, particularly in many tropical countries, increases the need to act fast to secure strong protected area networks. A recent study found 140 ecoregions where natural ecosystems were being converted at least 10 times more quickly than they were being protected (Hoekstra et al., 2005) and research has shown a correlation between a country's economic inequality and biodiversity loss (Mikkelson et al., 2007).

Changing Management

The philosophy and practice of modern conservation, which has been slowly emerging over the last 50 years or so, is characterized by a steadily increasing depth and complexity: from sites to ecoregions; species in danger to biodiversity; preservation of key sites to landscape approaches with multiple management; top-down to stakeholder driven. Conservation is also increasingly looking beyond protected areas to the management of whole ecosystems. At such scales, humans and other species need to learn to coexist, so conditions for both must be favourable.

Changing social conditions mean that many different stakeholders will now expect to have a say about whether a protected area is created or not and how such areas are managed will often depend on a complex process of negotiation, trade-offs and agreements. Bearing this in mind, when we talk about protected area 'managers' in this book we are referring to all those governance types outlined in Table 1.2, e.g. from government officials to local communities.

Effective protected area networks will increasingly only work if other benefits are recognized. This may be uncomfortable for some within the conservation movement, but it is the reality for protected area planners and managers in many parts of the world and this trend is likely to continue.

Protected areas are now one of the largest land-uses on the planet and our very success means that the expectations are growing all the time. How effectively we meet these will determine to a large extent whether the enormous increase in land and water under protection remains in perpetuity or if much of it is gradually degraded and, in time, degazetted.

Why This Book?

A lot of recent papers, books and articles have attempted to identify and quantify links between human benefits and the natural environment. Many of these suffer from a number of disadvantages. First, too many make claims that are vague or qualitative and, where hard numbers are given, these are often based on flimsy evidence. Readers soon recognize a small suite of case studies that are referred to time and again, at least some of which do not stand up to scrutiny. There is insufficient discussion about whether something that works in one situation can be transferred to others. Next, the type of benefits claimed from protected areas is often poorly defined and confused so that, for instance, compensation paid to a community for loss of goods and services is treated as being the same as direct benefits from tourist revenue or from increased fishing opportunities.

In response WWF and Equilibrium Research, with support from the World Bank and other partners, have been working since 2000 on a series of reports, tools and interlinked projects under the overall project title 'Arguments for Protection'. We wanted to achieve several things:

- separating myth from reality – understanding the benefits that protected areas can, and cannot, provide to human society;
- an expansion of evidence for benefits of protected areas away from a few well-used case studies;
- the development of new partnerships to build a greater constituency for protected areas;
- identification of important steps that could maximize these wider benefits;
- an increase in the security of existing protected areas and cogent arguments for new protected areas;
- support for the CBD Programme of Work on Protected Areas.

As researchers we came to protected areas relatively late, after years working on various sustainable management systems. We came to recognize that, important though the latter are, they will never deliver all the benefits that the world's species, including the human species, require. This book pulls together work over the last ten years looking at the wider role of protected areas and we hope it will contribute to setting the agenda for work on protected areas for at least the next ten. The chapters cover a wide range of benefits and each is arranged around a fairly standardized format looking at the values and associated benefits of the issue being discussed, followed by a review of the current and future role of protected areas and a discussion of management issues. Each chapter is supplemented by one or two more detailed case studies highlighting the benefits of specific protected areas or protected area systems in conserving the values discussed.

There is still much to be done to understand, quantify, manage, distribute and maximize the benefits protected areas can offer us all – but we hope that the information presented here provides a persuasive argument for why we need protected areas in a world where our activities continue to alter the natural environment around us at such an alarming rate.

References

Adams, C., Seroa da Motta, R., Arigoni Ortiz, R., Reid, J., Ebersbach Aznar, C. and de Almeida Sinisgalli, P. A. (2008) 'The use of contingent valuation for evaluating protected areas in the developing world: Economic valuation of Morro do Diabo State Park, Atlantic Rainforest, São Paulo State (Brazil)', *Ecological Economics*, vol 66, nos 2–3, pp359–70.

Balmford, A., Bruner, A., Cooper, P., Costanza, R., Farber, S., Green, R.E., Jenkins, M., Jefferiss, P., Jessamy, V., Madden, J., Munro, K., Myers, N., Naeem, S., Paavola, J., Rayment, M., Rosendo, S., Roughgarden, J., Trumper, K., and Turner, R. K. (2002) 'Economic reasons for conserving wild nature', *Science*, vol 297, no 5583, pp950–53.

Bennett, A. F. (1999) *Linkages in the Landscape: The role of corridors and connectivity in wildlife conservation*, IUCN, the World Conservation Union, Gland.

Bernard, F., de Groot, R. S. and Campos, J. J. (2009) 'Valuation of tropical forest services and mechanisms to finance their conservation and sustainable use: A case study of Tapantí National Park, Costa Rica', *Forest Policy and Economics*, vol 11, no 3, pp174–83.

Buckley, R. (2009) 'Parks and tourism', *PLoS Biology*, vol 7, no 6.

CBD (2004) *Programme of Work on Protected Areas*, Secretariat of the Convention on Biological Diversity, Montreal.

CBD (2006) *Global Biodiversity Outlook 2*, Convention on Biological Diversity, Montreal.

Coad, L., Burgess, N. D., Bomhard, B. and Besançon, C. (2009) *Progress Towards the Convention on Biological Diversity's 2010 and 2012 Targets for Protected Areas*, UNEP-WCMC, Cambridge.

Dudley, N. (ed.) (2008) *Guidelines for Applying Protected Area Management Categories*, IUCN, Gland.

Dudley, N. and Parrish, J. (2006) *Closing the Gap: Creating Ecologically Representative Protected Area Systems*, CBD Technical Series 24, Convention on Biological Diversity, Montreal.

Emerton, L. (ed.) (2005) *Values and Rewards: Counting and Capturing Ecosystem Water Services for Sustainable Development, Water, Nature and Economics*, Technical Paper No 1, IUCN, Ecosystems and Livelihoods Group Asia, Colombo.

Hoekstra, J. M., Boucher, T. M., Ricketts, T. H. and Roberts, C. (2005) 'Confronting a biome crisis: global disparities in habitat loss and protection', *Ecology Letters*, vol 8, pp23–9.

Ingraham, M. W. and Foster, S. G. (2008) 'The value of ecosystem services provided by the US National Wildlife Refuge System in the contiguous US', *Ecological Economics*, vol 67, pp608–18.

McCauley, D. J. (2006) 'Selling out on nature', *Nature*, vol 443, pp27–8.

MEA – Millennium Ecosystem Assessment (2005) *Ecosystems and Human Well-being: Synthesis*, Island Press, Washington, DC.

Mikkelson, G. M., Gonzalez, A. and Peterson, G. D. (2007) 'Economic inequality predicts biodiversity loss', *PLoS ONE*, vol 2, no 5.

Naidoo, R and Ricketts, T. (2006) 'Mapping the economic costs and benefits of conservation', *PLoS Biology*, vol 4, no 11.

Parks Forum (2008) *The Value of Parks*, Parks Forum, Victoria.

Rodrigues, A. S. L., Andelman, S. J., Bakarr, M. I., Boitani, L., Brooks, T. M., Cowling, R. M., Fishpool, L. D. C., da Fonseca, G. A. B., Gaston, K. J., Hoffmann, M., Long, J. S., Marquet, P. A., Pilgrim, J. D., Pressey, R. L., Schipper, J., Sechrest, W., Stuart, S. N., Underhill, L. G., Waller, R. W., Watts, M. E. J. and Yan, X. (2004) 'Effectiveness of the global protected area network in representing species diversity', *Nature*, vol 428, pp640–43.

SCBD (2008) *Protected Areas in Today's World: Their Values and Benefits for the Welfare of the Planet*, Technical Series no 36, Secretariat of the Convention on Biological Diversity, Montreal.

SQW Limited (2004) *The Economic Value of Protected Landscapes in the North East of England*, SQW Limited, Leeds.

UN (1972) *Stockholm Declaration*, United Nations, New York, NY.

2

Vital Sites: Protected Areas
Supporting Health and Recreation

Sue Stolton

Much of this book has been written or edited at our house in Wales, literally 100 yards or so south of the River Dyfi, which itself forms the southern border of the Snowdonia National Park. On numerous occasions when we have become too tired or too stressed to write anymore, we have thrown our walking boots into the back of the car and headed north to one of our favourite mountains for an afternoon of brisk physical exercise and mental relaxation. We have agonized over arguments and examples and even planned out chapter introductions like this one while clambering up the side of mountains like Cadair Idris and Rhinog Fawr, with nothing but a handful of birds for company. The national park system in England and Wales was at its origin based largely on the need for exercise and aimed to provide breathing space for people who spent most of their lives crowded into factories and cities. The link between physical exercise, mental well-being and exhilarating scenery has been recognized for centuries but it is only in the last 10 to 20 years that it has started to be codified by quantitative research and a precise terminology.

Sue Stolton

The Argument

The value

Human health is defined by the World Health Organization (WHO) as 'a state of complete physical, mental and social well-being and not merely the absence of disease or infirmity' (WHO, 1946). There are many paths to good health – and protected areas may not at first glance seem to be the most obvious. However, as this chapter will show, the links between our natural environment and health are many and varied.[1]

First, the bad news. One consequence of environmental degradation is a rapid increase in serious associated detrimental health impacts; WHO suggests that up to a quarter of all deaths would be avoidable simply by improved management of environmental conditions (Prüss-Üstün and Corvalán, 2006). For example, research has linked deforestation and forest fragmentation with the emergence of diseases such as HIV and Ebola, through increased contact between humans and primate carriers (Wilcox and Ellis, 2006). The increased prevalence of established diseases including malaria and leishmaniasis has also been linked to deforestation (Walsh et al., 1993). A major study in the Amazon established that mosquitoes carrying malaria were found in greater numbers in heavily deforested landscapes, regardless of human population density (Vittor et al., 2009). At the same time environmental degradation is also threatening some of the genetic materials that could help to provide medicines, thus creating a double blow for health. As the authors of a recent overview on human health and biodiversity observe: 'the current crisis of biodiversity loss represents nothing less than an enormous threat for biomedical research, the full magnitude of which we can now only guess' (Chivian and Bernstein, 2008). So by undervaluing our natural environment we are contributing to major health problems.

The benefit

Protected areas provide health benefits as a result of their environmental services, the biodiversity they contain and as places for mental and physical relaxation.

The biodiversity preserved in protected areas has the potential to address immediate health problems, either as traditional medicines (still the primary health-care option for many people) or as constituents of pharmaceuticals. More species of medicinal plants are harvested than of any other natural product (Hamilton et al., 2006) and over a quarter of all known plants have been used medicinally (Farnsworth and Soejarto, 1988). Many are obtained from protected areas – which are sometimes their last strongholds.

Medical drugs from natural products support an industry worth billions of dollars. As natural ecosystems come under pressure, the importance of protected areas as sites where researchers can find new genetic material is being recognized and is helping to pay for protected area establishment and management. The number of infectious diseases that are becoming resistant to existing pharmaceuticals makes the search for new drugs especially urgent. Forests are an acknowledged important repository of medicinal compounds from wild organisms (Colfer et al., 2006b), as are our oceans. Since the mid-1980s, over 2500 medically significant chemical compounds have been found in marine species (Tibbetts, 2004).

The fate of natural habitats, local medicinal practices, knowledge and traditions, and the well-being of communities are closely linked. Protected areas can provide the security needed to conserve resources, maintain sustainable management traditions and pass on knowledge about local medicines to younger generations (see Case Study 2.1 from Colombia).

Lastly, protected areas provide health benefits by their very existence. At a time when obesity has become a more serious health problem, on a global scale, than malnutrition, the role of exercise and personal responsibility for health is being widely acknowledged. In many places national parks and nature reserves provide some of the few spaces where people can take exercise in safe and pleasant surroundings. Conservation organizations and protected area managers are actively working with health authorities to encourage such approaches (see Case Study 2.2 from Australia). More recently, it has been recognized that beautiful landscapes and seascapes can also have important therapeutic benefits for the mind, and we describe below some innovative collaborations between protected area authorities and those responsible for people with mental-health or drug-dependency problems.

Current Contribution of Protected Areas

Protected areas can contribute positively to a wide range of health-related issues, which can be divided into four main areas: environmental benefits; sources of local medicines; sources of global medicines; and provision of direct health benefits.

Environmental benefits

Protected areas contribute two main environmental benefits as strategies for ensuring health and well-being: 'direct benefits' from conscious management of ecosystems against disease and 'indirect benefits' related to management activities that contribute to better health (e.g. provision of clean drinking water, soil stabilization, etc.) or for the resources that protected areas contain. Both are discussed below.

While ecosystem degradation can often spread disease, conscious ecosystem management can have a preventative effect. Avoiding deforestation or restoring natural vegetation can, for example, reduce the risk of malaria and certain other diseases (Oglethorpe et al., 2008). In Indonesia, the 32,000ha Ruteng Park on the island of Flores protects the most intact submontane and montane forests on the island. Researchers found that communities living near the protected area had fewer cases of malaria and dysentery, children missed school less because of ill health and there was less hunger associated with crop failure than in nearby communities without intact forests (Pattanayak et al., 2003). In an historical example, malaria was finally removed from Italy in the 1950s following an extensive eradication programme, which included long-term land-use planning. By the 1880s areas of maquis scrub in Tuscany had become severely degraded by human activities and grazing, creating a marsh exacerbating the spread of malaria. The Duna Feniglia State Nature Reserve was declared in 1971 in an area where a government-led reforestation process was initiated in the early 20th century to reduce mosquito habitat (Anon, 2006).

Traditional management of resources and habitats can also focus on plants with medicinal value. In West Africa, *Irvingia gabonensis* and *Ricinodendron heudelotii* have long been managed for their bark, which is used to treat diarrhoea and dysentery (Colfer et al., 2006b). In southern India, 55 specific Medicinal Plants Conservation Areas have been established by State Forest Departments to protect representatives of all major forest types and bio-geographical zones. Together they protect nearly 45 per cent of medicinal plant diversity (around 2500 species) of peninsular India (Medicinal Plant Conservation Network, 2009).

Indirect benefits related to management activities within protected areas can also contribute to better health through the protection of vital environmental services. The importance of protected areas in supplying sources of clean drinking water is discussed in Chapter 3.

Sources of local medicines

Traditional herbal medicines have been defined as: 'naturally occurring, plant-derived substances with minimal or no industrial processing that have been used to treat illness within local or regional healing practices' (Tilburt and Kaptchuk, 2008). Some traditional medicines are now traded globally but for many, particularly developing, countries, locally collected traditional medicines are a major resource for meeting primary health-care needs.

Ethnobotanical studies, which look at the cultural uses of plants, have been conducted in numerous protected areas and demonstrate their importance both for conserving a wide range of species and, in many places, also maintaining the knowledge of how they are used. Some examples of the number of medicinal plants used in 20 protected areas around the world are given below (Stolton and Dudley, 2010):

- Montseny Biosphere Reserve, Spain: 35 species;
- Arrábida Nature Park, Portugal: 156 species;
- Serra de Sao Mamede Nature Park, Portugal: 150 species;
- Cilento e Vallo di Diano National Park, Italy: 63 species;

Figure 2.1 *Women collecting medicinal plants in Kayan Mentarang National Park, Indonesia*
Source: © Alain Compost/WWF-Canon

- Kopaonik National Park, Serbia: 83 species;
- Piatra Craiului National Park, Romania: 63 species;
- Vikos-Aoos National Park, Greece: 100 species;
- Margalla Hills National Park, Pakistan: 50 species;
- Ayubia National Park, Pakistan: 21 species;
- Valley of Flowers National Park, India: 112 species;
- Nagzira Wildlife Sanctuary, India: 28 species;
- Gunung Leuser National Park, Indonesia: 158 species;
- Shey-Phoksundo National Park, Nepal: over 150 species;
- Langtang National Park, Nepal: 411 species;
- Endau-Rompin National Park, Malaysia: 52 species;
- Gunung Mulu National Park, Malaysia: 20 species;
- Cat Tien National Park, Vietnam: 120 species;
- Bale Mountains National Park, Ethiopia: 101 species;
- Isiboro-Sécure National Park, Bolivia: 38 species;
- Cumbres de Monterrey National Park, Mexico: 98 species.

Sources of global medicines

The links between global medicines and protected areas can be divided into two areas; firstly, protected areas can act as sources of material, primarily plants, used raw or in only lightly processed form; and, secondly, they can provide materials that are processed as components of pharmaceuticals.

In cases where commercial resource use is acceptable within a protected area, the key to success and equitable benefit-sharing lies in good management. This can also help to combat the well-documented problems of over-exploitation of medicinal plants – which is often illegal but common both inside and outside protected areas. Several international initiatives aim to conserve important plant species including the CBD's 'Global Strategy for Plant Conservation' (CBD, 2002) and the 'International Standard for Sustainable Wild Collection of Medicinal and Aromatic Plants' from the IUCN Species Survival Commission, BfN, WWF Germany and TRAFFIC (Medicinal Plant Specialist Group, 2007).

China provides the best example of traditional medicines which have become a major global business. Here, the traditional medicine industry accounted for 26 per cent of total pharmaceutical output in 2006. Many medicinal wild plants are collected beyond their regenerative capacity (Liou and Wasser, 2008). About 75 per cent of commercially harvested Chinese medicinal plant species occur in the mountains of the Upper Yangtze. A joint project by WWF, TRAFFIC and IUCN is working in this area aiming to balance resources for traditional Chinese medicine with conservation, in particular of panda habitat, and sustainable local livelihoods. One goal is to develop commercial partners who will buy certified 'panda friendly' products that bring higher incomes to local villages through managed harvest rather than 'resource mining' (Cunningham, 2009).

The use of complementary and alternative medicine is also increasing rapidly in the West. The potential to link effective conservation with medicinal plant collection in protected areas has been considered in detail in southeast Europe. In Prespa

National Park and Ohrid Protected Landscape in Albania, for example, more than 70 medicinal plant species are collected and exported, mainly to Germany. Proposals for a control and monitoring system, licensing and training for collectors and requirements for labelling of products have been developed (Schopp-Guth and Fremuth, 2001).

Developing new pharmaceutical drugs is a long, complex and costly process – but the rewards of finding a reliable cure can be enormous. The first challenge is the quest for new materials and one important area for research is bioprospecting, i.e. the search for wild species that contain chemicals with potential medicinal or commercial applications. Because all living things are remarkably similar, particularly at the genetic and molecular level, these 'natural' building blocks can provide vital leads to new treatments (Chivian and Bernstein, 2008).

Although over half of today's synthetic medicines originate from natural precursors, including well-known drugs like aspirin, digitalis and quinine, the systematic search for new plant compounds is a quite recent development (WHO, 2005). In the early 1980s no US pharmaceutical companies were researching plants in developing countries; by 2000 there were over 200 corporations and US government agencies studying rainforest plants for medicinal capacities and plant-based pharmaceuticals were estimated to earn over US\$30 billion per year (Zakrzewski, 2002).

Protected areas are viewed as reservoirs of potentially important compounds by the pharmaceuticals trade and bioprospecting in these areas is regarded as a good option for three reasons:

1   The establishment of clear agreements concerning resources is much easier when property rights are clearly established, as with state-owned properties.
2   Relatively simple governance structures, as is again the case with state-owned protected areas, simplify negotiations (although lack of wider stakeholder involvement can result in problems of equity of benefit-sharing).
3   High levels of both biodiversity and knowledge about wild species, e.g. park staff often know where rare species can be found (Columbia University, 1999).

Several pharmaceuticals have already been developed from compounds found in protected areas and more are in the pipeline, including:

• Animals: many animals serve as sources of medicines, with 23 per cent of the compounds in the 150 most commonly prescribed drugs in the US coming from animals in the 1990s (Grifo et al., 1997). A specific example is Angiotensin I, a drug to treat high blood pressure derived from the Brazilian arrowhead viper (*Bothrops jararaca*), which brought the US company that developed it (but not the people of Brazil) billions of US\$ profits annually (Sneader, 2005). A compound which has antimicrobial and fungicidal properties and may be useful for controlling fungal infections in humans was isolated from giraffe dung collected at the entrance of Etosha National Park in Namibia (US Patent, 1998).
• Plants: pharmaceutical products from tropical forest species include quinine from *Cinchona* spp.; cancer-treating drugs from rosy periwinkle (*Catharanthus roseus*); treatments for enlarged prostate gland from *Prunus africana* and diabetes

treatments from *Dioscorea dumetorum* and *Harungana vismia* (Colfer et al., 2006a). In 1987 collections of the forest liana *Ancistrocladus korupensis* were made in Korup National Park, Cameroon, by researchers from the US National Cancer Institute and a possible anti–HIV compound, michellamine B, was identified (Laird et al., 2003). Another possible anti-HIV compound was isolated from *Chrysobalanus icaco* subspecies *atacorensis* from Manovo-Gounda-St. Floris National Park, Central African Republic (Gustafson et al., 1991). Research in Cotapata National Park on the east side of the Andean Cordillera in Bolivia has led to the discovery of plants with antiplasmodial or antileishmanial activities (Acebey et al., 2007). A traditionally used malaria treatment from Madagascar is investigated by the Universite Pierre et Marie Curie-Paris. A compound isolated from the bark of *Strychnopsis thouarsii*, collected in Andasibe National Park, completely protected mice from malaria in experiments (Carraz et al., 2006).

- Micro-organisms: one of the most famous examples of micro-organisms from national parks is the thermophile *Thermus aquaticus*. Collected in a hot spring at Yellowstone National Park in the US in 1966, it helped in the development of the Polymerase Chain Reaction process which is used widely in medicinal applications (Stolton and Dudley, 2010). In Europe, the immunosuppressant property of cyclosporine was identified in a soil sample from the Hardangervidda National Park in Norway, collected in 1969. This was used in the drug Sandimmun and marketed in 1983 by Novartis; by 2000, it was one of world's most popular drugs with total sales of US$1.2 billion (Laird et al., 2003). Studies in Carlsbad Caverns National Park, New Mexico, led to the discovery of previously unknown bacteria on the walls and in the pools of several caves. By releasing enzymes that kill competitors, the bacteria compete fiercely with each other for the few available nutrients. Testing in the laboratory revealed that some of these enzymes attack leukaemia cells and may someday become instrumental in medical treatments (NPS, 2000).

Pharmaceutical companies initially usually only need quite small amounts of material so that collection can be consistent with conservation. However, links between protected areas and bioprospecting will only be equitable if there is clarity in the sharing of any benefits accrued from compounds discovered. There are already numerous examples of compounds being taken from protected areas without prior-informed consent and equitable benefit-sharing: i.e. biopiracy. This can either involve direct removal from a protected area or occur because the traditional knowledge of those living in or around a protected area has provided information that a species may have a medical use. At least 89 plant-derived medicines used in the industrial world were originally discovered by studying indigenous medicine (Beattie, 2003). Unfortunately, many examples given in this chapter (e.g. the patent received by Merck for an antibacterial compound collected from Etosha National Park, Namibia) illustrate not only the medicinal benefits from protected areas but the lack of sharing of these benefits with the original sources.

If truly equitable systems of benefit-sharing were agreed and implemented (see below) the rewards for developing countries could be notable. In the early 1990s a report for the United Nations Development Programme estimated the value of developing-country germplasm to the pharmaceutical industry as at least US$32,000 million per year; however, only a fraction of this amount has been paid for the raw materials and knowledge that local and indigenous people contribute (UNDP, 1994). Indeed, the complexities (and probably costs) involved in ensuring equitable partnerships with resource providers is sometimes leading pharmaceutical companies to move away from wild plants, with research activities directed instead at collecting microbes from the ocean floor, reviewing data stored in bioinformatics databases or other so-called 'troublefree' collecting sites (Hayden, 2005).

Provision of direct health benefits

Direct health benefits can be grouped as: i) those linked to the role of protected areas in providing a wide range of physical exercise; ii) issues related to mental health; and iii) a range of other well-being benefits linked to therapeutic activities. These three issues are also strongly linked with and contribute to overall well-being.

It has been calculated that in the US every US$1 invested in physical activity leads to a saving in medical cost of US$3.2 (Bird, 2004), as exercise has a major role in the prevention of chronic heart disease, strokes and vascular disease.

In Australia and the UK policies enshrine some of the principles and best practices developed to link human health and conservation needs. In Australia, Park Victoria's 'Healthy Parks Healthy People' message reinforces and encourages the connection between a healthy environment and a healthy society in all of the organization's activities (see Case Study 2.2).

In the UK, around 60 per cent of the population do not undertake sufficient physical activity to maintain good health (recommended as 30 minutes of moderate activity at least 5 days a week). Correcting this is a public health priority (Bird, 2004). Many protected areas actively promote outdoor activity programmes. For example, the British Trust for Conservation Volunteers runs a 'Green Gym' scheme across the country using the natural environment as a health resource. Evaluations have shown improvements in physical and mental health after participation. Many Green Gyms are active in national nature reserves. Attempts are also being made to reorientate the human-health agenda alongside biodiversity health. In a country where a national-ized health service is being pressurized by ill health related to lack of exercise, it is hoped that developing synergies between conservation and health policy will help to ensure both human well-being and conservation and restoration activities. The recent Policy Position Statement on 'Health and Wellbeing' by Natural England, the public body managing England's natural environment, looks at how this policy is implemented at ground level (Natural England, 2008).

Taking exercise in protected nature is not a new phenomenon. In Japan, Shinrin-yoku is the traditional practice of taking in the atmosphere and energy of the forest to improve health and reduce stress (Park et al., 2008). A recent study considered the psychological effects of Shinrin-yoku and found that immersion in the forest environment reduced hostility and depression and increased energy levels (Morita et al., 2007). As the Australian city of Sydney developed in the 18th and 19th centuries, so the value of the mountains to the west grew as a place of recreation. In what is now the Blue Mountains National Park and World Heritage site, a number of walking tracks were built in the 1830s and 1840s, the popularity of which increased dramatically with the completion of a rail connection in the 1860s. Public recreation reserves were gazetted from 1866 and in 1883 Katoomba Falls was protected following presentation of a public petition arguing their value for the 'health, morale and intellectual advancement' of the residents of Sydney (Stolton and Dudley, 2010).

Keoladeo National Park in India is located amidst the urban landscape of Bharatpur city. The forests and wetlands (which are internationally famous for their birds) attract hundreds of people who visit the park every morning to enjoy the fresh air, beauty and tranquillity. The park has designated a 2km stretch which 'morning walkers' enjoy every day between 5 and 7 a.m. During summer, when the daytime temperature in Bharatpur town can reach over 45°C, the number of morning walkers reaches almost 1000. The park management does not charge the usual entry fee for local people, who enjoy the vital environmental services of fresh, unpolluted air inside the park (Stolton and Dudley, 2010).

What many of us instinctively feel is the value of being in a natural landscape for our health and well-being has been the subject of recent research leading to a more rigorous theoretical understanding. The 'biophilia' hypothesis describes a bond between humans and other living systems; the term, popularized by E. O. Wilson, describes 'the connections that human beings subconsciously seek with the rest of life' (Wilson, 1984). Maller et al. (2006) reviewed published evidence supporting the assertion that contact with nature promotes health and well-being, and found the following statements were clearly demonstrated by research:

- There are some known beneficial physiological effects that occur when humans encounter, observe or otherwise positively interact with animals, plants, landscapes or wilderness.
- Natural environments foster recovery from mental fatigue and are restorative.
- There are established methods of nature-based therapy (including wilderness, horticultural and animal-assisted therapy among others) that have success healing patients who previously have not responded to treatment.
- The majority of places that people consider favourite or restorative are natural places, and being in these places is recuperative.
- Exposure to natural environments enhances the ability to cope with and recover from stress and recover from illness and injury.
- Having nature in close proximity, or just knowing it exists, is important to people regardless of whether they are regular 'users' of it.

In England, the Phoenix Futures Conservation Therapy Programme (CTP) has been helping the rehabilitation of people with substance misuse problems through active involvement in conservation projects in National Nature Reserves since 2001. Although the project notes the difficulty of assessing this type of activity; monitoring from mid-2007 to mid-2008 showed that 73 per cent of CTP attendees stayed in treatment for 12 weeks or more, compared to 49 per cent of non-participants (Le Bas and Hall, 2008). One of the participants in the scheme summed up the experience:

Figure 2.2 *Walking in Snowdonia National Park, Wales*

Source: © Nigel Dudley

> *My life has been on self destruct for at least ten years, I put all my efforts into harmful things for my body and mind … Ecology has just been a breath of fresh air to rekindle what I once had and can have again, only much improved. Not only does it give me what I need physically but mentally it is very therapeutic and is, and will, help my recovery.* (Phoenix Futures, 2009)

Future Needs: Resolving Some Remaining Tensions

We have shown the strong links between protected areas and our health. It would be disingenuous, however, to report only the positive benefits. Badly planned or managed protected areas can also increase some health problems. This is true for the spread of specific diseases but can also occur more generally if the creation of a protected area results in loss of homes or resources for dispossessed local communities:

- Forest animals can serve as hosts and vectors to a number of important diseases such as rabies, yellow fever, leishmaniasis and Chagas disease (Colfer et al., 2006a). Today, about three-quarters of all emerging infectious diseases[2] are, or have been, transmitted between animals and humans, with the pathogens usually traceable back to wildlife (Wilcox and Ellis, 2006). As protected areas become more isolated and animals possibly become overcrowded, concern has arisen over the evolution of parasite virulence and it has been suggested that conservation policies should address this problem, given the health risks currently posed by the spread of virulent viruses (e.g. avian influenza) (Lebarbenchon et al., 2006).

- Diseases can be transmitted between closely related species such as people and primates or cattle and buffalo. Transmission can take place when domestic animals graze with wild animals in or around protected areas or when tourists and field staff view primates. Zoonotic diseases are caused by infectious agents that are transmitted between (or shared by) animals and humans. For example, Ebola was transmitted from a chimpanzee (*Pan troglodytes*) in Côte d'Ivoire in the 1990s and more recently from western lowland gorillas (*Gorilla gorilla gorilla*) and chimpanzees (Kalema-Zikusoka, 2003).

- Protected area management can sometimes inadvertently be the cause of health problems. The fact that many rangers and managers stay away from home for long periods has been identified as a contributory factor in the spread of AIDS. In cases where communities are forcibly relocated to make way for protected areas this can cause health problems through exposure to new diseases. For example, when communities were relocated from the high plateau of Nyika National Park in Malawi, many went to the lowlands and succumbed to malaria, against which they had built up little natural resistance.

- There is a growing number of confrontations between humans and wild animals – a phenomenon termed 'Human Wildlife Conflict' (HWC). The main driver behind HWC is that growing population pressure leads to the poorest in society pushing agricultural frontiers to more marginal areas that are often sanctuaries for wildlife species. When wildlife loses its habitat and has reduced access to natural food sources it targets agricultural crops and livestock, and can destroy property and injure or kill people that get in its way. Conservation success, in terms of increasing animal numbers, can also lead to increased pressure at the boundaries of protected areas. These problems are likely being made worse by increased drought and/or floods, both manifestations of climate change (WWF, 2008).

- Resource use by indigenous, traditional and local people in protected areas is also not without its management challenges. Traditional systems to protect medicinal plants through taboos, seasonal and social restrictions and the nature of gathering equipment (Cunningham, 1993) can be disrupted by protected area management and legislation, which may abruptly forbid such use even if there has been a long previous history of sustainable use. This can cause local resistance to the protected area and can place unsustainable harvesting pressure on medicinal species outside the protected area.

Managing Protected Areas for
Health-related Objectives

Management of the health-related benefits of protected areas depends on the type of use, as discussed below.

Meeting both medicinal plant-resource use and conservation objectives often depend on ecosystem integrity, both to maintain species and from a cultural viewpoint (Montenegro and Stephens, 2006). There is a need to ensure that where legal resource extraction takes place in protected areas it follows principles of sustainable use, defined by the CBD as: 'the use of components of biological diversity in a way and at a rate that does not lead to the long-term decline of biological diversity, thereby maintaining its potential to meet the needs and aspirations of present and future generations' (CBD, 1992).

Putting such fine ideals into practice is not always easy; some conditions helpful in achieving sustainable harvesting of wild medicinal plants include:

- a defined area, under adequately strong tenure;
- presence of a responsible person or organization;
- a management plan or system, periodically reviewed;
- procedures to monitor harvested species and set management prescriptions for them;

Figure 2.3 *Production of herbs and medicinal plants for the local market in the buffer zone of the Ismailly Nature Reserve, Azerbaijan*

Source: © Hartmut Jungius/WWF-Canon

- procedures to ensure that harvesters are involved in preparation of the plan and setting of management prescriptions;
- procedures to ensure sustainable harvesting techniques (e.g. only taking so many leaves, or so much bark; cutting in a certain way; etc.);
- procedures to ensure good quality produce;
- procedures to ensure acceptable working conditions for harvesters (based on Hamilton, 2005).

Where such systems exist, protected areas can provide a sustainable resource for local medicines. In Bwindi Impenetrable National Park in Uganda, managers have been working with the local people to develop sustainable resource use after many years of conflict over access to resources. Community consultation meetings have developed recommendations for monitoring and community memorandums of understanding (MOUs) on resource use. Monitoring programmes for three plant species (*Ocotea usambarensis*, *Rytigynia kigeziensis* and *Loeseneriella apocynoides*) used for medicine and craft materials have been developed and resource use agreements made with the local community (Hockings et al., 2008).

Where resource use is linked to pharmaceutical development the key to developing equitable management models lies in benefit-sharing. The UN guide to *Biodiversity Access and Benefit-Sharing Policies for Protected Area* (Laird et al., 2003) provides best practice advice. The National Institute of Biodiversity of Costa Rica (INBio), a non-governmental and non-profit-making public body, has been a front runner in the development of bioprospecting research agreements. Since its inception in 1989 INBio has signed 19 agreements with industry and 18 with academic institutions. INBio's strategy is based on the premise that 'the best way to conserve biodiversity is to study it, value it, and utilize the opportunities it offers to improve the quality of life of human beings'. The agreements developed by INBio include: access (limited in time and quantity); equity and compensation (research costs and royalties); technology transfer (infrastructure and equipment); training of national scientists; and non-destructive uses. Each agreement has a workplan and budget that includes a 10 per cent donation to the government, which helps fund biodiversity conservation. Many of the protected areas in Costa Rica have been used for bioprospecting. For example, INBio has coordinated projects in Braulio Carrillo National Park with Merck & Co., Indena Spa, Phytera, Ehime Women's College of Japan, Harvard University, Utah University and the National Institute of Cancer in the US.

Other management activities are related directly to encouraging the role of protected areas in maintaining good health. There are more than a billion overweight adults worldwide and at least 300 million who are clinically obese (WHO, 2002). Managers are increasingly encouraged to use their protected areas as 'outdoor gyms'. Although this is clearly not a strategy for places with fragile environments or dangerous animals, for many managers the potential is considerable. Common features include:

- providing a safe and secure place to exercise and enjoy being in the fresh air;
- developing specific group walking and/or exercise activities (these initiatives are generally supported by publicity drives and involve park staff in leading walks);

- ensuring easy access to protected area facilities: this can range from waiving entrance fees to ensuring that park infrastructure, e.g. paths, gates etc., is accessible to people with different physical abilities. Some protected area systems now include exercise circuits and equipment on public trails, as in many Swiss reserves, or provide information on exercise, for example, Singapore reserves have a website listing exercise options.

In many countries protected areas also safeguard public health by ensuring vital ecosystem services. Approximately 3.1 per cent (1.7 million per year) of all deaths worldwide are attributable to unsafe water, sanitation and hygiene (WHO, 2002). As Chapter 3 illustrates, the link between protected areas and clean water represents perhaps one of the best 'win–win' opportunities for joint efforts to protect human health and biodiversity, for example, through the development of systems in which land-users are paid for the environmental services that they generate through management.

Box 2.1 *HIV/AIDS*

HIV/AIDS is the fourth biggest cause of mortality in the world (WHO, 2002). Although protected areas can contribute to the HIV/AIDS problem through choices made about staff deployment (see above), managers may also be able to make a positive contribution. Specifically:

- Conservation organizations and their local partners often work to improve communication and transportation infrastructures and resources in areas where they work. This can also help the work of local health and development organizations working on HIV/AIDS issues and can be particularly significant in remote areas.
- NGOs and protected area staff should have well-established contacts with local communities and organizations that can facilitate the work of health initiatives. Protected area agencies are increasingly running staff training programmes and extension work about the dangers of AIDS and about preventative measures.

In areas where HIV/AIDS is a substantial risk it is important for conservation organizations to assess organizational vulnerability in terms of staff, financial resources and management systems and to develop and implement workplace policies. Some guidance exists, such as the *Guidelines for Mitigating the Impacts of HIV/AIDS on Coastal Biodiversity and Natural Resource Management* developed by the Population Reference Bureau (Torell et al., 2007). At park level, for example, a vulnerability assessment carried out in Ankarafantsika National Park in Madagascar has been incorporated into the management strategy of the park. The park also has a trained officer as the HIV/AIDS Focal Point, who implements and coordinates related activities including: informing staff on HIV/AIDS; distributing free condoms to staff in the visitors' centre and in each field station; and holding HIV/AIDS information events in villages and hamlets around the park (Lopez et al., 2005).

Conclusions

Making the link between the environment and health has not happened overnight. In 1986, an international conference sponsored by WHO highlighted the need to bring the health and environment agendas together in a way that went beyond the normal responsibilities of countries' traditional health sectors. However, such changes of policy take time.

Although many protected areas across the world have been set up with the dual aims of conservation and recreation, few have specific health mandates. There are some exceptions and the examples given here show that policy agendas linking health and conservation can provide real benefits for both sectors. There is also a growing recognition of these links by some conservation NGOs. Conservation projects often partner with communities living in remote areas with high biodiversity in the developing world. Although conservation is the primary aim, it makes sense to link with, and sometimes work directly on, other development issues such as healthcare. These PHE (population-health-environment) projects integrate health and poverty-reduction strategies with conservation activities (see Case Study 7.1), seeking synergies to produce greater conservation and human well-being results than if they were implemented in isolated single-sector approaches (Oglethorpe et al., 2008).

These positive links, which are beginning to be recognized in the scientific literature and environmental and health policy around the world, continue to be undermined by habitat destruction and loss. Protected areas offer one of the most permanent and effective strategies for linking these two issues in practice and for the long term.

Case Study 2.1:
Protecting Medicinal Resources in Colombia

Sue Stolton and Emilio Rodriguez

In this world, God has left us everything surrounding us, the lands, waters, remedies for health. Now we have to look after them, if they finish, we will be finished as well.

This statement, made by an indigenous leader in Colombia, is well reflected by the recent declaration of a protected area in Colombia which focuses on preserving the shamanic tradition of local peoples and on the protection of the associated medicinal plants. The establishment of the Sanctuary of Flora Medicinal Plants Orito Ingi Ande was proposed by the indigenous Kofán communities and the traditional medicine-men of the Putumayo foothills, as part of their strategy to strengthen and restore their traditional culture and the associated landscapes.

Figure 2.4
A traditional medicine-man
Source: © Parques Nacionales, Colombia

Preserving biodiversity and culture

Orito Ingi Ande is in the Colombian Amazon Piedmont, the transition zone between Andean ecosystems and the lowlands. The Sanctuary is located in part of an ancestral territory of the Kofán and has long been an area of commercial exchange and socio-cultural relationships with other local indigenous communities (Parques Nacionales Naturales de Colombia, 2007). The area covers 10,200ha of tropical rainforest and Andean forest ranging from between 700 and 3300m above sea-level. The area is biologically rich containing an estimated 400 bird species and many species of amphibians, reptiles and mammals, such as the spectacled bear (*Tremarctos ornatus*) and the jaguar (*Panthera onca*), both endangered species (Parques Nacionales Naturales de Colombia, 2008).

The area is also important for medicinal plants, with over a hundred plants from the medicinal gardens of the area used by the local people. Two species in particular are inextricably linked with the local culture: the yoco (*Paullinia yoco*) and yagé (*Banisteriopsis caapi*). The yoco liana is one of the most highly regarded medicinal plants in northwestern Amazon. According to Jose Pablo Jaramillo, programme director of the Amazon Conservation Team (ACT) NGO, Colombia: 'Yoco can be considered a "keystone" species in terms of conservation, necessitating the protection of the surrounding ecosystem'. The whole culture and way of life of the various indigenous groups of the area is based on the ritual and sacred consumption of yagé. In consequence, anthropologists have named this region and its inhabitants the 'culture of yagé', which is regarded as one of the most purely preserved shamanic traditions in the world (Stolton and Dudley, 2010).

This part of the Amazon has been greatly affected by colonization. The indigenous peoples of the region have lost the majority of their territories, and deforestation has resulted in the loss of medicinal plants and the consequent impoverishment of cultures and traditional medical systems (Zuluaga Ramírez, 2005). However, the traditional healers, or Taitas, have long fought for the preservation of their culture. At a 1999 'Gathering of Taitas' in Yurayaco, in the foothills of the Colombian Amazon, 40 of the most prominent indigenous healers from 4 tribes met for the first time to discuss the future of their forests, their medicine and their people. The result was the Union of Traditional Yagé Healers of the Colombian Amazon (UMIYAC after its Spanish name) whose jointly signed declaration became the basis of this new alliance (AmazonTeam, 2009). They stated that:

> We consider yagé, our medicinal plants and our wisdom to be gifts from God and of great benefit for the health of humanity. This Gathering may be our last opportunity to unite and defend our rights. Our motivation is not economic or political. We are seriously determined to demonstrate to the world the importance of our values.
>
> We must regain possession of our territories and sacred sites. The forest is for us the fountain of our resources. If the forests disappear so will medicine and life.

The declaration of a floristic sanctuary, focusing on medicinal plants, is an initiative from this alliance and is seen as a means of combining the protection of the habitat and the biological resources with that of the traditional medicine systems, thus contributing to recovery of the area's natural, cultural and intangible heritage.

One strategy to protect the forests, their resources and the associated culture is through training and education for the followers of traditional medicine – to ensure that traditions are kept alive. This educational need was summarized by one member of the local community:

> *To lead a respectable life, children used to be taken to the 'taitas' to receive advice from them and for them to cure them drinking 'yagé'. It is necessary to guide young people and children not to lose the habits and for them to grow up and be educated with the ancestral values. Young people today don't care about earth, nature nor family, everything is getting lost.* (Stolton and Dudley, 2010)

Cosmovision

Orito Ingi Ande is the only protected area in Colombia primarily dedicated to the conservation of medicinal flora. However, it is much more than just an area set aside to conserve plant species. In the words of Juan Lozano, former minister for the Environment of Colombia:

> *The declaration of the Sanctuary Orito Ingi Ande is an important landmark in the history of the National Natural Parks of Colombia. The category of Sanctuary of Flora of Medicinal Plants harmonizes the western point of view of the conservation of biodiversity with the traditional integrated management of the Cosmovision of the Kofán People. The preservation and survival of their customs and traditions in the use and management of medicinal plants depends on the conservation of these territories.*

The protection of the area through its declaration as part of the National Natural Parks System is seen by the UMIYAC as an alliance to guarantee the perpetuity of the area and its values.

Case Study 2.2:
Parks Victoria (Australia)
'Healthy Parks, Healthy People' Initiative
John Senior

Parks Victoria is a statutory authority that manages a diverse array of environments extending over 4 million hectares in the state of Victoria, Australia. These areas include terrestrial and marine national and state parks and conservation reserves, as well as major metropolitan parks in Melbourne.

Like many protected area management agencies around the world, Parks Victoria needs to remain relevant to communities and governments in the midst of many other important considerations. Issues affecting education, health, security, transport, energy and water, among others, can overshadow parks when legislators are considering environmental priorities. However, there is no need to exclude one priority at the expense of another. Increasingly governments are encouraging more holistic strategies that foster partnerships between sectors and which involve collaborations that realign common interests. Parks Victoria's unique range and scale of responsibilities enable it to readily communicate with its urban constituencies about the value of biodiversity in relation to human well-being and thereby positively influence both their advocacy and visitor impact.

Strategic direction

On the basis of a research project carried out for Parks Victoria initially published in 2002 (and revised in 2008) by Deakin University's Faculty of Health and Behavioural Sciences (Maller et al., 2008), Parks Victoria has progressively adopted a 'Healthy Parks, Healthy People' approach to all aspects of its business. This philosophy seeks to reinforce and encourage the connection between a healthy environment and a healthy society, particularly as more people are now living in urban-dominated environments and have less regular contact with nature.

Progressively the organization has recognized that it has a clear role to play in enabling people to experience the health benefits associated with the precious natural environment. To achieve this role, new partnerships were required along with the need to dissolve disciplinary barriers and realign common interests with others, such as those within the health and community sectors. However, this kind of collaboration does not just happen; political support, champions, leadership, research and public awareness campaigns are all necessary to shift into a new park management paradigm.

Figure 2.5 *Ranger Roo plays a central role in promoting Park Victoria's 'Healthy Parks, Healthy People' message*

Source: © Parks Victoria

Changing management

Beginning as an awareness-raising campaign to highlight the connections between a healthy environment and a healthy community, 'Healthy Parks, Healthy People' has evolved into a new park management paradigm supported by many of Australia's leading park and health organizations.

The first challenge was to develop a genuine and effective message in line with Parks Victoria's core values. The message needed to trigger a perception in the minds of the public of an organization that exemplified the qualities and attributes of custodianship, environmental protection and a contribution to a civil society. The clear and simple slogan 'Healthy Parks, Healthy People' was used, implying that the environmental health of parks results in a healthy community and that spending active recreation time in a well cared for park environment can lead to greater health and fitness of both individuals and society. Broad-based awareness of this message was generated through an eight-week radio and print promotion programme, with activities supported by editorials in the national press.

Advancing the 'Healthy Parks, Healthy People' agenda also involved developing partnerships with health and other bodies, and with stakeholder groups. Support was sought and obtained from health bodies such as the Royal Australian College of General Practitioners, Asthma Victoria, the National Heart Foundation and Arthritis Victoria. Colourful posters and brochures were distributed to general medical practitioners' offices statewide, and more recently (in conjunction with Maternal and Child

Health Services and the Australian Breastfeeding Association) a congratulations card is provided to the mother of each new baby. These advise patients and mothers on the benefits of the natural environment and where to get more information about healthy activities in parks.

Community programmes which support people from diverse backgrounds have also been developed. These include a multilingual 'Park Note' translated into 33 languages, training for Parks Victoria Information Centre staff to increase their capacity to manage callers from non-English speaking backgrounds (including the use of interpreter services) and the provision of park information to the 'Welcome to Victoria Kit' (distributed annually to every new migrant child entering the education system). A new Volunteer Bilingual Park Guides programme in partnership with a number of community organizations has so far seen 11 graduating guides able to conduct tours in a second language including Turkish, Arabic, Spanish, Macedonian, Sudanese and Greek to assist communities in understanding and appreciating their local open spaces, flora and fauna. It is believed that this course is the first of its kind in Australia and the concept has created interest in other parts of Victoria, as a highly innovative approach to helping settlers gain a sense of belonging in their adopted home. Through partnering with the People & Parks Foundation, and in conjunction with the Variety Club, over 100 disadvantaged young people were able to be involved in camps which gave them an experience of nature.

A significant contributor to the success of 'Healthy Parks, Healthy People' to date has been its endorsement by staff. Across the organization, there is a growing appreciation of the relationship between a healthy parks system and a healthy society and programmes that demonstrate the broader role parks can play are beginning to grow from the 'grass roots'.

This Australian initiative has also been recognized and acknowledged internationally – by the Canadian Parks Council through its own version, called 'Healthy by Nature', and at the global level by IUCN using the theme 'Healthy Environments, Healthy People' at the 2008 World Conservation Congress.

The road ahead

Parks Victoria plans to advance the societal value of parks in Victoria by continuing to broaden the role parks play and to build awareness in Australia that parks are a vital part of a healthy and sustainable future. Thus, while recognizing that the connection of people to parks and to nature has a long history and is an enduring value, we need to ensure we are relevant to today's societal needs and to plan for the future. The contribution of nature to broader beneficial social outcomes can only enhance its value in the minds of decision-makers and lead to improved prioritizing and funding.

Notes

1. We recognize that the field of medical treatments is one where there is often enormous controversy and that the fact something is used as a medicine does not necessarily mean that it is effective (Goldacre, 2008). Analysis of the effectiveness of thousands of traditional, mainstream, alternative and complementary health products derived from nature is, however, beyond the scope of this chapter.
2. An infectious disease whose incidence has increased in the past 20 years and threatens to increase in the near future.

References

Acebey, L., Apaza, A., de Michel, R., Beck, S., Jullian, V., Ruiz, G., Gimenez, A., Chevalley, S. and Sauvain, M. (2007) 'The living library of the Cotapata National Park in Bolivia: an example of application of Bolivian law on the access to genetic resources', *Biodiversity and Conservation*, vol 17, no 8, pp1853–9.

AmazonTeam (2009) www.amazonteam.org/index.php/218/Indigenous_Gatherings, accessed 1 August 2009.

Anon (2006) 'Forestry and malaria control in Italy', *Unasylva*, vol 57, p224.

Beattie, A. J. (2003) 'New Products and Industries from Biodiversity', in R. Hassan, R. Scholes and N. Ash (eds) *Ecosystems and Human Well-being: Current State and Trends. Findings of the Condition and Trends Working Group*, Island Press, Washington, DC, US.

Bird, W. (2004) *Natural Fit: Can Green Space and Biodiversity Increase Levels of Physical Activity?*, RSPB and the Faculty of Public Health, Sandy.

Carraz, M. A., Jossang, J. F., Franetich, A. Siau, A., Liliane, C., Hannoun, L., Sauerwein, R., Frappier, F., Rasoanaivo, P., Snounou, G. and Mazier, D. (2006) 'A plant-derived morphinan as a novel lead compound active against malaria liver stages', *PLoS Medicine*, vol 3, no 12.

CBD (1992), 'Convention on Biological Diversity', www.biodiv.org.

CBD (2002) *Global Strategy for Plant Conservation*, CBD Secretariat, Montreal.

Chivian, E. and Bernstein, A. (2008) *Sustaining life: How Human Health Depends on Biodiversity*, Oxford University Press, New York, NY.

Colfer, C. J., Sheil, D., Kaimowitz, D. and Kish, M. (2006a) 'Forests and human health in the tropics: some important connections', *Unasylva*, vol 57, no 224.

Colfer, C. J., Sheil, D. and Kishi, M. (2006b) 'Forests and human health: assessing the evidence', *CIFOR Occasional Paper; No. 45*, Center for International Forestry Research, Bogor.

Columbia University, School of International and Public Affairs (1999) *Access to Genetic Resources: An Evaluation of the Development and Implementation of Recent Regulation and Access Agreements*, Environmental Policy Studies Working Paper no 4, Tides Center – Biodiversity Action Network, Washington, DC.

Cunningham, A. B. (1993) *African Medicinal Plants: Setting Priorities at the Interface between Conservation and Primary Healthcare*, People and Plants Working Paper 1, UNESCO, Paris.

Cunningham, A. B. (2009) 'Medicinal Plants and Panda Landscapes in China', in S. Stolton and N. Dudley (2010) *Vital Sites: The Contribution of Protected Areas to Human Health*, WWF International, Gland.

Farnsworth, N. R. and Soejarto, D. D. (1988) *Global Importance of Medicinal Plants*, Proceedings of an International Consultation, Chiang Mai, Thailand, Cambridge University Press, Cambridge.

Goldacre, B. (2008) *Bad Science*, Fourth Estate, London.

Grifo, F., Newman, D., Fairfield, A. S., Bhattacharya, B. and Grupenhoff, J. T. (1997) 'The origins of prescription drugs', in F. Grifo and J. Rosenthal (eds) *Biodiversity and Human Health*, Island Press, Washington, DC.

Gustafson, K. R., Munro, M. H. G., Blunt, B. W., Cardellina II, J. H., McMahon, J. B., Gulakowski, R. J., Cragg, G. M., Cox, P. A., Brinen, L. S., Clardy, J. and Boyd, M. R. (1991) 'HIV inhibitory natural products. 3. Diterpenes from *Homalanthus acuminatus* and *Chrysobalanus icaco*', *Tetrahedron*, vol 47, pp4547–54.

Hamilton, A. (2005) 'Resource assessment for sustainable harvesting of medicinal plants', paper presented at a side-event at the International Botanical Congress (Vienna) on Source to Shelf: Sustainable Supply Chain Management of Medicinal and Aromatic Plants, 21–2 July 2005.

Hamilton, A., Dürbeck, K. and Lawrence, A. (2006) 'Towards a sustainable herbal harvest: A work in hand', *Plant Talk*, vol 43, January, pp 32–5.

Hayden, C. (2005) 'Can pharmaceutical research give back?', *ReVista: Harvard Review of Latin America*, Winter 2005.

Hockings, M., Stolton, S., Dudley, N., James, R., Mathur, V., Courrau, J., Makombo, J. and Parrish, J. (2008) *Enhancing our Heritage Toolkit Assessing Management Effectiveness of Natural World Heritage Sites*, UNESCO, Paris.

INBio, www.inbio.ac.cr/en/default.html, accessed 1 August 2009.

Kalema-Zikusoka, G. (2003) 'Protected areas, human livelihoods and healthy animals: Ideas for improvements in conservation and development interventions', Southern and East African Experts Panel on Designing Successful Conservation and Development Interventions at the Wildlife/Livestock Interface: Implications for Wildlife, Livestock, and Human Health, AHEAD Forum, Durban, South Africa, 14–15 September 2003.

Laird, S., Johnston, S., Wynberg, R., Lisinge, E. and Lohan, D. (2003) *Biodiversity Access and Benefit-Sharing Policies for Protected Areas: An Introduction*, United Nations University Institute of Advanced Studies, Tokyo.

Lebarbenchon, C., Poulin, R., Gauthier-Clerc, M. and Frédéric, T. (2006) 'Parasitological Consequences of Overcrowding in Protected Areas', *EcoHealth*, vol 3, no 4, pp303–7.

Le Bas, B. and Hall, J. (2008) 'Conservation therapy – hands-on examples from National Nature Reserves', *Ecos*, vol 29, no 2.

Liou, C. and Wasser, R. (eds) (2008) *The State of Wildlife Trade in China*, TRAFFIC East Asia China Programme, Hong Kong.

Lopez, P., Bergmann, U., Dresrüsse, P., Fröde, A., Hoppe, M. and Rotzinger, S. (2005) 'Linking protected area management and HIV/AIDS prevention – experiences from Ankarafantsika National Park, Madagascar', *Parks*, vol 15, no 1, pp13–24.

Maller, C., Townsend, M., Pryor, A., Brown, P. and St Leger, L. (2006) 'Healthy nature – healthy people: "Contact with nature" as an upstream health promotion intervention for populations', *Health Promotion International*, vol 21, no 1, pp45–54.

Maller, C., Townsend, M., St Leger, L., Henderson-Wilson, C., Pryor, A., Prosser, L. and Moore, M. (2008) *Healthy Parks Healthy People. The Health Benefits of Contact with Nature in a Park Context: A Review of Current Literature – 2nd edition*, Deakin University and Parks Victoria, Melbourne.

Medicinal Plant Conservation Network, mpcn.frlht.org.in/index.htm, accessed 1 August 2009.

Medicinal Plant Specialist Group (2007) *International Standard for Sustainable Wild Collection of Medicinal and Aromatic Plants (ISSC-MAP). Version 1.0*, Bundesamt für Naturschutz (BfN), MPSG/SSC/IUCN, WWF Germany and TRAFFIC, Bonn, Gland, Frankfurt and Cambridge.

Montenegro, R. A. and Stephens, C. (2006) 'Indigenous health in Latin America and the Caribbean', *Lancet*, vol 367, no 3, pp 1859–69.

Morita, E., Fukuda, S., Nagano, J., Hamajima, N., Yamamoto, H., Iwai, Y., Nakashima, T., Ohira, H. and Shirakawa, T. (2007) 'Psychological effects of forest environments on healthy adults: Shinrin-yoku (forest-air bathing, walking) as a possible method of stress reduction', *Public Health*, vol 121, no 1, pp54–63.

Natural England (2008) *Policy Position: Health and Wellbeing Statement*, September 2008, Natural England, Sheffield.

NPS (2000) *Natural Resource Year in Review – 2000*, National Park Service, US Department of the Interior, Washington, DC.

Oglethorpe, J., Honzak, C. and Margoluis, C. (2008) *Healthy People, Healthy Ecosystems: A Manual for Integrating Health and Family Planning into Conservation Projects*, World Wildlife Fund, Washington, DC.

Park, B. J., Tsunetsugu, Y., Ishii, H., Furuhashi, S., Hirano, H., Kagawa, T. and Miyazaki, Y. (2008) 'Physiological effects of Shinrin-yoku (taking in the atmosphere of the forest) in a mixed forest in Shinano Town, Japan', *Scandinavian Journal of Forest Research*, vol 23, no 3, pp278–83.

Parques Nacionales Naturales de Colombia (2007) *Justificación para la Declaración del Area protegida*, Parques Nacionales Naturales de Colombia, Bogotá.

Parques Nacionales Naturales de Colombia (2008) 'The Sanctuary of Flora "Medicinal Plants Orito Ingi Ande" is born, Parques Nacionales Naturales de Colombia', Parques Nacionales Naturales de Colombia Press Release, Bogotá, 12 June, www.minambiente. gov.co/contenido/contenido.aspx?catID=718&conID=2188&pagID=182, accessed 1 August 2009.

Pattanayak, S. K., Corey, C. G., Lau, Y. F. and Kramer, R. A. (2003) *Forest Malaria: A Microeconomic Study of Forest Protection and Child Malaria in Flores, Indonesia*, Duke University, Durham, NC, available at: www.env.duke.edu/solutions/documents/forest-malaria.pdf, accessed 1 August 2009.

Phoenix Futures, www.phoenix-futures.org.uk/Filestore/Phoenix_Futures_CTP_PDF_Sept_2008.pdf, accessed 1 August 2009.

Prüss-Üstün, A. and Corvalán, C. (2006) *Preventing Disease through Healthy Environments – Towards an Estimate of the Environmental Burden of Disease*, WHO, Geneva.

Schopp-Guth, A. and Fremuth, W. (2001) 'Sustainable use of medicinal plants and nature conservation in the Prespa National Park area, Albania', *Medicinal Plant Conservation*, no 7, pp5–7.

Sneader, W. (2005) *Drug Discovery: A History*, John Wiley and Sons, Chichester.

Stolton, S. and Dudley, N. (2010) *Vital Sites: The Contribution of Protected Areas to Human Health*, WWF International, Gland.

Tibbetts, J. (2004) 'The state of the oceans, part 2: Delving deeper into the sea's bounty', *Environmental Health Perspectives*, vol 112, no 8, pp472–81.

Tilburt, J. C. and Kaptchuk, T. J. (2008) 'Herbal medicine research and global health: an ethical analysis', *Bulletin of the World Health Organization*, vol 86, no 8, pp577–656.

Torell, E., Kalangahe, B., Thaxton, M., Issa, A., Pieroth, V., Fahmy, O. and Tobey, J. (2007) *Guidelines for Mitigating the Impacts of HIV/AIDS on Coastal Biodiversity and Natural Resource Management*, Population Reference Bureau, Washington, DC.

UNDP (1994) *Conserving Indigenous Knowledge: Integrating Two Systems of Innovation*, Rural Advancement Foundation International, UNDP, New York, NY.

US Patent (1998) 'Patent no: 5801172 – Antifungal agent from sporomiella minimoides', www.patentstorm.us/patents/5801172/description.html, accessed 1 August 2009.

Vittor, A. Y., Pan, W., Gilman, R. H., Tielsch, J., Glass, G., Shields, T., Sánchez-Lozano, W., Pinedo, V. V., Salas-Cobos, E., Flores, S. and Patz, J. A. (2009) 'Linking deforestation to malaria in the Amazon: Characterization of the breeding habitat of the principal malaria vector, Anopheles darling', *American Journal of Tropical Medicine and Hygiene*, vol 81, pp5–12.

Walsh, J. F., Molyneux, D. H. and Birley, M. H. (1993) 'Deforestation: effects on vector-borne disease', *Parasitology*, vol 106, ppS55–75.

WHO (1946) *Preamble to the Constitution of the World Health Organization*, WHO, Geneva.

WHO (2002) *The World Health Report 2002: Reducing Risks, Promoting Healthy Life*, WHO, Geneva.

WHO (2005) *Ecosystems and Human Well-being: Health Synthesis*, WHO, Geneva.

Wilcox, B. A. and Ellis, B. (2006) 'Forests and emerging infectious diseases of humans', *Unasylva*, vol 57, no 224, pp11–18.

Wilson, E. O. (1984) *Biophilia*, Harvard University Press, Cambridge, MA.

WWF (2008) *Common Ground: Solutions for Reducing the Human, Economic and Conservation Costs of Human Wildlife Conflict*, WWF International, Gland.

Yeatts, D. S. (2006) *Characteristics of Thermal Springs and the Shallow Ground-Water System at Hot Springs National Park, Arkansas*, United States Geological Survey, Reston, VA.

Zakrzewski, P. A. (2002) 'Bioprospecting or biopiracy? The pharmaceutical industry's use of indigenous medicinal plants as a source of potential drug candidates', *University of Toronto Medical Journal*, vol 79, no 3, pp253–4.

Zuluaga Ramírez, G. (2005) 'Conservation of the biological and cultural diversity of the Colombian Amazon Piedmont: Dr. Schultes' Legacy', *Ethnobotany Research & Applications*, vol 3, pp179–88.

3

Running Pure: Protected Areas Maintaining Purity and Quantity of Urban Water Supplies

Nigel Dudley and Lawrence Hamilton

With its cool interior, low-level lighting and piped classical music, the cathedral-sized Basilica Cistern (Yerebatan Sarayı) is one of the most popular tourist destinations in Istanbul, providing a welcome escape from the heat and the crowds. Although the interior is beautiful, its origins are strictly utilitarian. The 336 marble columns create a vast tank, capable of holding 80,000m³ of water, the largest of several hundred underground cisterns that supplied the thirsty citizens of Constantinople, as Istanbul was formerly known. The city planners were careful not only to provide good water storage, but also to protect the source. Centuries ago all the drinking water for the city came from the Belgrad forest and was piped to the city's central square, Taksim. The Basilica Cistern was built in the 6th century, during the reign of Byzantine Emperor Justinian I to store water for the great palaces of the city. A thousand years later, the Ottoman court architect Mimar Sinan's magnificent Maglova Aqueduct also brought water from the edges of the forest to the centre of the old city.

Belgrad is broadleaved forest made up mainly of beech (Fagus sylvatica), hornbeam (Carpinus betulus) and oak (Quercus frainetto, Q. petraea, Q. robur). Today it is jointly managed for research and recreation, and for its importance as a water source. It is not exploited for timber or other resources, except for some thinning for research or to ensure good forest health. However, although Belgrad forest is officially protected, peripheral areas of forest are being replaced by illegal housing developments due to the rapid migration into the city and outward 'sprawl'. Nearly 6000ha of forest have been destroyed over the last 10 years in 872 incidents, some caused by intentional fires. Without a concerted effort to effectively protect the forest, much more is likely to be lost in the coming years. Recently, the Turkish government proposed an amnesty for settlers that have illegally occupied forest land. This could lead to further destruction of forest in the hope of a similar amnesty in the future. A forest that has protected a city's water resources for several thousand years is now under serious threat. Lack of awareness of the role of natural ecosystems providing vital services such as water is repeated world over.

Nigel Dudley

The Argument

The value

Water is, in theory, a quintessentially renewable resource. Water covers most of the world's surface and over much of the world it falls unbidden from the skies as rain or snow. Yet because of the carelessness and profligacy with which water resources have been used, the speed of human population growth and the increasing demands for water, the provision of adequate, safe supplies is now a major source of concern, expense, and international and intranational tension.

The poorest members of society, unable to afford safe water, suffer the greatest impacts. One in five people in the developing world live without a reliable water supply. Lack of clean water has dire short- and long-term health impacts including increased infant mortality, waterborne diseases, poor sanitation and impaired ability to work. This reduces industrial productivity and adds pressure on to health services.

As urbanization continues, these problems are likely to become more intense – a fact reflected in the UN Millennium Development Goal (2000) to: 'reduce by half, by 2015, the proportion of people without sustainable access to safe drinking water'. In order to meet this target in urban areas, more than 1 billion additional people in cities will need access to both water supply and sanitation over the next 15 years (UNESCO, 2003). However, current estimates suggest that rather than increased access to clean water, the impacts of climate change will mean an additional 1.8 billion people could be living in a water scarce environment by 2080 (UNDP, 2007).

Municipal authorities have a variety of ways of supplying drinking water, depending on where they are located, the resources available, social and political issues, and the willingness of the population to conserve water. The vast majority of cities get their drinking water by collecting or diverting existing freshwater sources, with minor amounts being extracted directly from rainwater or from the seas. All water-supply strategies contain their own challenges. Some countries are facing genuine shortages although in many others the problems relate more to access, transport and purity: for instance about 50 developing countries, mainly in Africa, still use less than 1 per cent of their available freshwater resources (Gujja and Perrin, 1999), but have serious problems in providing clean water. Some nations are finding it difficult to pay for or to organize the infrastructure needed to purify water and supply it to wells or individual households. Pollution creates major problems, with pollutants coming mainly from agriculture, sewage, industry and resource activities such as mining.

Until recently, the main focus of efforts to improve urban water sanitation and supply have focused on better distribution systems, treatment plants and sewage disposal. Although these issues remain of major importance, there is also increasing interest in the opportunities for purifying urban water through management of natural resources.

The benefit

Forested watersheds offer higher quality water than watersheds under alternative land uses, because all other land uses have a greater human footprint: more intensive management, less complete cover (hence more soil erosion and sediment) and more application of pollutants (such as pesticides, fertilizer or toxic waste). These quality impairers may enter the headwaters or the lower stretches of the watershed. Protected forest watersheds (no logging, agriculture or mining) are unquestionably the best guardians of water quality. While there are some contaminants that forests are less able to control – the parasite *Giardia*, for example – in most cases presence of forests will substantially reduce the need for treatment. The benefits that forests provide have been recognized for many years by companies that depend on high quality water; for example, the mineral water company Perrier-Vittel pays to restore forests in the catchment where it collects water in France (Johnson et al., 2002). Forested watersheds also have more water absorbing capacity than most other uses, reducing flood risk with their attendant sediment loads and inundation damage.

Where municipalities have protected forests for their water resources, quality issues have generally been the primary motivation. In Tokyo, for example, the Metropolitan Government Bureau of Waterworks manages the forest in the upper reaches of the Tama River to increase the capacity to recharge water resources, to prevent reservoir sedimentation, to increase the forest's water purification capacity and to conserve the natural environment. In Sydney, Australia, the Catchment Authority manages about one-quarter of the catchment as a buffer zone to stop nutrients and other substances that could affect the quality of water from entering storage areas (Dudley and Stolton, 2003). It is usually cheaper to prevent water from becoming polluted than to clean it up afterwards.

The situation with regard to the flow of water from catchments is more complex. Despite years of catchment experiments, the precise interactions between different tree species and ages, different soil types and management regimes are still often poorly understood, making accurate predictions difficult. In contrast with popular assumptions, many studies suggest that in both very humid and very dry forests transpiration/evaporation loss is likely to be greater from forests than from land covered with other types of vegetation; thus, less total water flows from forested catchments than, for example, from grassland or crops (Hamilton, 1983; Bruinjzeel, 1990). The evidence seems to suggest, however, that mountain cloud forests can capture fog or horizontal wind-driven precipitation, beyond what falls as vertical rain, and add it to the water budget (Hamilton et al., 1994). Conserved cloud forests are prime watershed cover. Some older natural forests (such as old Eucalyptus forests) can increase net water flow over younger forest, and some cities factor management of these forests into plans for maintaining adequate water supplies. In Melbourne, Australia, for example, where 90 per cent of the city's water supply comes from uninhabited mountainous areas, about 49 per cent of which are within National Parks, studies of rainfall and runoff data have concluded that the amount of water yield from forested catchments is related to forest age. It was found that forest disturbance can reduce the mean annual runoff by up to 50 per cent compared to that of a mature forest and can take as long as 150 years to recover fully (Dudley and Stolton, 2003). This is because evapotranspiration from older forests is lower per unit area than from younger forests.

Current Contribution of Protected Areas

Protected areas are an effective tool to maintain secure water supplies from forests. Historically, people have settled in areas rich with natural resources and today most of the world's population lives downstream of forested watersheds (Reid, 2001). The multiple benefits of these watersheds can be great; for example, in the Dominican Republic the Madre de las Aguas (the 'Mother of the Waters') Conservation Area, consists of five separate protected areas, which shelter the headwaters of 17 rivers that provide energy, irrigation and drinking water for over 50 per cent of the population (Dudley and Stolton, 2003).

In some parts of the world the need to safeguard these important functions of forests has long been recognized. The Celaque Mountain in Honduras is called 'Box of Water' in the Lencan language and has been worshipped for millennia as a God Mountain that supplies life-giving water. The mountain is the source of nine major rivers, which feed clean water to nearby cities and communities (Hamilton, 2008). In many countries population increases in the 19th and 20th centuries, with consequent colonization farther upslope, led to action to protect and/or manage water supplies. Since the foundation of the Munich waterworks in Germany, in around 1900, forest management and the issuing of forestry-licences has been focused on ensuring good water quality. Today, an area of 2900ha is managed primarily to maintain water quality (Dudley and Stolton, 2003).

Many important national parks and other wildlife reserves provide drinking water to towns and cities. In some cases the area was originally protected for scenic or wildlife values and its watershed benefits were only recognized later, as with the iconic Yosemite National Park in California which helps to supply high quality water to San Francisco. Sometimes the water values have been recognized from the beginning and watershed protection has been the major reason for protecting a forest. The cloud forests of La Tigra National Park (23,871ha) in Honduras provide more than 40 per cent of the annual water supply to the 850,000 people of the capital city, Tegucigalpa (Hamilton, 2008), and this was a major incentive for forest protection. The Angeles National Forest (Category VI, 265,354ha) in the US is one of 18 national forests in the Pacific Southwest Region created specifically to safeguard and preserve water supplies.

For some other cities, watershed protection has bought critical time for biodiversity by protecting remnant natural areas that would otherwise have disappeared and it is only later that the conservation values have been appreciated. This is the case in Singapore where the Bukit Timah National Park was initially protected to maintain urban water supplies but is now recognized as an important haven for wildlife and the only remaining area of natural forest on Singapore Island. In a few cases, the watershed values of protected areas still remain largely unrecognized and the downstream benefits are largely accidental (Dudley and Stolton, 2003).

A survey carried out for WWF and the World Bank in 2003 found that around a third (33 out of 105) of the world's largest cities obtain a significant proportion of their drinking water directly from protected areas (Dudley and Stolton, 2003). The cities were identified by population numbers, with 25 cities from the Americas, Africa, Asia and Europe and 5 from Australia. At least 5 other of the cities studied obtained water from sources that originate in distant watersheds that also include protected areas; and at least 8 more obtain water from forests that are managed in a way that gives priority to their functions in providing water. On the other hand, several of the top 100 cities are suffering problems with water supply because of degradation or pollution in watersheds, or draw water from forests that are being considered for protection because of their values to water supply. Far from being relegated to a few isolated examples, protecting forests to protect water is apparently already a major environmental service, as illustrated by the list of examples below:

- Mumbai, India: Sanjay Ghandi National Park;
- Jakarta, Indonesia: Gunung Gede Pangrango and Gunung Halimun;
- Karachi, Pakistan: at least six separate protected areas;
- Tokyo, Japan: Nikko National Park and Chichibu-Tama National Park;
- Singapore: Bukit Timah and the Central Catchment Area;
- New York, US: Catskill State Park;
- Bogotá, Colombia: Chingaza National Park;
- Rio de Janeiro, Brazil: 5 protected areas near the city and 15 further away protecting the catchment;
- Los Angeles, US: Angeles National Forest;
- Cali, Colombia: Farallones de Cali National Park;
- Brasília, Brazil: Brasilia National Park;
- Santo Domingo, Dominican Republic: at least six protected areas;
- Medellín, Colombia: Alto de San Miguel Recreational Park and Wildlife Refuge;
- Caracas, Venezuela: three national parks (see Case Study 3.1);
- Maracaibo, Venezuela: Perijá National Park;
- São Paulo, Brazil: at least six protected areas
- Salvador, Brazil: Lago de Pedra do Cavalo and Joanes/Ipitinga Environmental Protection Areas;
- Belo Horizonte, Brazil: eight separate protected areas;
- Madrid, Spain: Peñalara Natural Park and Cuenca Alta del Manzanares Regional Park;
- Vienna, Austria: Donau-Auen National Park;
- Barcelona, Spain: Sierra del Cadí-Moixeró and Paraje Natural de Pedraforca;
- Sofija, Bulgaria: Rila and Vitosha National Parks and a biosphere reserve;
- Ibadan, Nigeria: Olokemeji and Gambari Forest Reserves;
- Abidjan, Côte d'Ivoire: Banco National Park;
- Cape Town, South Africa: Cape Peninsula National Park and Hottentots Holland Nature Reserve;
- Nairobi, Kenya: Aberdares National Park;
- Dar es Salaam, United Republic of Tanzania: at least four protected areas;
- Durban, South Africa: Ukhlahlamba-Drakensberg Park;
- Harare, Zimbabwe: at least three protected areas;
- Johannesburg, South Africa: Maluti/Drakensberg Transfrontier Park and Ukhlahlamba-Drakensberg Park;
- Sydney, Australia: four protected areas;
- Melbourne, Australia: Kinglake, Yarra Ranges and Baw Baw National Parks;
- Perth, Australia: Yanchep National Park.

Figure 3.1 *Cayambe-Coca Nature Reserve Cloud Forest, Ecuador*

Source: © WWF-Canon/Kevin Schafer

Future Needs:
Recognizing the Role of Protected Areas

To be effective in maintaining water supply, protected areas also need to be well-managed; illegal degradation can undermine the potential benefits. From 2000 to 2005 the UN Food and Agriculture Organization estimated that forests were lost at a net rate of 7.3 million ha/year, almost entirely in the tropics (Perlis, 2009). In addition, the quality of much of the remaining forest is declining. The need for restoration is therefore of growing importance, including for ecosystem services. In Brazil the forests on the Tijuca Massif National Park, near Rio de Janeiro, were reforested with native species to restore water supplies (Da Cunha et al., 2001). However, the real value of watersheds is often underestimated or unrecognized and in theses cases restoration and protection initiatives often do not take place.

One way to ensure more active protection of water quality and quantity through forest protection is to raise awareness about the benefits of conservation (Emerton, 2005). Communities maintaining forests on their land are supplying services in terms of drinking water to other communities, sometimes a long way away, often without any recognition or compensation for benefits foregone. Although setting aside land for forest protection or restoration might be good for water, it could have severe implications for the lives of people who live there and who have their own ideas about what it should be used for. For example, Mount Elgon National Park in Uganda is an important source of drinking water and water services were a major incentive for protection. However, this caused conflict with local people who had used the forests for generations and abruptly found themselves excluded, creating problems that required considerable efforts to address (Scott, 1998). The Manupali catchment in the Philippines provides another example of potential conflict. The catchment is an upland area in the Mount Kitanglad Natural Park (Category II, 29,617ha) in Mindanao. Property rights are insecure. In the upper watershed there are overlapping claims between the Forest Department, the ancestral communities and the migrant farm communities. The boundaries of the municipalities surrounding the protected area also overlap with the public state forests. Thus, three types of management plans must be reconciled for land conflicts to be resolved (Swallow et al., 2001).

In many cases the economic case for managing ecosystem services can provide the impetus for sustainable forest management, forest protection and equitable benefit-sharing. Water regulation and supply has been estimated to be globally worth US$2.3 trillion (Costanza et al., 1997). At the national level, for example, a study calculated that the presence of forest on Mount Kenya saved Kenya's economy more than US$20 million by protecting the catchment for two of the country's main river systems, the Tana and the Ewaso Ngiro (Emerton, 2001). More systematic valuations of water supply are needed from protected areas to ensure their value is truly appreciated.

The issue for policy-makers is how to translate these values to help support particular types of land management and provide compensation to communities for the services that forests generate for others living further away. It is possible to collect user fees from people and companies benefiting from drinking water to help pay for the catchment benefits provided by protected area management. Payment for water services can also be one important way of helping negotiations with people living in or using watersheds to develop land-use mosaics that are conducive to maintaining high quality drinking-water supplies. Residents of the city of New York, for example, voted to support a package of incentives for protection and good management in the catchments upstream rather than invest in a new treatment plant (EPA, 1999). About 80 per cent of Quito's 1.5 million population receive drinking water from two protected areas; Antisana (120,000ha) and Cayambe-Coca Ecological Reserve (403,103ha). To control threats to the reserves, the government is working with a local NGO through the Antisana Fund, to protect the watersheds including stricter enforcement of protection to the upper watersheds and measures to improve or protect hydrological functions, protect waterholes, prevent erosion and stabilize banks and slopes (Troya and Curtis, 1998). The Nature Conservancy (TNC), which assisted in setting up this arrangement, is currently working on a similar scheme for Bogotá in Colombia (TNC personal communication, 2009). Such payment for environmental services (PES) schemes are getting an increasingly high profile but appear to work only if certain circumstances apply – particularly the presence of an identifiable source of money (such as a company) and a way of distributing benefits fairly among individuals (Pagiola et al., 2002).

Figure 3.2 *Monitoring water quality in Lake Nakuru National Park, Kenya*
Source: © Meg Gawler/WWF-Canon

Protected area managers, water companies and indeed general water users all need information about what particular forests can and cannot supply in terms of water needs and how such forests should be protected or managed to optimize the benefits. Many people have no idea where their tap-water comes from. Yet where there has been a debate and an information campaign – as in New York City and in Melbourne – support for catchment management is high. Better information about links between forests, protected areas and water supply could help to build a constituency for good watershed management.

Management Options

Forests offer a range of options for water provision, depending on their type, location and age, and on what users need. Cities may choose a number of different forest management options, including protection, sustainable management and, where necessary, restoration.

Greater understanding of ecosystem services and the provision of clear guidance to land and water managers is urgently required. Today those responsible for water supply and forest management are faced with a number of questions which need to be answered before any decisions are made about forests managed for water. These include.

- What are the most pressing needs regarding water supply? Are the pressures on water supply primarily driven by the need to get enough water, or a constant supply of water, or is the priority more to do with water quality?
- How is vegetation in the catchment likely to affect water quality and flow? This needs specialist analysis, although some general points can be made. For example, cloud forests are likely to increase water, old natural forests may also increase flow, compared with young forests and plantations which are likely to decrease flow. Presence of any type of forest is likely to increase quality. Individual cases need to be assessed, depending on soil, climate, forest types and age, and management regime.
- How about the soils? In shallow soils the role of vegetation is less than on deep soils where roots can exploit to greater depth. Soils that are shallow to bedrock produce 'flashy' flows and can neither accommodate nor store much precipitation. Slip-prone soil areas are aided by tree-cover to promote stability.
- What is the land use? Current status is important, but so are recent changes and likely future trends.

Answering these questions will help to determine what natural vegetation (and perhaps other land uses) in the catchment offers in terms of water supply and whether future changes are likely to increase benefits or create problems. With this information, more strategic analysis can help to plan optimum management interventions, answering questions like:

- What other demands are there on land in the catchment and how much might be available for water management? Are other pressures on land likely to improve or degrade water? How much land is available, partially or completely, for water management? Can current land uses be improved from the perspective of the water from the catchment? What impacts would these changes have for local people and what are their needs and wishes? Can catchment areas also be used for other land uses, such as tourism or recreation? In their natural state, catchments can be havens for biodiversity and its conservation, and for wilderness experiences.
- What are realistic management options? Present and future management options for land use, especially the establishment and maintenance of protected areas and forest restoration, should be analysed.

The analysis should tell whether the presence of forests can help supply the water quality and quantity required from the catchment and provide the information needed to make informed choices about a landscape mosaic that will fulfil both water needs and other needs from the watershed. Specific management interventions can then be developed (Dudley and Stolton, 2003).

Conclusions

Protected areas are not a panacea in terms of water supply, but they are clearly an important option to help to secure high quality urban water supplies in many situations. Lack of protection has already been identified as a problem in some cities while in others it seems that better catchment management would help to address urgent problems in water quality and in some cases also of supply. It should also be remembered that protection of forests for their watershed values has important and usually beneficial implications for biodiversity and other values.

Addressing the Millennium Development Goal on safe drinking-water will clearly require a wide range of initiatives. The potential for forest protection and good forest management to contribute the cheapest and purest water deserves far greater attention than it has received until now.

Case Study 3.1:
Protecting Water Supplies to Caracas, Venezuela

José Courrau

Caracas was founded in 1567 and quickly became one of the most prosperous Spanish colonial communities in South America. The city, which is located in the central section of the Coastal Mountain Range at 950m above sea-level, became the capital of the Venezuelan Republic in 1829. It has seen rapid, and mainly unplanned, urban growth; in 1997 the estimated population was 1.8 million, and continues to grow at a rate of 2.3 per cent a year. The trend of migration from the rural areas to the city has been difficult to stop. It is estimated that migration will cause more radial growth around the city, challenge the provision of basic services and create social and health problems. Hidrocapital, the Caracas water company, blames these issues for the growing pressures on the city's water resources (Hidrocapital, 2002).

Water supply

In 1600, the city's 2,000 inhabitants received water from a distribution system of clay pipes. This system was supplemented in 1675 by Franciscan priests who built a private aqueduct for the exclusive use of convents, monasteries and churches. These two water systems remained the main methods of water distribution for the next 200 years. The first officially managed aqueduct in Caracas was opened in 1874. This system consisted of a 46km canal connected to the Macarao River. Water was stored in a reservoir at El Calvario hill and from there distributed to central Caracas. The aqueduct provided 400 litres of water per second for Caracas, a record for the period.

Figure 3.3 *The city of Caracas continues to spread into the hillsides to accommodate its growing population*

Source: © Olga Sheean/WWF-Canon

For 50 years the aqueduct solved the water needs of the city. As the population increased only two aspects of the distribution system were improved: the 46km ground canal became a concrete canal and the reservoir at El Calvario was extended. As early as 1967 experts were predicting an exponential population growth in the capital with subsequent impacts on the demand for water (Azpurua et al., 1967).

In response the city authorities started to protect the sources of the major rivers which supplied water. Today the city receives water from several sources including three national parks: the Guatopo, the Macarao and the Avila National Parks.

The first area to be protected in 1926 was the Macarao National Forest. Located in the southeast of the city the area is part of the Coastal Mountain Range and includes the Macarao, San Pedro and Jarillo rivers. The 15,000ha area gained national park status in 1973. The park contains semi-deciduous forests, evergreen forests and coastal cloud forests. There are at least six species of birds with restricted distribution, such as the blue-chested hummingbird (*Sternoclyta cyanopectus*); other notable species include the puma (*Puma concolor*), howler monkey (*Alouatta seniculus*), three-toed sloth (*Bradypus variegatus*), deer (*Mazama americana*), peccary (Tayassu sp.), paují (Pauxi sp.), guacharaca (*Ortalis ruficauda*) and querrequerre (*Cyanocorax yncas*). The park contains the ruins of the first Caracas aqueduct.

The 122,464ha Guatopo National Park was declared in 1958. The water gener-ated in the park is collected in the Lagartijo, La Pereza, Taguacita, Cuira and Taguaza dams. The park consists of deciduous and evergreen forests. Palms include the small endemic palm *Asterogyne spicata*. Important animal species include the three-toed sloth, anteater (*Tamandua tetradactyla*) and endangered Giant armadillo (*Priodontes maximus*). Various carnivores have been reported, including the jaguar (*Panthera onca*) and honey bear (*Potos flavus*).

An area of 66,192ha was declared as El Ávila National Park in 1958 and extended to 85,192ha in 1974. It is located in the north-central part of Venezuela within the Coastal Mountain Range. The park includes several springs (Tocomé, Chacalito, Catuche, etc.) that carry water to the Tuy River. The main ecosystems protected in the park are evergreen forests, cloud forests and savannas (Dudley and Stolton, 2003).

The Guarico River provides a large amount of water for Caracas. It is protected under a less restrictive management category used in Venezuela named ABRAE (Area Under Regime of Special Administration), which is similar to a protective zone used for basin conservation. In addition to the water flowing from forests (as rivers) Caracas has a significant reservoir of underground water (Cañizalez et al., 2006).

Water management

Due to the serious financial limitations faced by the protected areas in Venezuela, in 1999 the agency responsible for protected area management, INPARQUES, started to consider charging the water companies for the direct services they obtain from the country's parks. However, this initiative has not yet been further developed (Cañizalez et al., 2006).

Today the city consumes an average of 17,000 litres of water per second and it is estimated that the average resident uses 500 litres of water per day. As the population grows, water availability is becoming a major concern. Over the last three years a series of 'conservationist committees' have been established by communities in the upper region of the watershed of the Guarico River, where the rivers that feed the Camatagua catchment are sourced. The flow from Camatagua catchment has been declining leading to water-rationing in some sectors of the capital. The main purpose of these committees is to control the use of the forest, to plant trees and to educate local people. However, the success of these committees has not been assessed or publicized. Recently, the government of Venezuela has confirmed the construction of a new catchment named Tuy IV which will collect water from the Cuira River.

References

Azpurua, Q., Pablo, P. and Rovati, G. (1967) 'El problema del agua en la Caracas del futuro: con especial referencia al abastecimiento de agua de los Valles del Tuy Medio', *Revista de Obras Públicas*, vol 115, no I, pp1267–87.

Bruinjzeel, L. A. (1990) *Hydrology of Tropical Moist Forests and Effects of Conversion: A State of Knowledge Review*, UNESCO, Paris, and Vrije Universiteit, Amsterdam.

Cañizalez, A., Peñuela, S., Díaz Martín, D., Elisa Febres, M., Caldera, O., Valderrama, O. and Mujica, E. (2006) *Gestión Integrada de los Recursos Hídricos en Venezuela: Una Visión del Sector, Basada en la Opinión de Expertos, para el IV Foro Mundial del Agua a Realizarse en México del 16 al 22 de Marzo de 2006*, Vitalis, Caracas.

Costanza, R., d'Arge, R., de Groot, R., Farberk, S., Grasso, M., Hannon, B., Limburg, K., Shahid Naeem, I., O'Neill, R., Paruelo, J., Raskin, R., Sutton, P. and van den Belt, M. (1997) 'The value of the world's ecosystem services and natural capital', *Nature*, vol 387, pp253–60.

Da Cunha, P., Menzes, E. and Teixeira Mendes, L. O. (2001) 'The mission of protected areas in Brazil', *Parks*, vol 11, no 3.

Dudley, N. and Stolton, S. (2003) *Running Pure: The Importance of Forest Protected Areas to Drinking Water*, WWF, Gland

Emerton, L. (2001) 'Why forest values are important to East Africa', *ACTS Innovation*, vol 8, no 2, pp1–5.

Emerton, L. (ed.) (2005) *Values and Rewards: Counting and Capturing Ecosystem Water Services for Sustainable Development*, IUCN Water, Nature and Economics Technical Paper no 1, IUCN, Gland.

EPA (1999) *Protecting Sources of Drinking Water Selected Case Studies in Watershed Management*, EPA 816-R-98-019, United States Environmental Protection Agency, Office of Water, Washington, DC.

Gujja, B. and Perrin, M. (1999) *A Place for Dames in the 21st Century?* WWF International, Gland.

Hamilton, L. S. (2008) *Forests and Water*, FAO Forestry Paper 155, FAO, Rome.

Hamilton, L. S. with King, P. N. (1983) *Tropical Forested Watersheds: Hydrologic and Soils Response to Major Uses or Conversions*, Westview Press, Boulder, CO

Hamilton, L. S., Juvik, J. O. and Scatena, F. N. (1994) *Tropical Montane Cloud Forests*, Ecological Studies Series, vol 110, Springer-Verlag, New York, Berlin, London, Paris and Tokyo.

Hidrocapital (2002) 'El laberinto del agua', *Vertientes: La Revista de Hidrocapital*, vol 2, no 9.

Johnson, N., White, A. and Perrot-Maître, D. (2002) *Developing Markets for Water Services from Forests: Issues and Lessons for Innovators*, Forest Trends, Washington, DC.

Nature Conservancy (2009) Personal communication with William Ginn, Chief Conservation Officer, Arlington, VA.

Pagiola, S., Bishop, J. and Landell-Mills, N. (eds) (2002) *Selling Forest Environmental Services: Market-based Mechanisms for Conservation and Development*, Earthscan, London.

Perlis, A. (2009) *State of the World's Forests 2009*, FAO, Rome.

Reid, W. V. (2001) 'Capturing the value of ecosystem services to protect biodiversity', in G. Chichilenisky, G. C. Daily, P. Ehrlich, G. Heal and J. S. Miller (eds) *Managing Human-dominated Ecosystems*, Monographs in Systematic Botany 84, Missouri Botanical Garden Press, St Louis, MI.

Scott, P. (1998) *From Conflict to Collaboration: People and Forests at Mount Elgon, Uganda*, IUCN, World Conservation Union, Nairobi.

Swallow, B. M., Garrity, D. P. and van Noordwijk, M. (2001) 'The effects of scales, flows and filters on property rights and collective action in watershed management', CAPRi Working Paper no 16, CGIAR System-wide Programme on Collective Action and Property Rights, International Food Policy Research Institute, Washington, DC.

Troya, R. and Curtis, R. (1998) *Water: Together We Can Care for It! Case Study of a Watershed Conservation Fund for Quito, Ecuador*, Nature Conservancy, Arlington, VA.

UNDP (2007) *Human Development Report 2007–2008*, UNDP, New York, NY.

UNESCO (2003) *Facts and Figures – Water and Cities*, www.wateryear2003.org/en/ev.php-URL_ID=5970&URL_DO=DO_TOPIC&URL_SECTION=201.html, accessed 9 August 2009.

4

Food Stores:
Protected Areas Conserving Crop Wild Relatives and Securing Future Food Stocks

Nigel Maxted, Shelagh Kell, Brian Ford-Lloyd and Sue Stolton

Since the time of the earliest botanical exploration, botanists have been drawn to the Akar fault valley in northwestern Syria. A beautiful horseshoe-shaped valley capping the northernmost end of Mount Lebanon, it is not only home to one of the most complete crusader castles left today, but is also a refugium for botanic diversity. I first visited the valley as a research student in 1986 in an attempt to rediscover the faba bean relative Vicia hyaeniscyamus, *thought by some to be synonymous with a related species from Palestine. Arriving at the site, the species was immediately located and the valley has been special for me ever since. In fact, the valley justifiably should be special to all humankind because recent analysis has shown that it contains the highest concentration of priority temperate crop wild relatives (CWR) anywhere in the world (Maxted and Kell, 2009a). However, worryingly, the area is being rapidly urbanized; therefore, protection of this unique site and its resources should be a global priority.*

Nigel Maxted

The Argument

The value

It has been estimated that there are approximately 284,000 species of flowering plants (Groombridge and Jenkins, 2002). Among many other benefits, plants provide an enormous reservoir of genetic diversity that is the foundation of agriculture and provides its continued support.

A wide range of genetic variation is needed within species to help them adapt to changing environmental conditions and to new pests and diseases. The plants we use as crops – either directly as food or as fodder for animals – draw on two sources for their resilience and adaptability. Firstly, on the broad genetic variation that exists in

---

Box 4.1 *Crop genetic diversity definitions*

Landraces: a dynamic population(s) of a cultivated plant that has historical origin, distinct identity and lacks formal crop improvement, as well as often being genetically diverse, locally adapted and associated with traditional farming systems and cultural values (Camacho Villa et al., 2005).

Crop Wild Relative: a wild plant taxon that has an indirect use derived from its relatively close genetic relationship to a crop; this relationship is defined in terms of the CWR belonging to gene pools 1 or 2, or taxon groups 1 to 4 of the crop (Maxted et al., 2006).

N.B. One method to establish the degree of crop relatedness is to apply the Gene Pool concept (Harlan and de Wet, 1971) – close relatives being found in the primary gene pool (GP1), more remote ones in the secondary gene pool (GP2), and very remote ones in the tertiary gene pool (GP3), and the three gene pools being established by the relative ease of hybridization with the crop. However, for the majority of crop complexes, particularly those in the tropics, the relative ease of hybridization between the crop and related wild species is unknown. So, as a pragmatic solution the taxonomic classification of the crop and other taxa in the same genus may be used (Maxted et al., 2006), such that: Taxon Group 1a – crop; Taxon Group 1b – same species as crop; Taxon Group 2 – same series or section as crop; Taxon Group 3 – same subgenus as crop; Taxon Group 4 – same genus; and Taxon Group 5 – same tribe but different genus to crop.

---

traditional varieties of crops themselves, developed over millennia of farmer experimentation (known as landraces); and secondly, genetic material from their wild relatives (or CWR). Both landraces and CWR serve as the world's repositories of crop genetic diversity and represent a vital source of genes for future food security. In light of the growing concern over the predicted impacts of both climate change and a massively growing world population on biodiversity and food security, taking action to conserve crop genetic diversity is no longer an option – it is a priority if humankind is to survive.

CWR are species closely related to crops (including crop progenitors) and are defined by their potential to contribute beneficial traits to crops, such as pest or disease resistance, yield improvement or stability (Maxted et al., 2006). However, like other wild plant species they are exposed to a growing threat of extinction and loss of genetic diversity. There are very few estimates of the loss of genetic diversity but Maxted et al. (1997d) estimated that between initial ratification of the CBD in 1993 and the 2010 Biodiversity Target date 25 to 35 per cent of plant genetic diversity will have been lost.

In the face of these threats, it is perhaps surprising that the diversity of CWR has not already been systematically conserved. Darwin observed, 'it appears strange to me that so many of our cultivated plants should still be unknown or only doubtfully known in the wild state' (Darwin, 1868). Instead, CWR have tended to fall through

---

Box 4.2 *Coffee conundrum*

Brazil's 'typica' coffee originates from the progeny of one tree, introduced from East Africa via the Caribbean. Such uniformity, and the susceptibility to disease which goes with it, means that landraces and CWR are of great importance as a source of wider genetic variation and potential crop traits. In the 1970s Latin American coffee plantations were under threat from rust disease. The plantations were saved because of information gained from a rust-resistant strain of coffee found in Ethiopia. However, despite their continuing importance as a genetic resource, the montane forests of Ethiopia and the *Coffea* species which grow in the forest understorey are under serious threat: about four-fifths have already been destroyed (Lewington, 1990).

---

the net; historically, they have not been a priority for agricultural conservationists as they are wild plant species, while at the same time, they have not been a priority for ecosystem conservationists as they are associated with agriculture. Yet they offer a practical example of how best to combine biodiversity conservation with the promotion of food security and poverty reduction – particularly necessary in areas such as South Asia and southern Africa where there is insufficient crop adaptation to meet the challenges of climate change and there is greatest food insecurity and poverty (Lobell et al., 2008).

Similarly, landraces have been seen as something for breeders to improve and standardize, as opposed to plants being celebrated and conserved for their historical, cultural and geographical qualities.

The benefit

It has been argued that the protected area and agrobiodiversity communities too often work in isolation (Maxted et al., 1997a); CWR conservation in protected areas has the benefit of directly linking ecosystem services and agrobiodiversity conservation to the benefit of both communities. Currently, there is only a handful of established protected areas where the genetic diversity of crops is actively conserved. However, in recent years there has been an increasing interest in CWR conservation and use following recognition of the following:

- CWR are increasingly threatened by the loss, degradation and fragmentation of their natural habitats (FAO, 1996 and 1998).
- They are often associated with disturbed habitats which are particularly threatened by climate change and are not being adequately conserved (Jain, 1975; Maxted et al. 1997c).
- Conservation of CWR species in existing protected areas offers an additional ecosystem service, thus increasing their overall value (Stolton et al., 2008).

- CWR offer the necessary, novel genetic diversity that can enhance crop productivity or commodity improvement, promote disease and pest resistance, and increase tolerance of adverse or marginal environments.
- Conventional and biotechnological breeding techniques have improved dramatically in recent years enabling more precise targeting of desirable traits, relatively easy transfer to the crop and fewer problems with the transfer of unwanted characteristics (Hajjar and Hodgkin, 2007).

These values are not simply theoretical. Pimentel et al. (1997) estimated that the introduction of new genes from wild relatives contributes approximately $20 billion towards increased crop yields per year in the US and US$115 billion worldwide, and a recent review of CWR use in crop improvement cited 291 articles reporting the identification and transfer of useful traits from 185 CWR taxa into 29 crop species (Maxted and Kell, 2009a). The review found that the degree to which breeders had used CWR diversity varies markedly between crops (notably, rice and wheat are the crops in which CWR have been most widely used), and the number of publications detailing the use of CWR in breeding has increased gradually over time – presumably as a result of technological developments for trait transfer (Figure 4.1).

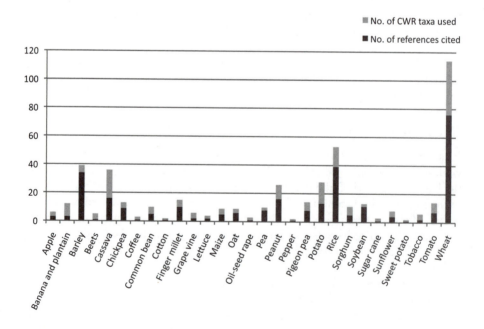

Figure 4.1 *The number of references reporting the identification and transfer of useful traits from 185 CWR taxa to 29 crop species, showing the number of CWR taxa used in each crop*
Source: Maxted and Kell, 2009b

The most widespread CWR use is in the development of disease and pest resistance (Maxted and Kell, 2009a). For example, CWR of potatoes (*Solanum* spp.) have been used to improve cultivated varieties since the 1900s, when genes from the Mexican *S. demissum* were used to breed resistance against the fungus that causes potato blight (Hijmans et al., 2000). During the 1970s, grassy-stunt virus severely reduced rice yields across Asia; after 4 years of research, during which over 17,000 cultivated and wild rice samples were screened, disease resistance was found in one wild population of *Oryza nivara* growing in Uttar Pradesh, India. Resistant rice hybrids containing the wild Indian gene are now grown across Asia (Shand, 1993).

Genes from wild relatives can also improve crop performance. For example, an endemic tomato (*Lycopersicon cheesmanii*) found in the Galápagos Islands has contributed significantly to commercial tomato cultivation by improving the crop's survival during long-distance transport. Yet a recent survey of tomato populations in the Galápagos found several populations of *L. cheesmanii* reported 30–50 years earlier had disappeared, mostly as a consequence of human activity, highlighting the need for active conservation (Nuez et al., 2004).

Current Contribution of Protected Areas

The need for *in situ* conservation

The development and endorsement of the CBD in 1992, the UN Food and Agriculture Organization (FAO) Global Plan of Action for Plant Genetic Resources in 1996 (FAO, 1996) and the subsequent International Treaty on Plant Genetic Resources for Food and Agriculture in 2001(FAO, 2001), as well as the CBD's Global Strategy for Plant Conservation (CBD, 2002), helped move the conservation of crop genetic diversity into the mainstream of international and national conservation concerns, particularly by refocusing activities on to *in situ* conservation (Maxted et al., 1997a; Meilleur and Hodgkin, 2004).

However, the number of CWR species of interest to the food and agriculture community may be much larger than previously recognized and therefore presents a daunting challenge to conservationists. For example, using a broad definition of a crop (i.e. any cultivated plant taxon) and CWR (i.e. any taxon within the same genus as a crop), Kell et al. (2008) found that around 83 per cent of Euro-Mediterranean flora comprises crop and CWR species. Using the same definition, Maxted and Kell (2009a) estimated that there are about 49,700 crop and CWR species globally. If only 77 major food crops are included then there are around 10,700 CWR of the most direct value for global food security. From the point of view of prioritizing species for conservation, this number can be further reduced to around 700 species that are the closest wild relatives of our major and minor food crops and thus of very high priority for worldwide food security (Maxted and Kell, 2009a).

Although historically the focus of CWR conservation has been *ex situ* in seed banks, analysis of European *ex situ* collections revealed that CWR taxa account for only 5.6 per cent of total germplasm holdings and further that these accessions represent 1095 CWR species, which is only 6 per cent of the 17,495 CWR species found in Europe (O'Regan, 2007). As well as this under-representation, the *ex situ* technique freezes adaptive evolutionary development, especially that which is related to pest and disease resistance (Maxted et al., 1997b). Practically, the conservation of the full range of the genetic diversity within all CWR species is not possible *ex situ*; therefore, *in situ* conservation is critical to secure CWR diversity (along with *ex situ* conservation as a back-up).

The change of emphasis from collecting cultivated material for *ex situ* conservation towards *in situ* conservation of locally adapted landraces and CWR has necessitated the research and development of new conservation methods (Hawkes, 1991). Two distinct approaches to *in situ* conservation have been developed:

1   Genetic Reserves (synonymous terms include genetic reserve management units, gene management zones, gene or genetic sanctuaries, crop reservations) conserving wild species in their native habitats with the objective of: 'management and monitoring of genetic diversity in natural wild populations within defined areas designated for active, long-term conservation' (Maxted et al., 1997c).
2   On-farm conservation which is defined as: 'the sustainable management of genetic diversity of locally developed landraces with associated wild and weedy species or forms by farmers within traditional agriculture, horticulture or agri-silviculture systems' (Maxted et al., 1997c).

Conservation of crop genetic diversity in protected areas

Protected areas provide one obvious tool for the conservation of crop genetic diversity in both genetic reserves and on-farm management systems. Many protected areas already play an important role in conserving socio-economically important plant species; however, in most of these protected areas, active CWR conservation is not being implemented. Further, Maxted and Kell (2009a) found that a high proportion of CWR of important food crops are not found within the boundaries of existing protected areas so, clearly, much more needs to be done to secure our crop genetic diversity *in situ*.

In cases where CWR are already known to occur within protected areas, CWR conservation should be promoted because: these sites already have an associated long-term conservation ethos and are less prone to short-term management changes; it is relatively easy to amend the existing site-management plan to facilitate genetic conservation of CWR species; and creating novel conservation sites particularly for CWR conservation would be avoided along with the cost of acquiring new land for conservation (Iriondo et al., 2008). However, many protected area managers are unaware, or only dimly aware, that the land under their stewardship contains important crop genetic diversity and thus could be important for our continued food security.

In theory, any type of protected area, as defined by the IUCN management categories (see Chapter 1), could be suitable for crop genetic diversity conservation. Examples of protected areas that play a role in conserving crop genetic diversity include the following:

- Strictly protected reserves (often small) set aside and left untouched to protect particular species under threat (category Ia). For example, the 89ha Erebuni State Reserve in Armenia, which was established to protect wild wheat CWR (*Triticum* spp.) (Avagyan, 2008).
- Large ecosystem-scale protected areas maintained to allow CWR to continue to flourish and evolve under natural conditions (category II). For example, the 1,716,295ha Manú National Park in Peru, where a number of commercially important or potentially important fruit tree species such as cocoa (*Theobroma cacao)* and 'sapote' (*Quararibea cordata)* grow in the lowland floodplain forests of the Manú River. It has been suggested that the forests of Manú 'probably include a disproportionate number of the general region's economically important plants, and they are exceptionally important to maintain germplasm for future programmes of genetic improvement' (Davis et al., 1994).
- Small reserves managed to maintain particular species (category IV), for instance through controlled grazing or cutting to retain important grassland habitat, coppicing to maintain woodland ground flora, or sometimes even intervening to restore the habitat of threatened CWR species, for example, the 3850ha Steckby-Lödderitzer Forest Nature Reserve in Germany is important for *in situ* conservation of wild fruit genetic resources and other CWR such as perennial ryegrass *(Lolium perenne)*.

A more deliberate approach may be needed inside protected areas to maintain landraces, along with the many CWR that are wild and weedy species often associated with disturbed ground (and thus well adapted to agricultural conditions).

Figure 4.2 *Relic stand of wild sorghum North Aïr, Niger*

Source: © WWF-Canon/John E. Newby

Figure 4.3 *Potato varieties in Peru*

Conservation of landraces is likely to be commonest in categories V and VI. One of the objectives of category V protected areas is 'To encourage the conservation of agrobiodiversity' (Dudley, 2008). Of course, this does not mean that all crops and livestock are suitable for conservation in protected areas, but that landraces may be a fitting target for management within protected areas, particularly if they are reliant on traditional cultural management systems and if such systems are compatible with 'wild biodiversity' (Phillips and Stolton, 2008). For example, the Garrotxa Volcanic Zone Natural Park in Spain has been actively managing crop genetic diversity since 1990, when surveys identified 53 traditional varieties of 8 species of fruit trees in the park (Bassols Isamat et al., 2008).

Protected areas which are managed as category VI aim to protect natural ecosystems and use natural resources sustainably – when conservation and sustainable use can be mutually beneficial (Dudley, 2008). In terms of crop genetic diversity, this means that they often protect both CWR and landraces. For example, the 1,360,500ha Sungai Kayan Sungai Mentarang National Park in the interior of Borneo is considered to hold a vast range of potentially useful and valuable genetic resources. The reserve contains many fruit wild relatives, and a large number of landraces (including rice varieties and fruit trees) are cultivated by indigenous peoples living in the park (Davis et al., 1994).

This dual approach to CWR and landrace conservation is also undertaken in the 456,000ha Aïr and Ténéré National Nature Reserve in Niger, which is the largest protected area in Africa and includes the volcanic massif of the Aïr Mountains and the surrounding Saharan desert of Ténéré. It contains an outstanding variety of landscapes, plant species and wild animals, including wild relatives of olive, millet, barley, wheat and sorghum, which have been the subject of genetic studies by the French Institute for Scientific Research and Cooperative Development and the International Board for Plant Genetic Resources (now Bioversity International). Conservation of landraces is also carried out in a number of traditional gardens maintained to conserve crop diversity within the nature reserve (Ingram, 1990).

The conservation of crop genetic diversity – in particular, diversity associated with traditional agricultural practices – is often most effectively achieved in areas managed by communities. For some communities the establishment of a protected area can help to protect indigenous or traditional lifestyles and farming practices, including the protection of landraces. However, not all Community Conserved Areas are protected areas and at present there is very little literature to draw on to provide examples of where such areas have been formerly recognized as part of a country's protected area system. For instance, the 'Potato Park' in Peru, where 1200 different traditional varieties of potato that are named, known and managed by local people, has not yet been recognized by the Peruvian National Parks agency, INRENA, as part of Peru's protected area network (Stolton et al., 2006).

To provide a snapshot of the link between crop genetic diversity conservation and protected areas, the University of Birmingham and WWF drew together data from 81 protected areas around the world that have links with crop genetic diversity (see Stolton et al., 2006). This list, although far from complete, provides a good indication of the potential importance of protected areas for conserving crop genetic diversity worldwide. Figure 4.4 shows the locations of these protected areas and a further 24 which have been recorded as containing populations of CWR of food crops of major importance for food security in one or more sub-regions of the world.

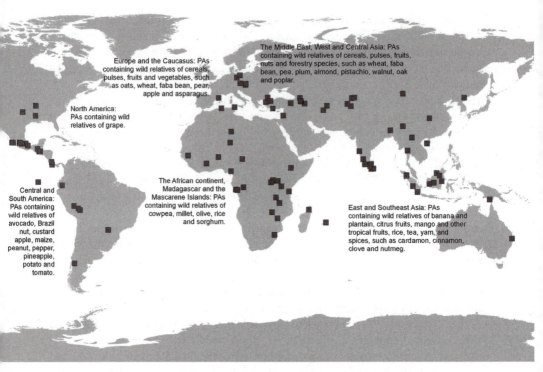

Figure 4.4 *105 global protected areas (PAs) known to contain CWR diversity*
Sources: Stolton et al., 2006; Maxted and Kell, 2009a

Future Needs: A Call for Protection

Despite the many good examples given above, our research has also revealed that there is a serious lack of *in situ* conservation of crop genetic diversity in protected areas on a global scale. Although some protected areas set up to conserve traditional landscapes or for sustainable use could be rich reservoirs of landraces, in practice results of survey work available for these areas still tends to concentrate on threatened or endemic wild species, leaving the breadth of cultivated species unrecorded. There is, therefore, clearly a need for further research in terms of landraces.

In relation to CWR the situation is of even greater concern. CWR are not spread evenly across the world, but are concentrated in relatively small regions often referred to as 'centres of crop diversity'. As a proxy for the assessment of their global conservation status, WWF and TNC compared levels of habitat protection and habitat loss in centres of crop diversity against global averages for terrestrial ecoregions (Stolton et al., 2008). The research identified 34 ecoregions that overlap with these centres of crop diversity and contain habitats particularly important for agrobiodiversity based on ecoregion descriptions and related literature. The extent of habitat protection was calculated as the percentage area of each ecoregion covered by a designated protected area according to the 2004 version of the World Database on Protected

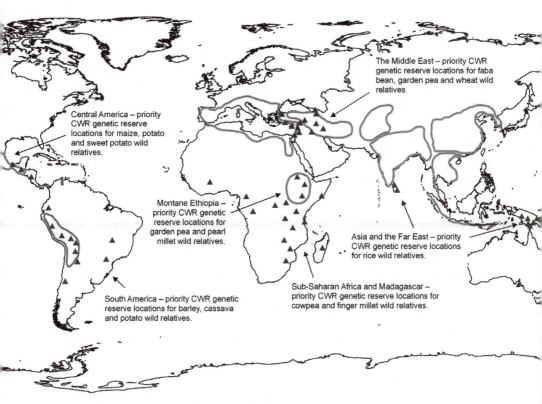

The Middle East – priority CWR genetic reserve locations for faba bean, garden pea and wheat wild relatives.

Central America – priority CWR genetic reserve locations for maize, potato and sweet potato wild relatives.

Montane Ethiopia – priority CWR genetic reserve locations for garden pea and pearl millet wild relatives.

Asia and the Far East – priority CWR genetic reserve locations for rice wild relatives.

South America – priority CWR genetic reserve locations for barley, cassava and potato wild relatives.

Sub-Saharan Africa and Madagascar – priority CWR genetic reserve locations for cowpea and finger millet wild relatives.

Figure 4.5 *Global priority genetic reserve locations for wild relatives of 12 food crops. The 'centres of crop diversity' (indicated by the enclosed lines) are likely to contain further priority sites for other crop gene pools*

Sources: FAO, 2009

Areas, excluding records that were identified as marine protected areas, lacked location data or had non-permanent status. A conservative estimate of habitat loss was derived by calculating the percentage area of each ecoregion classified as 'cultivated and managed areas' or 'artificial surfaces and associated areas' in the Global Land Cover 2000 (European Commission Joint Research Centre, 2000).

In total, 29 (82 per cent) of the 34 ecoregions that include major centres of crop diversity have protection levels of under 10 per cent, and 6 areas (18 per cent) have protection levels of 1 per cent or less. Furthermore, centres of crop diversity have experienced proportionately greater habitat loss. Globally, 21.8 per cent of land area has been converted to human dominated uses, whereas average habitat loss in centres of crop diversity is 35.9 per cent with a maximum of 76.6 per cent. That the world's centres of crop diversity have relatively little habitat protection and considerable habitat loss should be a clarion call for protected area strategies to maximize *in situ* conservation of priority and threatened CWR.

In response to the growing concern over conservation of CWR diversity, the FAO's Commission on Genetic Resources for Food and Agriculture has called for the development of a global network of *in situ* conservation areas for CWR. In a background study to support the Second Report of the State of the World's Plant Genetic Resources for Food and Agriculture and as a basis for updating the Global Plan of Action, Maxted and Kell (2009a) undertook gap analysis of 12 globally important food crop groups (finger millet, barley, sweet potato, cassava, rice, pearl millet, garden pea, potato, wheat, faba bean, cowpea and maize) and identified priority locations for CWR genetic reserve establishment in Africa, the Americas, the Middle East and Asia, and the Far East (see Figure 4.5). The authors found that a high proportion of priority CWR (i.e., the closest wild relatives and those under greatest level of threat) are not currently found within existing protected areas and that there is therefore an urgent need to instigate the establishment of further protected areas as well as to investigate the conservation management status of the CWR populations recorded within existing designated sites. The fact that a CWR occurs within a protected area does not mean that it is adequately conserved and protected area management plans may need to be adapted. Although further crop groups should be added, these priority sites can be used to begin recommendations for the establishment of the global network. While the results of the 12 crop complex analyses (with the exception of the Middle East and Eastern Congo) show few obvious opportunities for conservation of multi-crop gene pools in single genetic reserves, further research is likely to identify additional potential multi-taxon CWR genetic reserves.

The results of both studies highlighted the coincidence between the sites identified as needing greater protection and the centres of crop diversity, which are almost exclusively located in developing countries. These countries may have limited technical and financial resources to take responsibility for maintaining CWR genetic reserves; thus, the sustainable long-term funding of the global network of *in situ* conservation areas for CWR is a challenge that requires international attention.

Management Options for Food Security

The conservation of crop genetic diversity requires a range of responses. Many CWR species are found in pre-climax communities and anthropogenic habitats where human intervention may be essential to the maintenance of healthy populations, while conserving the diversity found in landraces often requires the maintenance of both the cultural and cultivation techniques used by farmers and of the broader social context within which they are farming (Louette and Smale, 1996; Vetelainen et al., 2006). A broad typology of different management approaches for protected areas is given in Table 4.1.

Whereas the presence of landraces in a protected area will be fairly obvious, even if the conservation requirements are not, the situation for CWR is often more complex; CWR have rarely been targeted for conservation management, which means that any protection that is afforded is passive (i.e. without active monitoring and management). Genetic diversity within and between individual CWR populations could thus be eroded and entire populations could even go extinct without

Table 4.1 *A typology of management approaches for protected area crop genetic diversity conservation*

Type of protected area	Management approach
Strictly protected areas and genetic reserves	Usually relatively small areas actively managed to preserve and promote the genetic diversity of CWR species, either as a separate reserve or as a zoned area within a larger protected area
Sustainable resource-use protected areas	Larger areas managed for a variety of values (e.g. wildlife, recreation and ecosystem services) containing important CWR and landraces and subject to particular management attention
Intensively managed areas	Protected areas, frequently small, where management is needed to maintain crop genetic diversity, either through interventions by protected area staff or by maintaining traditional agricultural systems
Extensively managed areas	Protected areas under some form of low intensity, extensive management, such as a Community Conserved Area or an area with landscape designation for protection, where CWR and landraces will be passively maintained

Box 4.3 *CWR – creating a baseline for conservation action*

Despite the steady increase in knowledge over the last 30 years about the location and status of wild species and which species should be categorized as CWR, global, regional and national overviews of the conservation status of CWR remain rare. The first step in ensuring the effective conservation of CWR is an inventory because this provides the critical baseline data for subsequent conservation planning. The first national inventories of CWR were probably those developed in the former Soviet Union (Brezhnev and Korovina, 1981) including Armenia, the latter of which has recently been expanded and extended (Gabrielian and Zohary, 2004). The UK (Maxted et al., 2007), Portugal (Magos Brehm et al., 2008) and Switzerland (Häner and Schierscher, 2009) have also recently completed national CWR inventories and similar efforts are underway in Germany, France and Italy (Meilleur and Hodgkin, 2004). At the regional level, projects mapping CWR are taking place in the Middle East, Bolivia, Guatemala, Paraguay and the US (Meilleur and Hodgkin, 2004), and a catalogue of crops and CWR of Europe and the Mediterranean Basin has been produced, which can be used to extract draft national inventories for the countries covered (Kell et al., 2005).

notice by those managing the protected area. Therefore, one urgent task is to carry out rigorous surveys and inventories of individual protected areas to find out what CWR (and landraces) are present and then to ensure that they are actively managed and monitored.

Guidelines specifically developed for managing crop genetic diversity conservation in protected areas were published by Iriondo et al. in 2008. Based on implementation experiences there are several approaches to establishing CWR genetic reserve networks (Maxted et al., 2007):

Global approach

This involves as a first step the prioritization of the major crop gene pools, identifying the most important CWR they contain and carrying out ecogeographic and genetic diversity surveys on the target taxa. The localities of the populations can be compared against the existing protected areas over a GIS platform to help identify candidate protected areas holding populations of interest. The ecogeographic features of the protected area add further information with regard to the potential adaptation genes that some of the populations may have. This type of analysis can also help identify gaps in the network of protected areas and other potential localities that fall outside of the network that should be conserved anyway. This approach was followed by the FAO when developing the network of *in situ* conservation areas for CWR (Maxted and Kell, 2009a).

National approach

A similar approach to that used to identify the global network could be taken at the regional or national level, but here the starting point need not be just the major crop gene pools present in the region or country but might be the entire flora of the region or country, as was the case for the recent identification of priority sites for the establishment of genetic reserves in the UK (Maxted et al., 2007). This approach is perhaps the most objective because CWR taxa targets are selected from the whole flora rather than those that a priori are considered a priority, i.e. the major crops. For the UK the 17 'best' sites identified to establish CWR genetic reserves contain 152 (67 per cent) of the 226 priority UK CWR species.

Monographic approach

Here the focus is a taxonomic group, a crop and its related CWR species. This approach involves identification of the CWR taxa within the target taxon. Depending on the number of CWR taxa identified, it then involves some form of prioritization possibly based on genetic or taxonomic closeness to the crop, the presence of desirable traits in the taxon or threat to individual species, followed by ecogeographic analysis and location of specific sites for the establishment of genetic reserves. This approach is exemplified by recent CWR studies for African cowpea (*Vigna* sp.) (Maxted et al., 2004) and wheat (*Aegilops* sp.) (Maxted et al., 2008).

Site-specific approach

The previous approaches may each be designated as top-down in the sense that you start with the goal of conserving CWR and then identify the locations where CWR are concentrated to establish genetic reserves within existing protected areas. The site-specific approach is the reverse where you have an existing protected area and wish to enhance its value by providing additional ecosystem services by designating it as a CWR genetic reserve. This would involve the local population or reserve manager identifying which CWR were present and amending the site management plan to prioritize the genetic conservation of key species.

There are clear differences between the four approaches to establishing CWR genetic reserve networks but it should be stressed that it is only by adopting these complementary approaches that the full diversity of CWR can be conserved.

Developing specific crop genetic diversity conservation in protected areas will generally require additional research and resources, and will impact on management practices. Below, four specific issues are discussed. More detailed guidance for identifying and managing crop genetic diversity in protected areas is given in detail in the report *Food Stores* (Stolton et al., 2006) and the guidelines contained in Iriondo et al. (2008).

Resource assessment

Managing in protected areas is likely to require additional resources, particularly if the populations are to be monitored at the genetic level; it is therefore important to identify likely costs and ways of meeting these. Resources will be needed for additional monitoring to ensure that the management regime is actually benefiting target populations, but there may also be costs associated with specific management interventions. Assessment should look beyond costs to include potential beneficiaries, particularly among local communities. In cases where there are clearly accepted and understood benefits in maintaining agricultural biodiversity, local people can sometimes offset a substantial amount of the costs through voluntary conservation and monitoring efforts.

Protected area design and management

Although there are many protected areas without fully up-to-date and well implemented management plans, most areas are managed in accordance with some form of planning document and many include a variety of zones in which different management objectives are followed. The design of crop genetic diversity conservation areas involves consideration of various factors, such as structure, size, whether a single large site or multiple smaller sites are best for the target taxon, the use of corridors, reserve shape, environmental heterogeneity and potential user communities. Individual species have specific design requirements. Practical experience of collecting CWR for *ex situ* conservation has shown, for example, that CWR often exist in small, isolated populations; therefore, sites with the largest populations should be selected and efforts taken in the management plans to encourage maintenance of as large a CWR population as possible. Practical examples of how genetic reserves were established for priority CWR species in Lebanon and the Palestinian Territories can be found in Al-Atawneh et al. (2008). As many CWR are associated with more disturbed habitats than plant species associated with climax vegetation, the management regime may necessitate conserving disturbance which results in the desired patchwork of diverse habitats. For the site management of the genetic reserves established to conserve CWR species in Lebanon and the Palestinian Territories, an appropriate level of grazing was required, though significant experimentation was needed before the appropriate level was identified (Al-Atawneh et al., 2008).

Resource use

The establishment and management of protected areas for their crop genetic diversity is not an end in itself. Because this type of conservation focuses explicitly on socio-economically important species, there is a direct link between genetic conservation and sustainable utilization. As a result, protected area managers will need to place greater emphasis on the requirements of stakeholders – the general public, and professional and traditional users of the site. However, there are no simple formulaic methods of achieving agreement about natural resource use: each protected area and each community needs to be approached individually.

Linkage to *ex situ* conservation and duplication

A safety back-up to ensure the conservation of the germplasm in the protected area, particularly in light of projected climatic changes and their potential impact on the protected area networks, can be put in place by sampling and depositing germplasm in appropriate *ex situ* collections. Although both *ex situ* and *in situ* techniques have their advantages and disadvantages they should not be seen as alternatives or in opposition to one another.

Conclusions

Protected areas can play an important role in the *in situ* conservation of crop genetic diversity. Although the links between food security and protected areas, or even the links between the biodiversity and agrobiodiversity communities, have rarely been made explicit, our research demonstrates that protected areas are important refuges for agrobiodiversity and as such help maintain agricultural systems and food security. It seems obvious that in a time of ecosystem instability that biodiversity and agrobiodiversity communities should work together and cooperation over crop genetic diversity conservation is a good means of drawing the two communities towards each other for mutual benefit. Just as botanic gardens in countries with colder climates often stimulate interest among the general public by including specimens of crops to show what a banana, coffee or rice plant looks like, so protected area managers can raise the profile of their sites by paying particular attention to native CWR species and advertising their presence to the potential user communities. Many protected areas also encompass cultivated lands and increasing recognition of the social, environmental and economic value of landraces adds an important dimension to the values of these areas.

However, despite this importance for future food security, CWR and landraces are generally not emphasized in protected area management plans and protected areas have not historically been viewed as part of a critical strategy for preserving agrobiodiversity. There is an urgent need to reverse this situation. The key messages from this chapter therefore are as follows:

- Many of the centres of diversity of our principal cultivated plants are poorly protected as are some specific high priority CWR populations; therefore, more designated protected areas are needed.
- Where crop genetic diversity and existing protected areas coincide, protected areas offer the most practical way forward for conserving a broad range of CWR diversity, which cannot be substituted with *ex situ* conservation.
- The role of protected areas in conserving crop genetic diversity could be greatly increased by raising awareness within protected area organizations.
- The promotion of the conservation of crop genetic diversity within existing protected areas may further enhance the public perception of protected areas and help to ensure longer term site security.
- There are already a few protected areas which are being managed specifically to retain landraces and CWR and there are many more protected areas that are known to contain populations essential to the conservation of plant genetic resources.

Overall, the estimated annual turnover of the commercial seed industry in Organisation for Economic Co-operation and Development (OECD) countries is US$13 billion (FAO, 1998) and the total commercial world seed market is assessed at approximately US$6000 million (International Seed Federation, 2009). If just a fraction of this sum was used to protect the resources breeders rely on to improve commercial seeds, and a small proportion of this went to the protected areas which conserve important crop genetic resources, many of the world's most under-resourced protected areas could receive a considerable boost to their budgets and thus their capacity for effective management.

Case Study 4.1:
Crop Genetic Diversity Protection in Turkey

Yildiray Lise and Sue Stolton

Turkey has the richest flora in the temperate zone. Nearly 9000 species were recorded in the *Flora of Turkey and the East Aegean Islands* in 1991 (Güner et al., 2000) but estimates put total species at between 10,000 and 12,000. One scientist has calculated that a new species is found in Turkey on average every 8 days and 20 hours (Plant Talk, 2003); indeed, between 2000 and 2007 an additional 470 taxa have been added to the flora (Özhatay et al., 2009). However, this plant diversity is under threat and some 4500 nationally rare species are listed in the 2 national Red Data Books (Ekim et al., 1989; 2000).

This rich biodiversity is the basis of the country's long history of agriculture and horticulture. Archaeological evidence traces the earliest agriculture back to Anatolia (which includes most of the modern republic of Turkey) almost 10,000 years ago (Harlan, 1992). Turkey is a major centre of the origin for cereals, with 25 CWR of wheat (*Triticum* and *Aegilops*), 8 of barley (*Hordeum*), 5 of rye (*Secale*) and 8 of oats (*Avena*); it also contains CWR of vegetable species including many brassicas, wild celery (*Apium graveolens*), wild beet (*Beta vulgaris* ssp. *maritima*), wild carrots (*Daucus* spp.) and wild lettuce (*Lactuca* spp.), and legumes such as wild lentils, peas and several chickpea species (*Cicer* spp.) (Açıkgöz et al., 1998).

Conservation status of cereal CWR

Cereals such as wheat and barley seem to have originated in or near woodlands and their wild progenitors can still be found in the oak forest belt of southeastern Anatolia and the pine, beech and Cilician fir forests of southern Anatolia. Forests once covered large parts of Turkey, but centuries of use and exploitation have reduced the area of large intact forest to some 12 per cent of the land area, mainly in the major mountain ranges in the north and south. Unfortunately these remaining forests receive little protection. Turkey has at least 12 different protected area categories covering more than 5.2 per cent of its landmass (Lise, 2008); however, the traditional focus of management is recreational, often to the detriment of ecological integrity.

Since the 1970s, there have been some attempts to ensure the conservation of the country's important CWR (Karagöz, 2008) institutionalized under a national plan for *in situ* conservation of plant genetic diversity (Kaya et al., 1998). Protected areas with specific management requirements adapted to individual plant species and environmental conditions, known as Gene Management Zones, have been introduced as a result of an '*In Situ* Conservation of Genetic Diversity Project'. They are natural or semi-natural areas with the primary objective of protecting genetic resources, while still allowing other economic activities, such as grazing and timber harvesting, as long as these do not threaten the primary objective (Anon, 2000).

The reserves were initially established in three locations:

1   Southeast Anatolia: Ceylanpınar State Farm for conservation of wild wheat, barley, lentil and chickpea germplasm (a total of 6 reserves).
2   Northwestern Aegean Region: Kazdagi National Park, which is rich in fruit progenitor, nut, ornamental and forest species (a total of 13 reserves).
3   Central Southern Anatolia: Bolkar Mountains, which lie at the extreme geographical limits of several species (a total of 5 reserves).

Following the publication of the national plan, an additional six reserves were established in the Lakes Region of Turkey (southwestern Anatolia) to protect 20 species (Karagöz, 2008).

Management aims to maximize maintenance of genetic diversity while allowing for continued adaptation to changing environmental conditions. Thus, discussion has centred on issues such as whether managers should intervene to promote colonization of annuals (e.g. many wild relatives of grains) in a given area or allow the natural succession of biennial and perennial vegetation. There are, however, no management authorities or plans in place for these reserves as yet (Karagöz, 2008).

Figure 4.6 *The Anti-Taurus mountain range in southeastern Anatolia*
Source: © Edward Parker/WWF-Canon

A national plan for *in situ* conservation of plant genetic diversity

A national plan for *in situ* gene conservation has been prepared. The target species in the plan include 57 agricultural plants (including field crops and fruit, vegetable, medicinal and aromatic species), 13 landraces and 25 forest tree species (Kaya et al., 1998).

The Ministry of Environment drafted legislation to adopt the strategy in 1999. However, the legislation was stalled due to disputes concerning responsibilities under the draft statute (Kaya et al., 1998). After many years the strategy was finally embedded into 'The National Biological Diversity Strategy and Action Plan' (Anon, 2007) under two specific goals:

- To identify, protect and benefit the components of genetic diversity, including the traditional knowledge, which have importance for Turkey.
- To identify, protect and monitor the components of biological diversity which have importance for agricultural biological diversity; to protect genetic resources which have actual and potential values for food and agriculture, and to ensure the sustainable use of such resources; and to ensure the fair and equitable sharing of the benefits arising out of the utilization of genetic resources.

The National Biological Diversity Strategy and Action Plan was enforced in 2008 upon its approval by the Ministry of Environment and Forestry.

Case Study 4.2:
Conservation of Endangered CWRs in Mexico's Sierra de Manantlán

Sue Stolton and Jorge Alejandro Rickards-Guevara

Maize is one of the world's major crops, cultivated globally on 130 million hectares. There are currently five recognized species of teocinte, the ancient ancestor of modern corn: *Zea diploperennis*, *Z. luxurians*, *Z. mays*, *Z. nicaraguensis* and *Z. perennis*. The maize gene pool consists mainly of cultivated *Z. mays* and the related wild species, which form an important genetic source for breeding and adaptation. *Zea diploperennis* and *Z. perennis* are perennial, while other species are annual. Virtually all populations of wild teocinte are either threatened or endangered (FAO, 1997). This case study tells the story of how two of these species have been saved from extinction.

Seeking Zea

In 1976, Dr. Hugh Iltis, Professor of Botany at the University of Wisconsin-Madison in the US, sent a New Year's card in the form of a poster to botanists around the world with a picture of *Zea perennis* against which he wrote 'extinct in the wild'. Wild populations of *Z. perennis* had last been seen in 1921 in western Mexico by two US Department of Agriculture botanists, who introduced the species to university greenhouses. Since then several other botanists had tried, and failed, to locate the wild population. A poster was placed on a bulletin board at the University of Guadalajara by a local taxonomist who urged her students: 'Go and find this teocinte, and prove that gringo Iltis wrong'. One undergraduate student took the challenge and went back to the plant's last known location in western Mexico and found the long-lost *Z. Perennis* (Stolton et al., 2006).

This one find led to an even more important discovery. On being told that *Z. perennis* was growing in another location the student, Rafael Guzman, collected more seed. However, this teocinte (known locally as '*milpilla*') turned out to be a new species – *Z. diploperennis*. Unlike *Z. perennis*, this species freely interbreeds with corn, which raised the possibility that the crop could be grown for several years from one rootstock and, perhaps more importantly, it appeared to be tolerant of seven corn viruses and the only member of *Zea* that is immune to three of them (Stolton et al., 2006).

Protection

Following this discovery, years of negotiations led eventually to the creation of the Sierra de Manantlán Reserve under the direction of the University of Guadalajara – the first protected area in Mexico established principally for the preservation of a wild crop relative, along with traditional agricultural systems and cultivars (Iltis, 1994). Steps towards protection began in 1984, when the State of Jalisco purchased land which included a large population of *Z. diploperennis*. The following year this area became the Laboratorio Natural Las Joyas de la Sierra de Manantlán, run by the University of Guadalajara. The area was recognized by UNESCO's Man and the Biosphere Programme in 1988 and is currently under the administration of the National Commission for Protected Areas (CONANP).

Apart from the Laboratorio Natural Las Joyas de la Sierra de Manantlán, none of the land in the Biosphere Reserve has been purchased by governmental authorities – at present 20 per cent is owned by indigenous communities, 40 per cent is community-owned ('*ejido*') lands and 40 per cent is privately owned (Sheean-Stone, 1989). Around 33,000 people live in the Biosphere Reserve, and some 400,000 rely on the Sierra's water catchment for industry, agriculture and other purposes (Stolton et al., 2006).

Understanding conservation management

The discovery of *Z. diploperennis* and the subsequent declaration of a biosphere reserve have together led to intensive research into the biodiversity, and specifically the flora of the reserve, which includes tropical humid forest and temperate grasslands. Over 2700 plant species have been recorded, of which 40 per cent are endemic to Mexico. Agricultural fields and associated secondary vegetation in hillsides and small valleys in the reserve and surrounding area have been found to contain CWR of beans (*Phaseolus coccineus* and *P. vulgaris)* as well as maize. The Sierra de Manantlán is also an important refuge for animals, including threatened species such as the jaguar (*Panthera onca*). So far, 108 species of mammals have been recorded in the region, at least 12 of which are endemic to montane areas of western Mexico and 2 subspecies are endemic to the reserve (Cuevas-Guzmán et al., 2009).

Protection strategies for *Z. diploperennis* began with gathering baseline information on the species' habitat requirements. Surveys revealed that all known *Z. diploperennis* populations were found near highland farming villages and that the plants invariably occur in clearings surrounded by pines, oaks and broadleaf cloud forest. *Z. diploperennis* was found in areas created by small-scale clearance for maize cultivation and subsequently abandoned, or in actively cultivated fields. Further research found that *Z. diploperennis* cover and stem abundance appeared to be highest in sites that had not been cultivated for at least 15 years. However, these sites also showed the first incursion of young woody trees that could eventually shade out the plant, suggesting that long-term conservation of the species would depend upon regular small-scale forest openings like those produced by shifting agriculture (Stolton et al., 2006).

Community knowledge

Sierra de Manantlán's success as a protected area is not just due to the work carried out by scientists and conservationists. Mexicans call teocintle the 'grain of the gods' and the crop is of great importance to food security in the region. The reverence accorded to the species has clearly helped to preserve its diversity.

The local rural communities in the region have considerable knowledge of the area's diversity and their agricultural practices have helped to retain species richness. The existence of *Z. diploperennis* and other CWR is likely to be due to the traditional agricultural practices of slash-and-burn cultivation ('*coamil*') and cattle-ranching. The management practices and objectives of the reserve thus stress the necessity of conserving traditional agricultural systems and it is planned to continue the *coamil* system in areas within the reserve, so that the *Z. diploperennis* populations can survive (Stolton et al., 2006).

References

Açıkgöz, N., Sabancı, C. O. and Cinsoym, A. S. (1998) 'Ecogeography and distribution of wild legumes in Turkey', in N. Zencirci, Z. Kaya, Y. Anikster and W. T. Adams (eds) *The Proceedings of International Symposium on* In Situ *Conservation of Plant Genetic Diversity*, Central Research Institute for Field Crops, Ankara.

Al-Atawneh, N., Amri, A., Assi, R. and Maxted, N. (2008) 'Management plans for promoting *in situ* conservation of local agrobiodiversity in the West Asia centre of plant diversity', in N. Maxted, B. V. Ford-Lloyd, S. P. Kell, J. Iriondo, E. Dulloo and J. Turok (eds) *Crop Wild Relative Conservation and Use*, CAB International, Wallingford.

Anon (2000) 'Cutting-edge conservation techniques are tested in the cradle of ancient agriculture: GEF Turkish project is a global model for *in situ* conservation of wild crop relatives', *Diversity*, vol 16, no 4.

Anon (2007) *The National Biological Diversity Strategy and Action Plan*, Ministry of Environment and Forestry General Directorate of Nature Conservation and National Parks Department of Nature Conservation National Focal Point of Convention on Biological Diversity, Ankara.

Avagyan, A. (2008) 'Crop wild relatives in Armenia: diversity, legislation and conservation issues, , in N. Maxted, B. V. Ford-Lloyd, S. P. Kell, J. Iriondo, E. Dulloo and J. Turok (eds) *Crop Wild Relative Conservation and Use*, CAB International, Wallingford.

Bassols Isamat, E., Falgarona Bosch, J., Mallarach Carrera, J.- M. and Perramon Ramos, B. (2008) 'Agrobiodiversity conservation in the Garrotxa Volcanic Zone Natural Park, Spain: Experience and recommendations for future directions', in T. Amend, J. Brown, A. Kothari, A. Phillips and S. Stolton (eds) *Protected Landscapes and Agrobiodiversity Values*, IUCN, Gland, and GTZ, Eschborn.

Biodiversity Leadership Awards (undated) www.biodiversityleadershipawards.org/manantlan. htm, accessed 1 August 2009.

Brezhnev, D. and Korovina, O. (1981) 'Wild relatives of cultivated plants', in *Flora of the USSR*, Lolos Publishers, Leningrad.

Camacho Villa, T. C., Maxted, N., Scholten, M. A. and Ford-Lloyd, B. V. (2005) 'Defining and identifying crop landraces', *Plant Genetic Resource: Characterization and Utilization*, vol 3, no 3, pp373–84.

CBD (2002) *Global Strategy for Plant Conservation*, www.cbd.int/programmes/cross-cutting/plant/, accessed 1 August 2009.

Cuevas-Guzmán, R., Benz, B. F. Jardel-Peláez, E. J. and Herrera-MacBryde, O. (undated) *Fact Sheet, Sierra de Manantlan Region*, Smithsonian Institution, SI/MAB Program, Washington, DC, www.nmnh.si.edu/botany/projects/cpd/ma/ma6.htm, accessed 1 August 2009.

Darwin, C. (1868) *The Variation of Animals and Plants Under Domestication*, John Murray Publishers, London.

Davis, S. D., Heywood, V. H. and Hamilton, A. C. (1994) *Centres of Plant Diversity. A Guide and Strategy for Their Conservation*, 3 volumes, IUCN, Cambridge, and WWF, Gland.

Dudley, N. (ed.) (2008) *Guidelines for Applying Protected Area Management Categories*, IUCN, Gland.

Ekim, T., Koyuncu, M., Erik, S. and Ýlarslan, R. (1989) *List of Rare, Threatened and Endemic Plants in Turkey According to IUCN Red Data Book Categories*, Turkish Association for Conservation of Nature and Natural Resources, Ankara.

Ekim, T., Koyuncu, M., Vural, M., Duman, H., Aytaç, Z. and Adigüzel, N. (2000) *Red Data Book of Turkish Plants*, Türkiye Tabiatini Koruma Derneği – Van Yüzüncü Yil Üniversitesi, Banşcan Ofset, Ankara.

European Commission Joint Research Centre, Institute for Environment and Sustainability (2002) *GLC 2000: Global Land Cover Mapping for the Year 2000*, bioval.jrc.ec.europa.eu/products/glc2000/glc2000.php, accessed 1 August 2009.

FAO (1996) *Global Plan of Action for the Conservation and Sustainable Utilization of Plant Genetic Resources for Food and Agriculture and the Leipzig Declaration*, www.fao.org/WAICENT/FaoInfo/Agricult/AGP/AGPS/Pgrfa/Pdf/GPAENG.PDF, accessed 1 August 2009.

FAO (1997) *The State of the World's Plant Genetic Resources for Food and Agriculture*, FAO, Rome.

FAO (1998) 'Crop Genetic Resource', *Biodiversity for Food and Agriculture*, FAO, Rome, www.fao.org/sd/EPdirect/EPre0039.htm, accessed 1 August 2009.

FAO (2001) *International Treaty on Plant Genetic Resources for Food and Agriculture*, FAO, Rome.

FAO (2009) 'The State of Diversity', *Second Report on the State of the World's Plant Genetic Resources for Food and Agriculture*, FAO CGRFA, Rome, pp8–25.

Gabrielian, E. and Zohary, D. (2004) 'Wild relatives of food crops native to Armenia and Nakhichevan', *Flora Mediterranea*, vol 14, pp5–80.

Groombridge, B. and Jenkins, M. D. (2002) *World Atlas of Biodiversity*, prepared by the UNEP World Conservation Monitoring Centre, University of California Press, Berkeley, CA.

Häner, R. and Schierscher, B. (2009) 'First step towards CWR conservation in Switzerland', *Crop Wild Relative*, vol 7, pp14–17.

Güner, A., Özhatay, N., Ekim, T., Hüsnü, K. and Baser, C. with the assistance of Hedge, I. (eds) (2000) *Flora of Turkey and the East Aegean Islands, 11* (Supplement 2), Edinburgh University Press, Edinburgh.

Hajjar, R. and Hodgkin, T. (2007) 'The use of wild relatives in crop improvement: a survey of developments over the last 20 years', *Euphytica*, vol 156, pp1–13.

Harlan, J. R. (1992) *Crops and Man*, American Society of Agronomy, Crop Science Society of America, Madison, WI.

Harlan, J. R. and de Wet, J. M. J. (1971) 'Towards a rational classification of cultivated plants', *Taxon*, vol 20, pp509–17.

Hawkes, J. (1991) 'International workshop on dynamic *in situ* conservation of wild relatives of major cultivated plants: summary of final discussion and recommendations', *Israel Journal of Botany*, vol 40, pp529–36, and in N. Maxted, B. V. Ford-Lloyd and J. Hawkes (1997) *Plant Genetic Conservation: The In Situ Approach*, Chapman & Hall, London.

Hijmans, R. J., Garrett, K. A., Huaman, Z., Zhang, D. P., Schreuder, M. and Bonierbale, M. (2000) 'Assessing the geographic representativeness of genebank collections: the case of Bolivian wild potatoes', *Conservation Biology*, vol 14, no 6, pp1755–65.

Iltis, H. (1994) 'New Year's card leads to newly discovered species of enormous economic potential', *R&D Innovator*, vol 3, no 6, June, www.winstonbrill.com/bril001/html/article_index/articles/101-150/article103_body.html, accessed 1 August 2009.

Ingram, G. (1990) 'Multi-gene pool surveys in areas with rapid genetic erosion: An example from the Aïr mountains, northern Niger', *Conservation Biology*, vol 4, pp78–90.

International Seed Federation (2009) www.worldseed.org/cms/medias/file/ResourceCenter/SeedStatistics/SeedTradeGrowth/Seed_Trade_Growth.pdf, accessed 1 August 2009.

Iriondo, J. M., Dulloo, E. and Maxted, N. (eds) (2008) *Conserving Plant Genetic Diversity in Protected Areas: Population Management of Crop Wild Relatives*, CAB International Publishing, Wallingford.

Jain, S. K. (1975) 'Genetic reserves', in O. H. Frankel and J. G. Hawkes (eds), *Crop Genetic Resources for Today and Tomorrow*, Cambridge University Press, Cambridge, pp379–96.

Kell, S. P., Knüpffer, H., Jury, S. L., Maxted, N. and Ford-Lloyd, B. V. (2005) *Catalogue of Crop Wild Relatives for Europe and the Mediterranean*, University of Birmingham, Birmingham, www.pgrforum.org/cwris/cwris.asp, accessed 2 September 2009.

Karagöz, A. (1998) '*In-situ* conservation of plant genetic resource in the Ceylanpınar State Farm', in N. Zencirci, Z. Kaya, Y. Anikster and W. T. Adams (eds) *The Proceedings of International Symposium on* In Situ *Conservation of Plant Genetic Diversity*, Central Research Institute for Field Crops, Ankara.

Karagöz, A. (2008) 'Status of plant genetic resources, significant for agriculture in Turkey', *2008 Annual Journal of Rural Environment*, Research Association of Rural Environment and Forestry, Ankara, pp26–42.

Kaya, Z., Kün, E. and Güner, A. (1998) 'National plan for *in situ* conservation of plant genetic diversity in Turkey', in N. Zencirci, Z. Kaya, Y. Anikster and W. T. Adams (eds) *The Proceedings of International Symposium on* In Situ *Conservation of Plant Genetic Diversity*, Central Research Institute for Field Crops, Ankara.

Kell, S. P., Knüpffer, H., Jury, S. L., Ford-Lloyd, B. V. and Maxted, N. (2008) 'Crops and wild relatives of the Euro-Mediterranean region: making and using a conservation catalogue', in N. Maxted, B. V. Ford-Lloyd, S. P. Kell, J. Iriondo, E. Dulloo and J. Turok (eds) *Crop Wild Relative Conservation and Use*, CAB International, Wallingford, pp69–109.

Lewington, A. (1990) *Plants for People*, National History Museum, London.

Lise, Y. (2008) 'Climate change and protected areas: Wilderness Areas', *Yeşil Atlas*, no 74–83, December 2008, DBR Publications, Istanbul (in Turkish).

Lobell, D. B., Burke, M. B., Tebaldi, C., Mastrandrea, M. D., Falcon, W. P. and Naylor, R. L. (2008) 'Prioritizing climate change adaptation needs for food security in 2030', *Science*, vol 319, pp607–10.

Louette, D. and Smale, M. (1996) *Genetic Diversity and Maize Seed Management in a Traditional Mexican Community: Implications for* In Situ *Conservation of Maize*, NRG Paper 96–03, CIMMYT, Mexico.

Magos Brehm, J., Maxted, N., Ford-Lloyd B. V. and Martins-Loução, M. A. (2008) 'National inventories of crop wild relatives and wild harvested plants: Case-Study for Portugal', *Genetic Resources and Crop Evolution*, vol 55, no 779–96.

Maxted, N., Ford-Lloyd, B. V. and Hawkes, J. G. (eds) (1997a) *Plant Genetic Conservation: The* In Situ *Approach*, Chapman & Hall, London.

Maxted, N., Ford-Lloyd, B. V. and Hawkes, J. G. (1997b) 'Complementary conservation strategies', in N. Maxted, B. V. Ford-Lloyd and J. G. Hawkes (eds) *Plant Genetic Conservation: The* In Situ *Approach*, Chapman & Hall, London, pp20–55.

Maxted, N., Ford-Lloyd, B. V., Jury, S. L., Kell, S. P. and Scholten, M. A. (2006) 'Towards a definition of a crop wild relative', *Biodiversity and Conservation*, vol 14, pp1–13.

Maxted, N., Hawkes, J. G., Ford-Lloyd, B. V. and Williams, J. T. (1997c) 'A practical model for *in situ* genetic conservation', in N. Maxted, B. V. Ford-Lloyd and J. G. Hawkes (eds) *Plant Genetic Conservation: The* In Situ *Approach,* Chapman & Hall, London, pp545–92.

Maxted, N., Hawkes, J. G., Guarino, L. and Sawkins, M. (1997d) 'The selection of taxa for plant genetic conservation', *Genetic Resources and Crop Evolution*, vol 44, no 337–48.

Maxted, N. and Kell, S. P. (2009a) *Establishment of a Global Network for the In Situ Conservation of Crop Wild Relatives: Status and Needs*, FAO Commission on Genetic Resources for Food and Agriculture, Rome, p266.

Maxted, N. and Kell, S. P. (2009b) 'CWR in crop improvement: To what extent are they used?', *Crop Wild Relative*, vol 7, pp7–8.

Maxted, N., Mabuza-Dlamini, P., Moss, H., Padulosi, S., Jarvis, A. and Guarino, L. (2004) 'An ecogeographic survey: African Vigna', *Systematic and Ecogeographic Studies of Crop Genepools*, vol 10, IPGRI, Rome.

Maxted, N., Scholten, M. A., Codd, R. and Ford-Lloyd, B. V. (2007) 'Creation and use of a national inventory of crop wild relatives', *Biological Conservation*, vol 140, pp142–59.

Maxted, N., White, K., Valkoun, J. Konopka, J. and Hargreaves, S. (2008) 'Towards a conservation strategy for Aegilops species', *Plant Genetic Resource: Characterization and Utilization*, vol 6, no 2, pp126–41.

Meilleur, B. A. and Hodgkin, T. (2004) '*In situ* conservation of crop wild relatives: status and trends', *Biodiversity and Conservation*, vol 13, pp663–84.

Nuez, F., Prohens, J. and Blanca, J. M. (2004) 'Relationships, origin, and diversity of Galápagos tomatoes: implications for the conservation of natural populations', *American Journal of Botany*, vol 91, no 86–99.

O'Regan, F. (2007) 'An examination of the European internet search catalogue (EURISCO) with special reference to the quality of passport data and crop wild relatives', unpublished MSc thesis, University of Birmingham, Birmingham.

Özhatay, N., Kültür, Ş. and Aslan, S. (2009) 'Check-list of additional taxa to the Supplement Flora of Turkey IV', *Turkish Journal of Botany*, vol 33, pp191–226.

Plant Talk (2003) 'Important plant areas of Turkey documented', *Plant Talk*, November 2003.

Phillips, A. and Stolton, S. (2008) 'Protected landscapes and biodiversity values: An overview', in T. Amend, J. Brown, A. Kothari, A. Phillips and S. Stolton (eds) *Protected Landscapes and Agrobiodiversity Values*, IUCN, Gland, and GTZ, Eschborn.

Pimentel, D., Wilson, C., McCullum, C., Huang. R., Dwen, P., Flack, J., Tran, Q., Saltman, T. and Cliff. B. (1997) 'Economic and environmental benefits of biodiversity', *BioScience*, vol 47, pp747–57.

Shand, H. (1993) *Harvesting Nature's Diversity*, FAO, Rome.

Sheean-Stone, O. (1989) 'Mexico's wonder weed', *WWF Reports,* Gland.

Stolton, S., Boucher, T., Dudley, N., Hoekstra, J., Maxted, N. and Kell, S. (2008) 'Ecoregions with crop wild relatives are less well protected', *Biodiversity*, vol 9, nos 1–2, pp52–5.

Stolton, S., Maxted, N., Ford-Lloyd, B. V., Kell, S. P. and Dudley, N. (2006) *Food Stores: Using Protected Areas to Secure Crop Genetic Diversity*, WWF International, Gland.

Vetelainen, M., Negri, V. and Maxted, N., (2009) *European Landraces: On-farm Conservation, Management and Use,* Technical Bulletin 15, Biodiversity International, Rome.

5

Nursery Tales: Protected Areas Conserving Wild Marine and Freshwater Fish Stocks

Nigel Dudley and Sue Stolton

The mountains of the Norwegian Lofoten Islands are like a child's drawing: harsh, elongated pyramids rising up directly from the sea, still snow-capped in late May. Wooden fishing houses are squeezed into any flat land along the shore and sometimes, as with the place where we are staying, overflowing on stilts into the harbour. Huge triangular racks hold rows of fish drying in the 24-hour light of midsummer and the smell of salt and cod fills the air. These are some of the richest fishing seas in Europe and every evening we eat huge, fresh Atlantic cod that one of our housemates catches from a tiny rowing boat out in the bay; probably the finest fish we can recall eating anywhere in the world.

Keeping out foreign fishing fleets is one of the main reasons that Norway has always refused to join the European Union. However, all this bounty was recently under threat. A combination of climate change and overfishing led to a catastrophic collapse in the Atlantic cod stocks during the 1980s and 1990s. Complete disaster was only averted by the introduction of catch quotas and spawning closures in 1995, which has led once again to a steady increase in the cod population. Here, protection has little to do with the niceties of biodiversity conservation, but was an emergency measure to safeguard a fishing industry that is centuries old.

Nigel Dudley

The Argument

The value

Nearly 40 per cent of the global population now lives within 100km of a coast, and many of these people depend on the productivity of the sea. However, the Millennium Ecosystem Assessment has assessed that: 'The use of two ecosystem services – capture fisheries and freshwater – is now well beyond levels that can be sustained even at current demands, much less future ones' (Millennium Ecosystem Assessment, 2005).

Increased fishing pressure depletes fish stocks and causes rising poverty and decreasing food security. Specifically, in many cases poor coastal communities have seen their traditional fish stocks reduced by the actions of large offshore trawlers from far away. An estimated 250 million people in developing countries are directly dependent on small-scale fisheries for food and income; according to the FAO, fish account for '19 per cent of the protein intake in developing countries, a share that can exceed 25 per cent in the poorest countries and reach 90 per cent in isolated parts of coastal or inland areas and in small island developing states' (Béné et al., 2007).

Marine ecosystems are complex, consisting of a myriad of species that interact with each other, with people and with their environment. These ecosystems are under increasing pressure from fishing and associated damage, pollution, invasive species and diseases, climate change, mineral exploitation, coastal development and tourism. Overfishing has long been regarded as the most significant threat to marine ecology and human food supply (Pauly et al, 2005), however, the threat of climate change and ocean acidification may present an even more significant challenge.

Unfortunately, we are only at the start of understanding how marine systems interact. Fishery managers have tended to treat species as isolated targets, separate from other species and from their habitats. Of over 800 species exploited in US marine waters, the status of over 60 per cent was unknown to the National Marine Fisheries Service in 1998; in many other countries data on marine species is even more rudimentary. A series of policy and legislative blunders, resulting from ignorance and often compounded by political cowardice, has created a crisis in many marine fisheries and policy-makers are looking for solutions to a growing problem. Marine protected areas (MPAs) represent one of the simplest ways to rebuild fish stocks by simultaneously protecting target species, their habitats and the ecological processes that underpin fish production (Roberts and Hawkins, 2000).

The benefit

With the global crisis in fish stocks, small-scale fishing communities are extremely vulnerable; marine protected areas with regulated and sustainable small-scale fishing activities generally increase the amount of fish landed within two years of establishment. In theory larger and more representative systems of protected areas can provide an even greater range of benefits. It has been estimated that an ambitious target of conserving 20 to 30 per cent of the world's seas could create around 1 million jobs, increase the sustainability of a global marine fish catch (worth around US$70–80 billion per year) and ensure the sustainability of marine ecosystem services with a gross value of roughly US$4.5–6.7 trillion a year (Balmford et al., 2004).

Box 5.1 *Freshwater fisheries*

Although this chapter concentrates on marine fisheries, inland (i.e. freshwater) fisheries are extremely important sources of nutrition and income around the world. For example, Cambodia's inland fisheries have an annual value of up to US$500 million with 60 per cent coming from Tonle Sap Lake (a UNESCO Man and Biosphere reserve) (ICEM, 2003) – see also Case Study 5.1 on Lake Malawi.

Current Contribution of Marine Protected Areas: Helping Fisheries Recover

In a broad review undertaken for WWF, Roberts and Hawkins (2000) identified five main benefits of MPAs to fisheries.

1 Enhancing the production of offspring to restock fishing grounds

MPAs create sheltered conditions that help to enhance fish-breeding and overall population. Three factors are important: fish size, habitat and life-cycle. Firstly, MPAs help conserve fish of all ages. Overfishing often removes most of the older members of the population, but bigger fish generally produce many more eggs than smaller ones and are thus disproportionately important for breeding. For example, one 10kg red snapper (*Lutjanus campechanus*) produces over 20 times more eggs at a spawning than ten 1kg snappers. Secondly, some species, especially those that are attached or have limited powers of movement (e.g. oysters, clams and abalones) only reproduce successfully at high population densities. Protecting these species' habitat can thus enhance reproduction (Roberts and Hawkins, 2000). Thirdly, MPAs can ensure that species are protected at vulnerable stages of their life-cycle, in particular fish nurseries and spawning grounds, thus increasing the chances that fish reproduce before being caught. This approach has been used in Florida Bay where lobsters are protected in reserves until they are large enough to migrate to the reefs where they may be captured. The Florida Keys National Marine Sanctuary is a 9850 km^2 MPA protecting mangroves, seagrass and coral reef habitats, including a network of 24 fully protected zones. Monitoring results show increases in the number and size of heavily exploited species such as spiny lobster within these zones (Keller et al., 2003).

Researchers conclude that fish density, and thus presumably reproduction, is generally higher inside MPAs, particularly when surrounding areas are heavily fished (Pérez-Ruzafa et al., 2008). A review of 112 independent studies in 80 different MPAs found strikingly higher fish populations inside the reserves compared with surrounding areas (or the same area before an MPA was established). Relative to reference sites, population densities were 91 per cent higher, biomass 192 per cent higher, and average organism size and diversity 20–30 per cent higher in MPAs, usually between one and three years after establishment. These trends occurred even in small MPAs (Halpern, 2003).

2 Allowing spillover of adults and juveniles into fishing grounds

Since most fish have free-floating larvae or eggs, the offspring of protected animals can drift out of reserves – restocking distant fishing grounds. As fish stocks build up inside reserves, juvenile and mature fish move out to populate nearby areas. Six factors affect spillover: the success of protection; the time that the MPA has been established; intensity of fishing outside the MPA; mobility of species; boundary length of the reserve (greater edge to area ratio increased spillover); and boundary porosity, with out-migration encouraged if there is continuous habitat type (Roberts and Hawkins, 2000).

3 Preventing habitat damage

Most fishing creates some damage: trawling and use of dynamite are the most serious but even line-fishing results in disturbance and litter that can damage bottom-living communities.

4 Promoting development of natural biological communities

(which may be different from communities in fishing grounds)

For example, in Chile the establishment of an MPA led to a replacement of mussel beds with barnacles, due to the recovery of a predatory snail, *Concholepas concholepas*, which controlled the former (Castilla and Duran, 1985).

5 Facilitating recovery from catastrophic human disturbance

Healthy ecosystems are more resistant to major disruptions than ecosystems weakened by over-exploitation. Studies of recovery of coral reefs from major disturbances found that healthy reefs, with good populations and reproduction rates, are more resilient and recover relatively quickly, while reefs suffering from multiple stresses show little or no recovery (Connell, 1997).

A body of evidence for the effectiveness of MPAs in increasing fish numbers and spillover effects is developing rapidly (see Table 5.1).

Figure 5.1 *The sergeant major (Abudefduf saxatilis) damselfish, Fiji*
Source: © Cat Holloway / WWF-Canon

Table 5.1 *Impact of MPAs on fisheries – some recent research examples from around the world*

MPA	Increase in fish numbers	Spillover
Medes Islands MPA, Spain (Stelzenmüller et al., 2008)	✓	✓
Columbretes Islands Marine Reserve, Spain (Stobart et al., 2009)	✓	✓
Côte Bleue MPA, France (Claudet et al., 2006)		✓
Cerbere-Banyuls and Carry-le-Rouet MPAs in France, and Medes, Cabrera, Tabarca and Cabo de Palos MPAs in Spain (Goni et al., 2008)		✓
Nabq Managed Resource Protected Area, Egypt (Ashworth and Ormond, 2005)	✓	✓
Mombasa MPA, Kenya (McClanahan and Mangi, 2000)		✓
Malindi and Watamu Marine National Parks, Kenya (Kaunda-Arara and Rose, 2004)	✓	✓
Saldanha Bay, Langebaan Lagoon, South Africa (Kerwath et al., 2009)	✓	✓
Apo Island, Philippines (Abesamis and Russ, 2005)	✓	✓
Wakatobi Marine National Park, Indonesia (Unsworth et al., 2007)	✓	
Monterey Bay National Marine Sanctuary; Hopkins Marine Life Refuge; Point Lobos State & Ecological Reserve; Big Greek Marine Ecological Reserve, US (Paddack and Estes, 2000)	✓	
Soufriere Marine Management Area, St Lucia (Roberts et al., 2001)	✓	✓
Abrolhos National Marine Park, Brazil (Francini-Filho and Leão de Moura, 2008)	✓	
Rottnest Island, Western Australia (Babcock et al., 2007)	✓	

Note: not all studies above looked at both fish numbers and spillover

Figure 5.2 *Fishing below a rompong in Wakatobi Marine National Park,*
Southeast Sulawesi, Indonesia

Source: © WWF-Canon/Jikkie Jonkman

Figure 5.3 *Park rangers removing fishing net caught on the reef*
in Wakatobi National Park, Indonesia

Source: © Robert Delfs/WWF-Canon

Future Needs: The Urgency of Protection

Despite the fact that MPAs are increasingly recognized as a vital conservation tool, there are far less protected areas in marine environments than on land. Currently, about 12 per cent of marine coastal (intertidal) areas are protected, but only 4 per cent of the marine shelf (i.e. areas of over 200m depth) receive protection (Coad et al., 2009). Also, it is estimated that up to 80 per cent of the world's MPAs have little or no management. Of particular concern is the lack of protection for coral reefs and mangrove forests, the high seas, particularly sensitive areas at risk from shipping activities and breeding grounds for commercially important fish (WWF, undated).

Coral reefs and mangroves are two of the world's most endangered ecosystems. They are also important breeding sites for many fish. It is probable that there are few, if any, pristine coral reefs left in our oceans and it has been predicted that 15 per cent of reefs will be lost by 2030 and possibly a further 20 per cent in 20 to 40 years (Wilkinson, 2008). Indeed, coral-reef declines have exceeded 95 per cent in many locations, creating intense interest in the potential role of protected areas (Mumby and Steneck, 2008). MPAs can address some but not all of the problems facing corals, but they do have a role to play as outlined in Table 5.2.

Table 5.2 *Status of knowledge about the effects of fully protected marine reserves on fisheries in coral reef areas*

Reserve impact	Status of science
Increased fish and invertebrate biomass within borders	Confirmed and widely reported
Adult spillover to support adjacent fishery	Confirmed by a few studies but not others
Larval spillover to provide demographic support to nearby fished reefs	Expected but not demonstrated
Increased coral recruitment (Caribbean)	Confirmed by a few studies
Enhanced biodiversity	Mixed results (positive, negative and no impact reported)

An FAO study concluded that the current mangrove area worldwide has fallen below 15 million ha, down from 19.8 million ha in 1980 and that mangrove deforestation continued, albeit at a slightly lower rate in the 1990s (1.1 per cent per annum) than in the 1980s (1.9 per cent per annum). This reflects that in recent years most countries have banned conversion of mangroves for aquaculture and require environmental impact assessments prior to large-scale conversion for other uses (Wilkie and Fortuna, 2003).

Box 5.2 *The Coral Triangle*

Covering nearly 6 million km^2 of ocean across six countries in the Indo-Pacific, the Coral Triangle is an important focus for conservation initiatives. More than half of the world's coral reefs, 75 per cent of coral species, 40 per cent of coral-reef fish species and 6 of the 7 species of marine turtles can be found in the triangle. The area is part of a wider region that contains 51 of the world's 70 mangrove species and 23 of the 50 seagrass species.

The Coral Triangle supports livelihoods and provides income and food security, particularly for coastal communities. Resources sustain more than 120 million people in the area. Total annual values from coral reefs, mangroves and other natural habitats within the Coral Triangle have been estimated at over US$2.3 billion; marine resources also contribute to a growing nature-based tourism industry valued at over US$12 billion annually. Crucially, the Coral Triangle is the spawning and nursery ground for principle market tuna species that populate the Western and Central Pacific Ocean: yellowfin, albacore, bigeye and skipjack. The Western and Central Pacific Ocean supplies close to 50 per cent of the global tuna catch, representing half of the world's canned tuna and one-third of the Japanese sashimi market. Tuna fisheries are critically important to the commerce and food security of the region.

In May 2009, the six Coral Triangle governments (Indonesia, Malaysia, Papua New Guinea, the Philippines, the Solomon Islands and Timor Leste) launched a 'Regional Plan of Action' for the next decade at the World Ocean Conference in Indonesia. This is the most detailed plan for ocean conservation ever seen and the fruit of an ambitious partnership – the Coral Triangle Initiative on Coral Reefs, Fisheries and Food Security launched in 2007 in Bali.

Only about 6 per cent of the near-shore and continental-shelf habitats in the Coral Triangle are legally protected (see Case Study 5.2 on the Philippines); it is not surprising therefore that one of the major action points is the development of marine protected area networks (WWF, 2009).

Most of the world's oceans are outside national jurisdiction. These high seas are also often in desperate need of protection. Fishing, oil and gas exploration and mining threaten their biodiversity. Deep sea fish, such as orange roughy or deep sea perch (*Hoplostethus atlanticus*) are highly vulnerable to fishing and an entire population may be hauled up in a single trawl.

Although reserves have proved extremely successful in preserving individual fish populations much more protection is needed to halt serious declines worldwide. For reserves to recover exploited species they must be large enough to protect animals from fishing by encompassing their full ranges of movement. The best solution is often a network protecting carefully selected inshore and offshore habitats, the full range of habitat types and species, and including consideration of the requirements of migratory species and the influences of ecological processes within ocean basins. For example, if giant clams in one area grow from larvae produced many kilometres away, it will be necessary to protect both the adult habitat and the source of larvae (Wells and Hildesley, 1999). Finally, without long-term financing MPAs will not achieve their management aims or be able to enforce boundaries and closed areas or undertake monitoring of marine biodiversity.

Management Options

MPAs present particular management challenges that need different approaches to protected areas on land, for example:

- MPAs are designated in a fluid three-dimensional environment; in some instances, different management approaches may be needed at different depths.
- There are usually multidirectional flows (e.g. tides, currents).
- Tenure is rarely applicable; marine areas are usually considered to be 'the commons' to which anyone has a right of use and access.
- Full protection may only be necessary at certain times of the year, for example, to protect breeding sites.
- Controlling entry to, and activities in, MPAs is frequently very difficult to regulate or enforce, and to be effective boundaries or restrictions need management arrangements that are well publicized, readily understood and enforced.
- MPAs are subject to the surrounding and particularly 'down-current' influences, with most if not all 'upstream' activities occurring outside the management control limits of the MPA.
- The scales over which connectivity occurs can be very large (Dudley, 2008).

MPAs which aim to conserve fish stocks need to be developed with local fisherfolk to ensure success. Examples of community involvement in marine conservation occur around the world. In particular, many small community-managed MPAs have been set up in the Pacific and Southeast Asia. These currently are not always recognized as MPAs by the national agencies. One example is Western Samoa, where a network of over 50 small village fish reserves has been established under the Village Fisheries Management Plan (Wilkinson, 2002). A study of MPAs in the Caribbean found that nearly all include stakeholder consultation and about 55 per cent have active and formal mechanisms for stakeholder input. Fishing and tourism are two of the main ways in which MPAs benefit local communities.

Fisheries are important for local livelihoods, and only 15 per cent of MPAs completely ban fishing. However, zoning is practised: close to 40 per cent of active MPAs where information was available employed zoning as a tool for fisheries management (Geoghegan et al., 2001). Fish are the most important source of animal protein for villagers living in and around protected areas in central and southern Lao People's Democratic Republic. Therefore, the sustainability of fisheries is critical to food security. In Lao PDR, Fish Conservation Zones (FCZs), which are 'no-take' zones, are the most important co-management tool for fisheries. These zones have

Figure 5.4 *Small pelagic fish are dried by villagers living around Lake Malawi National Park*
Source: © John E. Newby/WWF-Canon

been established in areas that have been selected using indigenous knowledge. Since their establishment, villagers have reported significant increases in stocks of over 50 fish species (Baird, 2000).

Conclusions

Although still only representing a fraction of the world's protected areas MPAs have clearly shown that they can play a role in maintaining biodiversity and providing refuges for marine species. Most crucially, by protecting important habitats from damage by destructive fishing practices and other human activities, and allowing damaged areas to recover, they provide areas where fish are able to spawn and grow to their adult size. This can have the knock-on effect of increasing fish catches (both size and quantity) in surrounding fishing grounds. When this occurs MPAs can help to maintain the many local cultures, economies and livelihoods which are intricately linked to the marine environment.

Case Study 5.1:
Freshwater Fishery Sustainability in Lake Malawi, East Africa

Sue Stolton

Lake Malawi is the third largest lake in Africa. It is about 560km long and up to 75km wide and borders three countries: Malawi, Mozambique and Tanzania. The lake has the highest fish species diversity of any lake in the world, estimated at some 800 species. Most of these species belong to the Cichlidae family, of which more than 90 per cent are endemic to Lake Malawi (Munthali, 1997). The shallower south of the lake supports a rich fishery and accounts for about 60 per cent of the lake's annual fish catch (Weyl et al., 2005).

Protecting fish stocks

Lake Malawi National Park is found to the south of the lake. The park, which lies on and around the Nankumba Peninsula, includes Boadzulu, Mpande, the Maleri Islands and seven other offshore islets, as well as an aquatic zone which extends 100m offshore from all of these areas. The park was designated in 1980 and was the world's first freshwater underwater protected area. It remains unique in Africa for being established primarily to protect the rich aquatic life of the lake, especially the small brightly coloured rocky-shore tilapiine cichlids and the larger haplochromine cichlids which provide most of the food fish. The peninsula also forms the only freshwater national park in the world that is also declared as a World Heritage site (Chafota et al., 2005).

Lake Malawi is an important source of food, income and employment for the thousands of people living in the lake basin, which is one of the poorest regions on the planet. Fisheries provide nearly 75 per cent of the animal protein consumed by people in Malawi and is a significant source of employment (Munthali, 1997). Five shoreline villages, Chembe, Masaka, Mvunguti, Zambo and Chidzale, are included within enclaves of the protected area (UNEP-WCMC, 2005).

The lake's fish have been exploited by traditional methods for many years. Although commercial fishing, using purse seining, began in the lake in 1935, a significant fishing industry was not established until 1968 with the introduction of trawling. There is striking evidence of changes in fish populations since that time. Studies carried out in the 1970s showed significant changes in the species composition of catch as the trawl fishery intensified, with larger cichlid species disappearing from the catches and smaller species increasing in abundance (Kasuloa and Perrings, 2006). Overall the annual fish yield declined from 21,000 tonnes in 1971 to 9000 tonnes in 1983 (Ogutu-Ohwayo and Balirwa, 2006). By the late 1980s studies found cichlid species such as *Lethrinops mylodon* and *L. macracanthus*, which had declined substantially in the 1970s, had become locally extinct and many other species had declined. A one-year moratorium on trawling in the southwest arm of the lake between 1992 and 1993 had a marked effect in increasing both fish biomass and species composition (Kasuloa and Perrings, 2006).

Management cycles

Management of the fisheries in Lake Malawi has to a certain extent gone full circle. In pre-colonial times the lake's resources were under a common property regime and the fishery was regulated by family heads, village headmen and chiefs. The first fishing regulations were introduced in 1930, prohibiting fishing by traps, weirs and poisoning and excluding foreign commercial fishers from operating within two miles of traditional fishing grounds. However, enforcement of the regulations was lax. A fisheries department was established in Malawi in 1946 to regulate fishing and the fish-trade, and to conduct research. This implicitly transferred the control and ownership of the lake's resources from the communities to central government. The Fisheries Act of 1974 was supposed to implement the government's policy of maximizing sustainable yield from stocks that could be economically exploited in national waters. However, policing of the act was again unsuccessful due to lack of trained staff and patrol equipment, and the low level of penalties for non-compliance. The 1990s saw a change in emphasis, with the Fisheries Conservation and Management Act (1997) recognizing the benefits of co-management to utilize local knowledge and skills. The Act stipulates that co-management is developed through legally binding agreements between the government and recognized fisher associations (Kasuloa and Perrings, 2006). Between 1997 and 2000, about 267 beach village committees were formed but most have not been trained in management issues (Makuwila, 2001).

Protected area management

Lake Malawi National Park has been zoned to allow traditional seine fishing methods aimed at catching migratory fish in limited areas, although in most of the protected area the resident fish are completely protected (UNEP-WCMC, 2005). In 2002, the average annual fish catch was reported as being about 30,000 tonnes; with 92 per cent of the catch made by artisanal fishing and 8 per cent by the mechanized commercial fishing sector (Weyl et al., 2005). For communities in the enclaves of the national park Village Natural Resource Committees have been developed to work with the park authorities (UNESCO, 2000).

Although rising populations and demand for fish remain a threat to the lake's fishery the changing management and governance structures seem to be working. Research has found that the national park has higher species diversity than neighbouring areas where fishing takes place. Furthermore, in southern and central parts of the lake, outside the protected area, fish sanctuaries, controlled by traditional authorities, local communities and private companies, have also reported higher fish catches and potentially more diverse fish communities (Drill, 2008).

Case Study 5.2:
Managing and Monitoring Success:
The Story of Tubbataha Reefs, Philippines

Edgardo Tongson and Marivel Dygico

Nestled within the Coral Triangle at the centre of the Sulu Sea, the Tubbataha Reefs are the largest coral atoll formations in the Philippines covering an area of 100km². The nearest land mass of size is mainland Palawan, with the capital of Puerto Princesa City lying 150km northwest of Tubbataha. The tidal shifts and wind-driven surface currents of the Sulu Sea create ideal conditions for larval dispersal. So, despite the reef's relative isolation, the currents help carry larvae of corals and fish from Tubbataha to the surrounding reefs, especially on the eastern side of Palawan, which supports the biggest human population in the province.

Changing resource use

The islands of Cagayancillo are the nearest human settlement to Tubbataha and are home to the traditional users of Tubbataha's resources. At the start of the 1980s,

Figure 5.5 *Two-toned Gorgonian fan coral* (Paramuricea placomus) *in Tubbataha Reef*
Source: © Jürgen Freund/WWF-Canon

Cagayanon fishers started to perceive the pressure of overfishing in their immediate surroundings. Threats came from increased commercial fishing and seaweed farming. In 1989, the near pristine condition of the reefs deteriorated due to illegal fishing, including the use of explosives, indiscriminate dropping of anchors and unscrupulous collection of wildlife. Fishers from China and Taiwan also encroach into the Sulu Sea to catch turtles and fish, including sharks, using destructive methods (Tongson and Cola, 2007).

The reefs also began attracting the attention of researchers. They started to formally record the richness of the reef – which has nearly 400 species of corals (85 per cent of all coral species in the Philippines and about half of all coral species in the world), 479 species of fish, 79 species of algae, 10 species of seagrass, 7 species of breeding seabirds, 9 species of whales and dolphins, and 2 species of marine turtles. However, their studies in the 1980s also documented the increasing evidence of damage wrought on the reefs and their wildlife populations (Dygico, 2006).

Protection and governance

Calls for the protection of Tubbataha began in the mid-1980s and in August 1988 the Tubbataha Reef National Marine Park was declared, the first MPA in the country. This proclamation transferred Tubbataha's management jurisdiction from the municipal government of Cagayancillo to the national government. It banned the collection and gathering of corals, wildlife and any marine life, and outlawed the disturbance and destruction of the habitat. In 1993 the reef was declared a World Heritage site, the only purely marine World Heritage site in Southeast Asia today.

One negative effect of proclaiming Tubbataha's protection was that the wealth of its fisheries were advertised, making it an attractive target for unscrupulous fishers. Although the declaration of the MPA put Tubbataha off-limits to fishing, in reality fishing continued within the MPA boundaries.

The effective conservation of Tubbataha took several years to reach. The key to success was the development of locally based management involving the local community and stakeholder equity among all the different groups using Tubbataha, i.e. the big fishers, small fishers, divers, boat operators, conservation NGOs, government and academic researchers (Tongson and Cola, 2007). The Tubbataha Protected Area Management Board (TPAMB) has 17 members, from government agencies, local government, the Philippine Navy and Coast Guard and NGOs. All these organizations have local offices based in Puerto Princesa and Cagayancillo, enabling the members to attend quarterly meetings. Decisions are made by consensus. The Tubbataha Management Office (TMO) is the implementing arm of the TPAMB, overseeing the day-to-day operations of park management. The TMO is headed by a park manager, and several staff are recruited from nearby areas. In 1998, a park management plan was prepared following consultations with the local government and fishers; the plan is regularly updated to reflect monitoring and assessment results.

Effective management

As monitoring and assessment systems were developed and refined in the MPA the results of effective management and protection have been recorded. Hard coral cover increased and fish biomass doubled from 166 tonnes per km^2 in 2004 to 318 tonnes per km^2 in 2005 due to increases in fish size. This increase indicates that spawning stocks are maintained within the boundaries of the park, the effects of which are felt beyond the boundary. Indeed, perceived fish catches outside the MPA reported by fishers during focus group discussions were said to have increased from 10kg/day to 15–20kg/day for the period 1999–2004 (Tongson and Cola, 2007). Furthermore, the comparatively high fish biomass in the nearby reef of Jessie Beazley, which has doubled since 2000, is attributed to its proximity to Tubbataha which allowed fish migration. Jessie Beazley is only about 20km from Tubbataha. Basterra reef, some 70km farther to the south, is totally unprotected and suffers badly from fishing pressure (Dygico, 2006).

The monitoring data showing the importance of Tubbataha as a spawning ground for fisheries in the Sulu Sea helped convince commercial fishers to respect the no-take policy and local people to appreciate the management of the MPA. On its own initiative, the local community has established five MPAs as part of its coastal resources management programme (Tongson and Cola, 2007).

It is not just biodiversity which has benefited from the MPA. Socio-economic information was gathered in Cagayancillo to determine the impact of conservation on the people who were directly using the reef's resources before they were declared a no-take zone. A local participatory evaluation conducted in April 2005, reviewed income records and found an impressive 90 per cent increase between 2002 and 2004. Other indicators such as land and home ownership, hygiene facilities and access to electricity all increased between 2000 and 2004 (Dygico, 2006).

Many conservation projects fail because local stakeholders share a disproportionate burden of the cost arising from a no-take zone compared to benefits accruing to global and national stakeholders and more powerful groups. Tubbataha Reefs has demonstrated that reconciling competing interests, based on the sharing of costs and benefits that all stakeholders consider satisfactory and equitable, is an effective model for conservation and development (Tongson and Cola, 2007).

References

Abesamis, R. A. and Russ, G. R. (2005) 'Density-dependent spillover from a marine reserve: Long-term evidence', *Ecological Applications*, vol 15, pp1798–1812.

Ashworth, J. S. and Ormond, R. F. G. (2005) 'Effects of fishing pressure and trophic group on abundance and spillover across boundaries of a no-take zone', *Biological Conservation*, vol 121, no 3, pp333–44.

Babcock, R. C., Phillips, J. C., Lourey, M. and Clapin, G. (2007) 'Increased density, biomass and egg production in an unfished population of Western Rock Lobster (*Panulirus cygnus*) at Rottnest Island, Western Australia', *Marine and Freshwater Research*, vol 58, pp286–92.

Baird, I. (2000) *Integrating Community-Based Fisheries Co-Management and Protected Areas Management in Lao PDR: Opportunities for Advancement and Obstacles to Implementation*, Evaluating Eden Series, Discussion Paper no 14, IIED, London.

Balmford, A., Gravestock, P., Hockley, N., McClean, C. J. and Roberts, C. M. (2004) 'The worldwide costs of marine protected areas', *Proceedings of the National Academy of Sciences of the United States of America*, vol 101, no 26, pp9694–7.

Béné, C., Macfadyen, G. and Allison, E. H. (2007) *Increasing the Contribution of Small-Scale Fisheries to Poverty Alleviation and Food Security*, FAO Fisheries Technical Paper 481, FAO, Rome.

Castilla, J. C. and Duran, L. R. (1985) 'Human exclusion from the rocky intertidal zone of central Chile: the effects on *Concholepas concholepas* (Gastropoda)', *Oikos*, vol 45, pp391–9.

Chafota, J., Burgess, N., Thieme, M. and Johnson, S. (2005) 'Lake Malawi/Niassa/Nyasa Ecoregion Conservation Programme: Priority Conservation Areas and Vision for Biodiversity Conservation', WWF SARPO, Harare.

Claudet, J., Pelletier, D., Jouvenel, J. Y., Bachet, F. and Galzin, R. (2006) 'Assessing the effects of marine protected area (MPA) on a reef fish assemblage in a Northwestern Mediterranean marine reserve: identifying community-based indicators', *Biological Conservation*, vol 130, pp349–69.

Coad, L., Burgess, N. D., Bomhard, B. and Besançon, C. (2009) *Progress towards the Convention on Biological Diversity's 2010 and 2012 Targets for Protected Areas*, UNEP-WCMC, Cambridge.

Connell, J. H. (1997) 'Disturbance and recovery of coral assemblages', *Proceedings of the 8th International Coral Reef Symposium, Panama*, vol 1, pp9–22.

Drill, S. L. (2008) 'The use of protected areas for biodiversity and stock conservation in an East African lake', *Reconciling Fisheries With Conservation*, American Fisheries Society Symposium, vol 49, pp1253–62.

Dudley, N. (ed.) (2008) *Guidelines for Applying Protected Area Management Categories*, IUCN, Gland.

Dygico, M. (2006) *Tubbataha Reefs, A Marine Protected Area That Works*, WWF-Philippines, Quezon City.

Francini-Filho, R. B. and Leão de Moura, R. (2008) 'Dynamics of fish assemblages on coral reefs subjected to different management regimes in the Abrolhos Bank, eastern Brazil', *Aquatic Conservation in Marine and Freshwater Ecosystems*, vol 18, pp1166–79.

Geoghegan, T., Smith, A. H. and Thacker, K. (2001) *Characterization of Caribbean Marine Protected Areas: An Analysis of Ecological, Organizational and Socio-Economic Factors*, CANARI Technical Report no 287, CANARI, Tobago.

Goni, R., Adlerstein, S., Alvarez-Berastegui, D., Forcada, A., Renones, O., Criquet, G., Polti, S., Cadiou, G., Valle, C., Lenfant, P., Bonhomme, P., Pérez-Ruzafa, A., Sanchez-Lizaso, J.

L., García-Charton, J. A., Bernard, G., Stelzenmüller, V. and Planes, S. (2008) 'Spillover from six western Mediterranean marine protected areas: evidence from artisanal fisheries', *Marine Ecology-Progress Series*, vol 366, pp159–74.

Halpern, B. S. (2003) 'The impact of marine reserves: do reserves work and does reserve size matter?', *Ecological Applications*, vol 13, pp117–37.

ICEM (2003) *Regional Report on Protected Areas and Development. Review of Protected Areas and Development in the Lower Mekong River Region*, ICEM, Indooroopilly, Queensland.

Kasuloa, V. and Perrings, C. (2006) 'Fishing down the value chain: Biodiversity and access regimes in freshwater fisheries – the case of Malawi', *Ecological Economics*, vol 59, pp106–14.

Kaunda-Arara, B. and Rose, G. A. (2004) 'Effects of Marine Reef National Parks on fishery CPUE in coastal Kenya', *Biological Conservation*, vol 118, pp1–13.

Keller, B. D., Delaney, J. and Causey, B. (2003) 'Monitoring changes in the fully protected zones of the Florida Keys National Marine Sanctuary', *Proceedings of the Gulf and Caribbean Fisheries Institute*, vol 54, pp694–701.

Kerwath, S. E., Thorstad, E. B., Næsje, T. F., Cowley, P. D., Økland, F., Wilke, C. and Attwood, C. G. (2009) 'Crossing invisible boundaries: The effectiveness of the Langebaan Lagoon Marine Protected Area as a harvest refuge for a migratory fish species in South Africa', *Conservation Biology*, vol 23, pp653–61.

McClanahan, T. R. and Mangi, S. (2000) 'Spillover of exploitable fishes from a marine park and its effect on the adjacent fishery', *Ecological Applications*, vol 10, no 6, pp1792–1805.

Makuwila, M. (2001) *The Use and Management of Lake Malawi/Niassa/Nyasa: A Socio-economic Perspective on the Malawian Side*, WWF, Gland.

Millennium Ecosystem Assessment (2005) *Ecosystems and Human Well-being: Synthesis*, Island Press, Washington, DC.

Mumby, P. J. and Steneck, R. S. (2008) 'Coral reef management and conservation in light of rapidly evolving ecological paradigms', *Trends in Ecology and Evolution*, vol 23, no 10, pp555–63.

Munthali, S. M. (1997) 'Dwindling food-fish species and fishers' preference: problems of conserving Lake Malawi's biodiversity', *Biodiversity and Conservation*, vol 6, pp253–61.

Ogutu-Ohwayo, R. and Balirwa, J. S. (2006) 'Management challenges of freshwater fisheries in Africa', *Lakes & Reservoirs: Research and Management*, vol 11, pp215–26.

Paddack, M. J. and Estes, J. A. (2000) 'Kelp forest fish populations in marine reserves and adjacent exploited areas of central California', *Ecological Applications*, vol 10, pp855–70.

Pauly, D., Watson, R. and Alder, J. (2005) 'Global trends in world fisheries: impacts on marine ecosystems and food security', *Philosophical Transactions of the Royal Society Biological Sciences*, vol 360, pp5–12.

Pérez-Ruzafa, A., Martín, E., Marcos, C., Zamarro, J. M., Stobart, B., Harmelin-Vivien, M., Polti, S., Planes, S., García-Charton, J. A. and González-Wangüemert, M. (2008) 'Modelling spatial and temporal scales for spill-over and biomass exportation from MPAs and their potential for fisheries enhancement', *Journal for Nature Conservation*, vol 16, no 4, pp 234–55.

Roberts, C. M., Bohnsack, J. A., Gell, F., Hawkins, J. P. and Goodridge, R. (2001) 'Effects of marine reserves on adjacent fisheries', *Science*, vol 294, pp1920–23.

Roberts, C. M. and Hawkins, J. P. (2000) *Fully-protected Marine Reserves: A Guide*, WWF Endangered Seas Campaign, Washington DC, and Environment Department, University of York, York.

Stelzenmüller, V., Maynou, F. and Martín, P. (2008) 'Patterns of species and functional diversity around a coastal marine reserve: a fisheries perspective', *Aquatic Conservation: Marine and Freshwater Ecosystem*, vol 19, no 5, pp554–65.

Stobart, B., Warwick, R., Gonzalez, C., Mallol, S., Diaz, D., Renones, O. and Goni, R. (2009) 'Long-term and spillover effects of a marine protected area on an exploited fish community', *Marine Ecology-Progress Series*, vol 384, pp47–60.

Tongson, E. and Cola, R. (2007) 'Negotiating stakeholder agreements for conservation: The case of Tubbataha Reefs, Philippines', *Science Diliman*, vol 19, no 1, pp46–62.

UNEP-WCMC (2005) *Lake Malawi National Park, World Heritage Site Fact Sheet*, UNEP-WCMC, Cambridge.

UNESCO (2000) *Periodic Report for Lake Malawi Natural World Heritage Site*, whc.unesco.org/en/list/289/documents/, accessed 14 August 2009.

Unsworth, R. K. F., Powell, A., Hukom, F. and Smith, D. J. (2007) 'The ecology of Indo-Pacific grouper (Serranidae) species and the effects of a small scale no take area on grouper assemblage, abundance and size frequency distribution', *Marine Biology*, vol 152, pp243–54.

Wells, S. and Hildesley, W. (1999) 'Future developments in marine protected areas', in S. Stolton and N. Dudley (eds) *Partnerships for Protection*, Earthscan, London.

Weyl, O. L. F., Nyasulu, T. E. and Rusuwa, B. (2005) 'Assessment of catch, effort and species changes in the pair-trawl fishery of southern Lake Malawi, Malawi, Africa', *Fisheries Management and Ecology*, vol 12, pp395–402.

Wilkie, M. L. and Fortuna, S. (2003) *Status and Trends in Mangrove Area Extent Worldwide*, Forest Resources Assessment Working Paper no 63, FAO, Rome.

Wilkinson, C. R. (ed.) (2002) *Status of Coral Reefs of the World 2002*, Australian Institute of Marine Science, Townsville, Queensland.

Wilkinson, C. R. (ed.) (2008) *Status of Coral Reefs of the World: 2008*, GCRMN/Australian Institute of Marine Science, Townsville, Queensland.

World Bank (2004) *Saving Fish and Fishers: Toward Sustainable and Equitable Governance of the Global Fishing Sector*, Report no 29090-GLB, Agriculture and Rural Development Department, World Bank, Washington, DC.

WWF (2009) www.worldwildlife.org/what/wherewework/coraltriangle/, accessed 2 September 2009.

WWF (undated) *MPA Management: How is Your MPA Doing?*, WWF International, Gland, assets.panda.org/downloads/12investinginpeople.pdf, accessed 2 September 2009.

6

Natural Security:
Protected Areas and Hazard Mitigation

Jonathan Randall, Sue Stolton and Glenn Dolcemascolo

*The Swiss Alps are a haven for both walkers and biodiversity. Bright yellow signs mark well-maintained footpaths through forests full of wild boar (*Sus scrofa*) and chamois (*Rupicapra rupicapra*), up steep mountain slopes and on to the wildflower meadows of the high Alps. The forests feel natural and, to the casual eye, ageless, but neither is true. In fact, most of the trees were planted comparatively recently. Around 150 years ago the Swiss government recognized that deforestation was leading to serious avalanches, landslides and flooding, and introduced a rigorous system of protection and restoration (McShane and McShane-Caluzi, 1997). Following a serious flood in 1987, further steps were taken to use forests as protection against natural hazards, through the Federal Ordinances on Flood and Forest Protection. Swiss scientists and land managers identified four main stages of natural hazard management:*

- *hazard assessment;*
- *defining protection requirements;*
- *management planning;*
- *emergency planning (Lateltin et al., 2005).*

They recognized healthy forests as a major component of disaster prevention and forests in the Alpine region. Now, 17 per cent of Swiss forests are managed to protect against avalanches and floods; services which have been valued at US$2–3.5 billion per year (ISDR, 2004).

Sue Stolton

The Argument

The value

More people are affected by disasters than by war (Christian Aid, 2007); in 2008 at least 36 million people were displaced by natural disasters, including over 20 million displaced by climate-related disasters (OCHA, 2009). Natural disasters as a result of earthquakes and extreme climatic events are increasing, partly because climate change is creating more unsettled weather and partly because human societies, particularly in poor countries, are becoming less able to cope with sudden events that can lead to disasters. As the number of lives lost and the economic and social toll rise, the focus on disasters within the international community has also sharpened. A steady stream of reports, conferences and agreements have highlighted the impacts of natural disasters, calling for better disaster management in the short-term and implementation of disaster reduction strategies in the long-term. Since 2000 much of this work has been led by the International Strategy for Disaster Reduction (ISDR), which provides a framework to coordinate actions to address disaster risks at the local, national, regional and international levels. At a policy level the Hyogo Framework for Action, endorsed by UN member states at the World Conference on Disaster Reduction, Kobe, Japan, in 2005, means that all signatory countries commit to make major efforts to reduce their disaster risk by 2015.

Box 6.1 *When are 'natural disasters' natural?*

'Strictly speaking, there is no such thing as a natural disaster, but there are natural hazards, such as cyclones and earthquakes ... A disaster takes place when a community is affected by a hazard ... In other words, the impact of the disaster is determined by the extent of a community's vulnerability to the hazard. This vulnerability is not natural. It is the human dimension of disasters, the result of the whole range of economic, social, cultural, institutional, political and even psychological factors that shape people's lives and create the environment that they live in.' (ISDR, 2004)

The literature on disaster management has increasingly made links between disasters and the health of natural ecosystems. Put simply, if natural systems are degraded and the effectiveness of ecosystem services are reduced, then the consequences of natural hazards such as heavy rain, hurricanes, earthquakes or drought are likely to be exacerbated and can lead to a disaster. It is likely that if natural systems are compromised, either locally through activities such as deforestation or wetland drainage, or globally due to the impacts of climate change, the impacts of the disaster are likely to increase.

And it is clear that natural systems are being compromised. The Millennium Ecosystem Assessment notes that: 'Changes to ecosystems have contributed to a significant rise in the number of floods and major wild fires on all continents since the 1940s' (Millennium Ecosystem Assessment, 2005). This increase is indeed significant; between 1900 and 1940 about 100 disasters per decade were reported (ICSU, 2005). Between 1975 and 2008, the figures show a substantial rise. The International Emergency Disasters Database EMDAT recorded 8866 events killing 2,283,767 people during this period. Of these, 23 mega-disasters killed 1,786,084 people, mainly in developing countries. In other words, 0.26 per cent of the events accounted for 78.2 per cent of the mortality. Even taking into account that some of this increase is probably due to better reporting, the upward trend is hard to ignore.

The concept of ecosystem resilience is defined as the ability of a system to undergo, absorb and respond to change and disturbance while maintaining its functions (Carpenter et al., 2001). The detailed mechanisms by which natural ecosystems can absorb or deflect natural hazards are complex and variable and still surprisingly poorly understood by the scientific community. However, local communities and land managers have long recognized the importance of including disaster management and mitigation strategies as part of land-use protection. Today, ecosystem management is a vital component of disaster risk reduction, a management regime to which protected areas can clearly contribute (ISDR, 2009).

The benefit

The potential benefits of disaster prevention and mitigation must be considered in the context of the high costs to human life, health, culture and property by not taking action to reduce the risk of disasters. Although few of us could be considered totally safe from natural disaster, some areas of the world are more disaster prone than others. Overall about 75 per cent of natural disasters between 1970 and 1997 occurred in the Asia and the Pacific region, mostly in the poorest of developing countries (UNEP, 2002), and more than 95 per cent of all deaths as a result of natural disasters are in least developed nations (Pilon, 1998). Vulnerability increases as populations rise, urbanization increases and more people move to high-risk areas such as floodplains, coastal zones, small islands and steep slopes. Impacts are also linked to poor planning control in relation to infrastructure development, lack of early warning systems and inability to deal with the effects of disasters in terms of, for example, providing rapid medical care and clean water.

Economic losses from weather and flood catastrophes have increased tenfold over the past 50 years. However, as with social costs and deaths, the economic impacts of disasters are also uneven and disasters often have the most significant impacts on already vulnerable economies. At present, billions of dollars are spent on the aftermath of disasters and less on disaster prevention, although experience shows that spending on pre-disaster mitigation is far better value and more effective at reducing impacts on human communities. Studies have shown that US$1 invested in risk reduction can save between $2 and $10 in disaster response and recovery cost (IFRC, 2007).

Ecologists, engineers and disaster risk managers are trying to balance development, conservation and disaster preparedness, and are increasingly drawing on traditional approaches. For example, communities on the coast of Vietnam are very vulnerable to storm damage. Since 1994 local community forests in northern parts of the country have been planting and protecting mangrove as a way of buffering against storms. An initial investment of US$1.1 million saved an estimated US$7.3 million a year in sea-dyke maintenance. During typhoon Wukong in 2000 the project areas remained relatively unharmed while neighbouring provinces suffered significant losses of life and property (Brown et al., 2006).

The importance of conservation to both disaster mitigation and the economics of disaster mitigation has been illustrated in academic analyses. Sathirathai and Barbier (2001) estimate the coastal storm protection value of mangroves in Thailand at between US$27,264 and US$35,921 per hectare. Seidl and Steffens Moraes (2000) have valued the environmental resources of the Pantanal Conservation Complex at over US$15.5 billion per year. More specific annual values have been estimated at: US$120.5 million in terms of climate regulation, US$4,703.61 million for disturbance regulation and US$170.7 million in relation to erosion control (Schuyt and Brander, 2004). From a global perspective, one influential study in 1997 estimated that the planet's annual ecosystem services could be valued at between US$16–$54 trillion, with an estimated average of US$33 trillion, which was 1.8 times the current global gross national product (Costanza et al., 1997). As currently some 11 per cent of the world is managed as a protected area it would stand to reason that a considerable portion of this US$33 trillion might be attributed to the services provided by protected areas.

While we have noted that the original intent of creating several protected areas was to maintain their environmental services, today these services are rarely described in the literature or in many cases even recognized. Disaster mitigation seldom appears explicitly in management plans and it seems likely that opportunities to use protected areas to buffer against natural disaster are being lost as a consequence.

Current Contribution of Protected Areas: Balancing Natural Systems with Disaster Prevention

Many ecosystems are adapted to withstand extreme climatic events. In fact, such events may be necessary to maintain ecosystem health and vitality. For instance, fire can germinate seeds and provide space for regrowth, floods can bring fertility and even small landslides and avalanches can open up the forest canopy and stimulate regeneration. However, recognizing that natural systems are often resilient is not the same as assuming that these natural ecosystems buffer human societies against disaster. The fact that a forest fire is an ecologically sustainable way of maintaining vitality on an ecosystem scale is not necessarily much comfort to people who have had their homes burnt down. Floodplains can often absorb floods but this will not be looked on kindly by people who are living there. It also appears that at certain scales of hazard, natural ecosystems are likely to be overwhelmed, so that, for example, forests can and do help to reduce minor floods but are less effective at mitigating once-in-a-century floods. If we want natural ecosystems within protected areas to mitigate disasters in ways that are convenient for ourselves, then this function and value will need to be reflected in the management plans and budgets of protected areas.

Where properly planned and budgeted, protected areas can play three direct roles in preventing or mitigating disasters arising out of natural hazards:

1 Maintaining natural ecosystems, such as coastal mangroves, coral reefs, floodplains and forests that may help to buffer against natural hazards.
2 Maintaining traditional cultural ecosystems that have an important role in mitigating extreme weather events, such as agroforestry systems, terraced crop-growing and fruit-tree forests in arid lands.
3 Providing an opportunity for active or passive restoration of such systems where they have been degraded or lost.

These strategies are examined with respect to the mitigation of a variety of major hazards below.

Flooding

Natural or semi-natural habitats can help to mitigate flooding by:

- floodplains providing space for floodwaters to disperse without causing major damage;
- natural vegetation absorbing the impacts of floods.

Floodplains have evolved as a result of frequent immersion. They contain specialized ecosystems and are often particularly fertile due to constant deposition of new soil and nutrients. The human tendency to alter floodplains accelerated during the 20th century as rivers were increasingly dammed and channelled. The dykes and levees that were built to restrain water and channel it further downstream destroyed natural flooding patterns. The human impacts of flooding have been increased by people choosing to locate their settlements on floodplains, thereby transforming what were once harmless or beneficial flood events into major disasters.

There is now increasing recognition that protecting, or where necessary, restoring natural flows, including beneficial flooding regimes, can provide a cost-effective method of addressing flood problems. The science of integrated river basin management (IRBM) – the process of coordinating conservation, management, development and use of water, land and related resources within a given river basin – seeks to improve catchment planning and is also a valuable tool for preventing disastrous floods. Part of this simply involves setting aside flood-prone areas for uses other than industry, crops or housing; for example, as temporary pasture or as protected areas. In many cases this may involve restoring traditional flooding patterns and removing dykes and barriers to provide space for flood waters to escape and reduce downstream impacts (see Case Study 6.2).

For example, the Wetlands Reserve Program in the US aims to restore, enhance and protect wetlands. By the end of 2006 nearly 750,000ha of land was included in the programme. In England, the state conservation body Natural England has argued that the restoration of peat bogs, natural floodplains and lowland marshes should be 'not a replacement for, but a necessary complement to existing flood defences'. Creating protected areas on floodplains, including through the restoration of natural flooding patterns, can have a dual benefit by restoring native wildlife and providing space for floodwaters to disperse without causing damage. Protected areas can consist of strictly protected nature reserves or protected landscapes (e.g. IUCN category V) where traditional cultural management systems such as grazing continue to take place (Stolton et al., 2008).

In terms of reducing flood risk, establishing a protected area can be a win–win option by addressing a gap in global conservation and simultaneously reducing risks to human populations. Inland waters are currently badly under-protected. The UN-ISDR *Guidelines for Reducing Flood Losses* recommend that 'Alternate use of flood-prone land should be considered where possible. It is better to have the land zoned and used for purposes such as parks, nature areas or ecological reserves than to try and ensure that future development is flood proofed' (Pilon, 1998). The Whangamarino Ramsar site in New Zealand is the second largest bog and swamp complex remaining in North Island and is a good example of the value of protecting

Figure 6.1 *The Kinabatangan floodplain is the largest remaining forested floodplain in Sabah, Malaysia*

Source: ©WWF-Canon/Hartmut Jungius

floodplains. The wetland has a significant role in flood control (the value of which has been estimated at US$601,037 per annum at 2003 values) and sediment trapping (Schuyt and Brander, 2004). Values rise in years when there is flooding and it is estimated that flood prevention in 1998 was worth US$4 million alone. There have been 11 occasions when the wetlands have been needed to absorb floods since 1995 (Department of Conservation, 2007). The site is also of considerable biodiversity value and more botanically diverse than any other large low-lying peatland in North Island.

Natural vegetation may play a role in absorbing the impacts of flooding but its contribution is still a subject of active debate. Overall, the scientific literature suggests that removal of forest cover leads to a decrease in evapotranspiration losses and runoff concentration times, the net effect being greater water surpluses and more rapid runoff, thus increasing flood risk (Jones, 2001). The role of natural vegetation has also been recognized by the UN Task Force on Flood Prevention and Detection, whose members submitted a report to the UN Economic Commission for Europe stating that: 'Natural wetlands, forested marshlands and retention areas in the river basin should be conserved, and where possible restored or expanded' (UNECE, 2000).

An analysis of flood data from 56 developing countries found a significant link between forest loss and increased flood risk (Bradshaw et al., 2007). These findings certainly justify the policies of numerous governments which link deforestation with flooding. Deforestation has long been anecdotally blamed for increased flooding in tropical or mountainous regions (Stolton et al., 2008). Logging bans in Thailand in 1985 and in China in 1998 were both in direct response to disastrous floods (although in both cases the particular floods that triggered the political response may have been too large for forests to control). Similarly, in Madagascar there is mounting concern that increased rates of deforestation are causing greater flooding in the eastern half of the island where the monsoon rains are particularly severe. Increased protection is seen as one response. Mantadia National Park, for example, protects the watershed of the Vohitra River. An analysis of the economic benefits of the park to farmers in the region, due to reduced flooding as a consequence of reduced deforestation, found that conversion from primary forest to swidden (an area cleared of vegetation for cultivation) can increase storm flow by as much as 4.5 times. It has been concluded that the net value of forest protection within upper watersheds in terms of reduced crop damage from floods in agricultural plots in lower basins was US$126,700 in 1997 (to put this figure into perspective the authors note that in 1991 Madagascar had per capita GNP of US$207) (Kramer et al., 1997).

Landslides, avalanches and rock falls

Natural vegetation, particularly forests, conserved in protected areas can also prevent and mitigate sudden earth and snow movements by:

- stabilizing soil and packing snow in a way that prevents slippage;
- slowing the movement and extent of damage once a slip is underway.

Figure 6.2 *A landslide that left 3000 homeless in West Papua, Indonesia*
Source: © WWF-Canon/Alain Compost

The concept that at least a proportion of landslides, avalanches and rock falls can be effectively controlled by maintaining vegetation on steep slopes has been recognized and used as a practical management response for hundreds of years (Rice, 1977). Conversely, forest clearance can dramatically increase the frequency of, for example, shallow landsliding on steep slopes. The potential of vegetation to reduce landslides is not unlimited. Local geology, slope and weather patterns are all major and often dominant criteria. Benefits of vegetation are likely to be strongest in the case of small or shallow landslides and mud- and snow-slips; huge, catastrophic events will not be stopped. Similarly, forests have only limited potential to stop or divert an avalanche or landslide once it is in motion.

The 72,00ha, category V Jiuzhaigou Nature Reserve forms the core of the Jiuzhaigou Valley World Heritage site in Sichuan, China. Government policy had focused on accelerating development through timber extraction and tourism. However, a combination of lack of downstream irrigation water and major flooding led to a ban on commercial logging in 1998 along with the adoption of sustainable forestry policies. In 1996 a plan was agreed to reduce agricultural land in the buffer zone and plant trees on steep slopes; residents have received compensation for giving up farmland (Stolton et al., 2008).

Storm surge and coastal erosion

Protected areas can also help to retain natural vegetation, reefs and landforms that can help block sudden incursions by seawater.

The role of mangroves in providing coastal defences against surges, rough seas and other abrupt forms of coastal activity is increasingly being recognized. Some countries have introduced restoration programmes in recognition of their coastal protection role as in Bangladesh (Saenger and Siddiqi, 1993). Such restoration efforts are being repeated around the world (Field, 1999). In Bangladesh, the world's top natural disaster hotspot in terms of mortality rate according to the World Bank (Dilley et al., 2005), the effective protection of the Sundarbans, the largest mangrove forest in the world, helps to protect southwest Bangladesh from cyclones. The mangroves' extensive root systems and the mineral-rich waters in which they grow also support a large variety of species and the spawning grounds they support are critical to the survival of local fisheries. These root systems also help to stabilize wet land and coastlines and contribute to the Sundarbans' role of buffering inland areas from the cyclones (Paul, 2009). In Bhitarkanika Conservation Area, India, the services provided by the mangrove ecosystem and the estimated cyclone damage avoided in three selected villages, taking a cyclone of 1999 as a reference point, were valued by assessing the socio-economic status of the villages. In the villages protected by the mangroves, adverse factors were lower (i.e. damage to houses) and positive factors higher (i.e. crop yield) than villages not sheltered by mangroves (Badola and Hussain, 2005).

Similarly, healthy and intact coral reefs are acknowledged as providing protection from storm surge (Moberg and Folke, 1999), as well as from more frequent

Figure 6.3 *Encroachment of housing on the mangrove forest near*
Hol Chan Marine Reserve, Belize

Source: © WWF-Canon/Anthony B. Rath

coastline erosion (Frihy et al., 2004). Mature sand dunes and coastal wetland areas also provide valuable buffering capacity. Unfortunately, a large proportion of coral reefs have suffered high levels of damage from over-exploitation and are now facing severe threats from bleaching as a result of global warming of the seas.

In Sri Lanka, for example, coral reefs are under threat. Even in protected areas, they are vulnerable because management capacity has been too weak to prevent destructive fishing techniques from being used (Caldecott and Wickremasinghe, 2005). Reef damage in Sri Lanka has led to erosion on the south and west coasts estimated at 40cm a year. The cost of replacing the coastal protection provided by these reefs has been calculated as being somewhere between US$246,000 and $836,000 per km (UNEP-WCMC, 2006), a figure far higher than that needed adequately to manage a protected area. Coral reefs and other shoreline systems are high on the list of habitats requiring protection and marine protected areas are often considered as 'ecological insurance' against acute and chronic disturbances (Wilkinson et al., 2006). Offshore barrier islands also offer important protection from storm surges as the shallow water around the islands slows the surge of water, reducing its strength as it reaches shore.

Drought and desertification

Protected areas can provide barriers against the impacts of drought and desertification by:

- reducing pressure (particularly grazing pressure) on land and thus reducing desert formation;
- maintaining populations of drought resistant plants to serve as emergency food during drought or for restoration.

Droughts cause immediate problems of their own and also, in combination with factors such as changes in grazing pressure and fire regimes, create an increased tendency for desertification, even in parts of the world where this has not previously been the case. The disasters associated with drought and desertification are usually slower-moving than the calamities associated with sudden influxes of earth or water but may have an even higher casualty rate in the long term.

The protection of natural vegetation may be the fastest and most cost-effective way of halting desert formation. Morocco is basing the establishment of eight national parks on the twin objectives of nature conservation and desertification control. It is developing co-management governance structures so that local stakeholders can be involved in decision-making; the need to protect dunes and other slopes to stop soil erosion is now more generally recognized by local people (Stolton et al., 2008). In Mali, the role of national parks in desertification control is also recognized and protected areas are seen as important reservoirs of drought-resistant species (Berthe, 1997). In Djibouti, the Day Forest has been made a protected area and regeneration projects have been initiated to prevent further loss of this important forest area and attendant desert formation (UNCCD, 2006).

Fire

Protected areas can protect against fire by:

- limiting encroachment into the most fire-prone areas;
- maintaining traditional cultural management systems that have controlled fire;
- protecting intact natural systems that are better able to withstand fire.

Incidence of fire is increasing around the world, caused by a combination of warmer climates and human actions. The role of protected areas is often complex and depends more than in most of the other cases discussed here on the particular social and ecological circumstances as well as on management choices and implementation.

In fire-prone areas, where natural fire is an expected and necessary part of ecosystem functioning, protected area management may have to be a trade-off between what would be ideal for nature and what is acceptable for neighbouring human communities. Many protected areas in savannah grasslands and dry tropical forests use prescribed burning to stimulate some of the impacts of wildfire without allowing the hottest and most dangerous fires to develop. In countries like Australia this reduces the threat of large-scale fires moving out into surrounding farmland and settlements. In other cases, control of grazing pressure by livestock can help to maintain frequent 'cool fires' on grassland, which prevent the build-up of inflammable material, thus reducing the threat of serious fires.

As ecosystems become more vulnerable to fire because of climate change or land-use practices, human-induced fire becomes increasingly likely to create natural disasters. Evidence suggests, for example, that forest areas cut for timber are at greatest risk of fire because the debris left behind dries out rapidly, acting as kindling. For example, although the Indonesian forest fires of 1982–3 had major impacts on Kutai National Park (198,629ha, category II), studies of the area found that fire killed more trees in secondary forest than in primary forest. Selectively logged forests suffered comparatively more damage due to the opening up of the canopy which created a drier climate with logging debris providing fuel for fires. In the more mature, protected forests, fire swept through the undergrowth only affecting larger trees where fire crept up vines (MacKinnon et al., 1997).

Hurricanes and typhoons

Protected areas can help to address problems of hurricanes and typhoons through:

- their role in mitigating floods and landslides;
- directly buffering communities and land against the worst impacts of storm events (e.g. storm surge).

Extreme storm events are an annual hazard in some parts of the world, and are anxiously tracked by citizens in regions such as the Caribbean where they have wreaked increasing destruction over the last few decades. Some of the side effects of hurricanes and typhoons, such as flooding, landslides and coastal damage, are described separately in this chapter. As with the other disaster-related discussion there has been a debate about whether or not natural vegetation, including forests, can help to absorb the main impacts of such storms and thus reduce effects on people, crops and property.

Hurricane Jeanne, which impacted several Caribbean islands in 2004, is a frequently cited example of how environmental management can greatly reduce the impact of cyclones on people and property. High rates of rainfall from Jeanne resulted in 7 flood-related deaths in Puerto Rico, 24 in the Dominican Republic and over 3000 in Haiti. Researchers concluded that the main reason for the difference was related to rural–urban migration and the consequent change in forest cover, particularly in mountain regions. Forest cover in Haiti has been reduced through planned and unplanned deforestation to less than 3 per cent. Seventy years ago, forest cover in Puerto Rico was similarly degraded and severe erosion and floods were common, but today forest cover has increased to almost 40 per cent and a similar process of forest recovery is underway in the Dominican Republic (Mitchell and Grau, 2004). The percentage of land cover in protected areas is markedly different as well, with Haiti having only 0.3 per cent cover while the Dominican Republic has 24.5 per cent (Stolton et al., 2008). It is possible that the human tragedy that unfolded in the wake of Hurricane Jeanne could have been substantially avoided if forest cover and protection had been in place. As Salvano Briceno, Director of the ISDR, stressed:

> *Environmental degradation has been the main cause of the devastating floods, which occurred last year in Haiti and the Philippines. The entire United Nations system, together with member states, national and regional organizations, have to commit themselves fully to disaster risk reduction policies if we want to avoid a re-emergence of such events there or anywhere else in regions often prone to natural disasters.*
> (UN/ISDR, 2005)

Future Needs: Recognizing the Role of Protected Areas in Planning and Management

The intensity of some hazards (in particular extreme weather events) and the vulnerability of human communities to natural disasters are both increasing. One reason for this increased vulnerability is environmental destruction and the consequent losses of ecosystem services. Many natural systems – including floodplains, forests, coastal mangroves and coral reefs – have the potential to reduce natural hazards. They do not provide total protection – the largest disasters will usually overwhelm natural defence systems – but they can and do play a role in reducing the number of lives lost and the economic costs of disasters. This is especially true in the increasingly frequent medium-scale disasters that escape international attention but continually erode development gains (ISDR, 2009).

The current exploitation and inadequate protection of coastal mangrove forests, coral reefs, freshwater ecosystems including estuaries, and upstream forests have left many areas extremely vulnerable to disaster. Protected areas have a key role to play in protecting against natural disasters by maintaining these important natural habitats in good condition. These functions deserve wider recognition, and should be included in protected planning and funding strategies.

Management Options

Until the 1970s, the international community considered disasters as exceptional circumstances: the once-in-a-hundred-years events which local capacity alone could not be expected to cope with and where external emergency relief was essential. The concept of disaster preparedness was developed during the 1970s and 1980s and truly established in the 1990s, which was declared the International Decade for Natural Disaster Reduction, one of the principal goals of which was to institutionalize the culture of disaster prevention.

There is now considerable and welcome recognition of the role of ecosystem services in disaster mitigation by many governments and international organizations. Tools to maximize the benefits are becoming available and efforts are increasingly being made to address risk reduction through ecosystem-based management. However, comparatively little best-practice guidance exists as yet to help implement the various declarations and agreements that have been developed. As the ISDR notes, 'Although the inherent links between disaster reduction and environmental management are recognized, little research and policy work has been undertaken on the subject. The intriguing concept of using environmental tools for disaster reduction has not yet been widely applied by many practitioners' (ISDR, 2004).

Perhaps one reason for this gap in best-practice guidance is that it is hard to develop generic management strategies when is comes to questions of environmental stability and hazard mitigation. In 1982, a review of 94 experiments on water balance and flow routing found that deforestation tends to increase runoff and flood peaks. The authors noted, however, that it was hard to develop management best practices or predictions from these studies as each catchment was unique and much depended on the type of the forest cover, climate and physical characteristics of the area studied (Bosch and Hewlett, 1982).

Community involvement in disaster management is important. In Honduras, for example, the Ibans Lagoon, part of the 525,000ha Río Plátano Man and Biosphere Reserve (category II) is home to three indigenous groups – the Miskito, Pech and Tawahka – as well as members of the Garífuna ethnic group and Ladinos from other parts of Honduras. One of the pressing concerns for these communities is the erosion of the narrow coastal strip between lake and ocean caused by the waves from both the lagoon and the sea, particularly during bad weather. This erosion has been exacerbated by the removal of shore vegetation, including mangroves, for firewood and house-building or to provide easier access to the lagoon for boat-landings and washing. Like much of the Caribbean, Honduras can be affected by tropical storms and hurricanes, which increase the risk of erosion and flooding. In 2002, MOPAWI, a Honduran NGO, began working with the communities of the coastal strip to identify the scale of the environmental problems and ways to tackle them. During a series of workshops involving men, women and children from 15 different communities, participants developed a community action plan for the management and protection of the lagoon and its associated ecosystems. Workshop participants gave highest priority to reforesting the lagoon shore with mangrove and other species in order to reduce erosion and improve fish habitats. The community has subsequently implemented these conservation activities (Simms et al., 2004).

Indeed, many local communities around the world are already using ecosystem-based adaptation to reduce the impact of climate change, including in various disaster-response strategies (see, for example, Mumba, 2008). It is sometimes professional development agencies that have more difficulty in integrating responses across disciplines.

Win–win situations, as in Honduras, can only be achieved when local communities understand the complex interactions between natural systems and disaster mitigation and cooperatively agree on the actions needed. Hurricane Katrina, the massive cyclone that devastated the Louisiana Gulf Coast in the US, was probably one of the best reported disasters that the world has ever known, with television and web viewers around the globe able to watch the tragedy unfold. The live coverage focused attention on the levees which let the flood waters in. The story of Katrina, however, begins not on 29 August 2005 when the hurricane made landfall, but decades earlier in the 1930s, when the construction of levees for flood control began fundamentally to alter coastal prairies and marshes in Louisiana. In the wake of the hurricane local communities demanded that existing levees be reconstructed and upgraded to afford increased protection against future hurricanes. At the same time, communities requested that the local, state and federal governments take steps to stem the loss of marshes and wetlands that provide disaster management, economic, ecological and recreational benefits. Unfortunately, these are conflicting aims as the presence of levees, and other human activities such as oil and gas exploration, have greatly altered the hydrological regime. In order for the wetlands and barrier islands of the area to achieve their full potential in buffering the impacts from future hurricanes, innovative, long-term solutions are required that combine land conservation with the systematic re-establishment of the regional hydrological regime. Such solutions also require broad community support and engagement (Stolton et al., 2008): indeed, without full and informed community participation many of the responses discussed in this chapter are likely to fail.

The important role of forests in reducing disaster risk should be an integral part of any forest management plan in disaster-prone regions. The maintenance of forest cover for disaster risk reduction should include consideration of both the area under trees and the quality of the forest that remains. Maintaining healthy forests can have both immediate impacts on disaster mitigation as well as addressing some of the underlying causes of disasters. A detailed study of the Batticaloa district of Sri Lanka following the Indian Ocean Tsunami found that although the tsunami was about 6m high when it reached shore and penetrated up to 1km inland, the mixed landscape, comprising beach, mangrove-fringed lagoon, coconut plantation, scrub forest and home gardens, seems to have absorbed and dissipated much of the tsunami's energy. By the time the wave reached the village it was less than 40cm high and caused no loss of life. The mangroves are comprised of a band of trees 5–6m deep, of which the first 2–3m (mainly *Rhizophora apiculata* and *Ceriops tagal*) were severely damaged by the tsunami. The inner 3–4m of mangrove vegetation, however, was much less damaged. The study concluded that mangrove restoration, particularly in the first 300m on both sides of the lagoon, should be a high priority due to their importance, both from a biodiversity and environmental security point of view (Caldecott and Wickremasinghe, 2005).

Conclusions

Our vulnerability to disaster has been increased by environmental destruction and the consequent losses of ecosystem services. Many natural systems – including floodplains, forests, coastal mangroves and coral reefs – have the potential to reduce natural hazards. They do not provide total protection but they can and do play a role in reducing the number of lives lost and the economic costs of climate-related hazards and earthquakes.

Recognition of the role that ecosystem services play in disaster mitigation is mixed. Many local people instinctively link declining environmental quality with increasing vulnerability to hazards, but these links have often not been made explicit in local planning, or governments have been ineffective in controlling the causes of environmental decline. Continuing debate about the role of ecosystem services is to some extent undermining efforts to develop a concerted response aimed at protecting and improving environmental services against natural hazards. Government and inter-governmental responses have a tendency to separate out actions against climate change, natural disasters, poverty reduction and conservation, for example, whereas the most effective responses usually need to consider these and other aspects simultaneously. Better integration could itself be a valuable step towards increasing the efficiency with which ecosystem services are employed in risk reduction.

There is, therefore, an urgent need to stop the degradation of ecosystem services and to ensure their long-term protection, particularly where a high risk of disaster coincides with environmental degradation. Protection and restoration of ecosystems will sometimes require trade-offs: e.g. restoration of natural floodplains may help control floods but may also mean relocation for some families. Similarly, protection of coastal habitats can help reduce storm surges but may reduce valuable tourism projects. Such losses need to be balanced against reduced damage and loss of life from floods and landslides, and more sustainable local development.

The emergence of compelling new economic analyses of the costs and benefits of ecosystem management for reducing risk are making it easier to build a case and convince decision-makers. However, to make the case as strongly as possible, managers of protected areas must partner with disaster risk managers to advocate for integrated solutions. More importantly, they must work together in designing solutions to reduce vulnerability. Experience has shown that when they work together, engaging each other in planning and implementing programmes, multiple benefits in community resilience can be achieved.

Case Study 6.1:
Environmental Degradation and
the Indian Ocean Tsunami of 2004

Sue Stolton and Anita van Breda

Tsunamis are caused by seismic disturbances and can result in the largest and most powerful waves on earth. On 26 December 2004 an earthquake deep in the Indian Ocean began a chain reaction that led to one of the worst natural disasters of recent history. The first area to be hit was the coast of Aceh Province in Sumatra, Indonesia. Over the following hours, a tsunami wreaked havoc on the coastal areas of 12 countries in the Indian Ocean.

The tsunami caused immense social, economic and environmental devastation in areas that were already suffering from poverty. It killed more than 280,000 people, left over 1 million homeless and caused over a US$1 billion worth of damage (Wilkinson et al., 2006). The disaster galvanized communities across the world to lend support, with the aid pledged to affected countries topping US$11 billion (HPN and ODI, 2005).

The initial earthquake off Sumatra was the world's largest seismic event in the last 40 years. Its effects were always going to be great, but impacts were worsened by poor land-use planning and environmental degradation.

Figure 6.4 *Devastated coastal area in Aceh province, Indonesia, after the 2004 tsunami*
Source: © WWF-Canon/Yoshi Shimizu

Mitigating the impacts

Computer modelling has suggested the importance of vegetation in dissipating the power of tsunamis (Danielsen et al., 2005) and research into the buffering effects of coral reefs has demonstrated that a sufficiently wide barrier reef within 1–2m of the surface reduces by up to 50 per cent the distance inland a wave travels, depending on the nature of the tsunami, geometry and health of the reef and its distance from shore (Kunkel et al., 2006). Field evidence is limited, however, because although many storms reach shore every year, powerful tsunamis are rare. Thus, there are fewer opportunities to study their impacts and mitigating factors. Studies in Japan have noted the role of forests in limiting the effects of tsunami damage and have made recommendations regarding forest area required to both mitigate and reduce tsunami impacts (Harada and Imamura, 2005; Shuto, 1987).

Research carried out following the 2004 tsunami is helping to improve understanding of land-management options and to highlight the role of protected areas to ensure future earthquakes do not result in such a major disaster:

- Detailed studies in Hikkaduwa, Sri Lanka, where the reefs are protected in a marine park, noted that the tsunami damage reached only 50m inland and waves were 2–3m high. At Peraliya, just 3km to the north, where reefs have been extensively affected by coral mining, the waves were 10m high, and damage and flooding occurred up to 1.5km inland (Fernando et al., 2005).
- A study of about 250km (19 locations) on the southern coast of Sri Lanka and about 200km (29 locations) on the Andaman coast of southern Thailand found that two mangrove species, *Rhizophora apiculata* and *R. mucronata*, and *Pandanus odoratissimus*, a tree that grows in beach sand, were effective in providing protection from tsunami damage due to their complex aerial root structure (Tanaka et al., 2007).
- In the Maldive Islands, the coastal vegetation provided important protection to the residents (Keating and Helsley, 2005). Much of the tsunami's force was dissipated in areas where the coast was fronted by a dense hedge of native shrubs such as magoo (*Scaevola sericea*). An impact survey carried out by UNEP concluded that: 'In general, natural shorelines and land surfaces fared better during the tsunami than did developed features. Tsunami impacts were greatest where villages or cultivated fields directly abutted the sea with little or no coastal protection. Wherever a fringe of natural coastal forest or mangroves had been left untouched there was a marked reduction in erosion and destruction of buildings' (UNEP, 2005a).
- The conclusions of a major report on the status of coral reefs throughout the tsunami-affected area found that: 'coral reefs absorbed some of the tsunami energy, thereby possibly providing some protection to the adjacent land, however, mangroves and coastal forests afforded the most protection to infrastructure on the land and probably reduced the loss of life in these areas' (Wilkinson et al., 2006).

The future – what role can protected areas play in hazard mitigation?

Evidence for the benefits of coral reefs and mangroves for shore protection is currently less for tsunamis than it is for storms, but clearly in some cases there is evidence of mitigation offered through ecosystems services. Unfortunately, some of this potential may soon be lost. Coral and mangrove communities are declining fast and coastlines are changing. Currently, only 9 per cent of the total area of mangrove in the world is protected and there are no accurate figures for coral reef protection (UNEP-WCMC, 2006).

The most logical approach to ensure coastal protection through ecosystem services would be the protection of remaining natural habitats where these are under threat, followed, where appropriate, by restoration of degraded areas. A critical step would be to ensure effective management of those protected areas that have already been declared. Although many countries of the Indian Ocean have designated marine protected areas to conserve coral reefs, few have effective management plans or enforcement of legislation, with the result that resources continue to decline. Of the damage to natural systems caused by the tsunami it is predicted that most coral reefs will recover naturally in five to ten years, provided that other stress factors are removed, and mangrove forests that have only been slightly damaged will re-seed themselves and recover (Wilkinson et al., 2006). Mangroves more severely damaged will need more active restoration and many of the countries affected by the 2004 tsunami are already restoring mangroves.

Such responses have been recommended by UNEP and FAO. In February 2005, at a meeting on coastal zone rehabilitation and management organized by UNEP in Egypt the 'Cairo Principles' for post-tsunami rehabilitation and reconstruction were adopted (UNEP, 2005b). Principle 3 calls for the conservation, management and restoration of wetlands, mangroves, spawning areas, seagrass beds and coral reefs. Similar activities were called for by the FAO in 2006, with experts calling for urgent action to be taken to protect existing coastal forests, rehabilitate degraded ones and plant new forests and trees in sites where they are suitable and have the potential to provide protection (FAO, 2006).

Finally, it should go without saying that disaster mitigation through ecosystem services is only one of many strategies for disaster risk reduction and preparedness. Thousands of lives, for example, could have been saved had a tsunami early-warning system been established in the Indian Ocean (Alverson, 2005).

Case Study 6.2:
Restoration and Protection Plan to
Reduce Flooding in the Lower Danube

Orieta Hulea and Christine Bratrich

The Danube is a truly European river. The continent's second-longest river, it originates in the forests of Germany and flows eastwards for a distance of 2800km before emptying into the Black Sea via the Danube Delta in Romania. The river flows through or borders ten countries and its drainage basin includes parts of nine more countries.

The Danube's watershed covers more than 800,000km², of which only about 7 per cent is protected. A comparison of former natural floodplains (i.e. the floodplains as they were about 300 years ago) and the recent floodplains (i.e. the area remaining between flood protection dykes and/or natural terraces) of the Danube and some of its tributaries indicates a dramatic loss of water retention areas, which is contributing to increased flood occurrence. Overall, the middle and lower Danube has lost about 70 per cent of its former floodplains, and its tributary rivers the Tisza and Sava have lost nearly 90 per and 70 per cent of floodplains respectively (Schwarz et al., 2006). Agriculture and forestry dominate the watershed (67 per cent and 20 per cent respectively) and over 10 per cent of the watershed is developed. Wetlands represent only 1 per cent of the watershed (Revenga et al., 1998).

Figure 6.5 *The Danube delta in Romania*

Source: © Michel Gunther/WWF-Canon

The last ten years have seen a cycle of devastating floods in the Danube's watershed. The first serious flooding event this century was in the summer of 2002, following a period of unusually low pressure across much of Europe. The Danube, along with many other rivers in central Europe, flooded and over 100 people lost their lives. The estimated economic costs were huge, some 10 billion euros in Germany, 3 billion in Austria and 2 billion in the Czech Republic (Swiss Re, 2002). The next serious flood event in 2005 was the result of heavy rainfall in the upper Alpine catchment of the river. The main flood wave which reached the middle Danube was only a negligible 3–5 year event, failing to reach the lower Danube at all. Nevertheless, flash floods in Bulgaria and parts of Romania destroyed many villages. In 2006 flooding along the lower Danube reached a near once-in-a-hundred-year event. In the entire Danube basin at least 10 people lost their lives and up to 30,000 people were displaced, with overall damage estimated at more than 0.5 billion euros. The floods were limited to the middle and lower Danube and mostly driven by snowmelt (Schwarz et al., 2006).

Causes of the disaster

Since the 1970s the lower Danube has largely been disconnected from its large floodplains and many side channels have been closed, in particular on the Romanian side. This has considerably reduced the discharge capacity of the river system, forcing floodwaters to overflow and break the dykes as during the 2006 floods (Schwarz et al., 2006). Satellite images and GIS-measurements show that the floods were restricted to the river's former floodplains. Although the immediate cause was rapid snow melt and heavy rain, the disaster was really the result of years of ill-conceived planning and investment, which placed property, agriculture and industrial development in the path of the flood waters. The Romanian Prime Minister, Călin Popescu-Tăriceanu, publicly blamed the flooding on the country's system of dykes, built in the 1960s and 1970s under communism in order to reclaim land for agriculture (BBC, 2006).

The cutting off of side-channels, riverbank enforcement, construction of dykes and drainage of wetlands for agricultural purposes altered the dynamics of the floodplain and wetlands. Consequently, their ecological value and ability to miti-gate natural hazards decreased dramatically. Floodplain ecosystems provide a broad range of services such as the provision of fish, reeds, wood, drinking water, nutrient reduction/storage and, of course, flood risk mitigation. In the lower Danube, WWF has estimated the added value of a restored floodplain using a range of parameters for economic values (i.e. fish, reed, pasture/cattle) and ecological values (i.e. water storage, nutrient removal, sediment retention, habitat for birds and fish, aesthetic value). The benefits of restored floodplains were calculated as having an overall value of about 500 euro per ha per year (Schwarz et al., 2006).

Mitigating the impacts

WWF analysed the impacts of the 2006 floods in four of the most affected areas in Romania (the Baltas of Bistret, Potelu, Calarasi and the island Calarasi-Raul), which together comprise at least 75 per cent of the area flooded. The research concluded that if restoration activities had been implemented and the capacity of the river had been increased through reconnecting side-channels and widening the riverbed, the flood level would have been lowered by up to 40cm during the flood (Schwarz et al., 2006).

The river reclaimed its former floodplain during the 2006 flooding, so logically the restoration of this floodplain will help lead to sustainable and sufficient solutions to flooding in the future. Indeed, proposals for increased restoration of degraded habitats and protection of floodplains have been slowly developing for some time. Foremost among these is the Lower Danube Green Corridor Agreement facilitated by WWF and signed by Bulgaria, Moldova, Romania and Ukraine in 2000. The signing parties pledged to establish a Lower Danube Green Corridor (LDGC) composed of a minimum commitment of 773,166ha of existing protected areas, 160,626ha of proposed new protected areas and 223,608ha to be restored to the natural flood-plain. Management ranges from:

- areas with strict protection;
- buffer zones with differentiated protection, in which selected human activities are permitted and degraded areas restored;
- areas where sustainable economic activities could be developed (WWF, 2000).

One major outcome is the development of a network of protected areas (including Natura 2000 sites), representing 70 per cent of the total LDGC area in the four countries. The mosaic of protected areas includes Ramsar sites, Biosphere Reserves, a World Heritage site (Srebarna Lake) and national/nature parks (e.g. Balta Mica a Brailei). However, so far only 7 per cent of the restoration commitment has been accomplished, and the largest wetland areas that have been converted to agricultural polders are still waiting to be reconnected to the river, including those at Potelu, Seaca-Suhaia-Zimnicea, Gostinu-Prundu-Greaca, Kalimok-Tutrakan, Pardina and Sireasa. If progress had been quicker the 2006 floods might not have been such a major disaster.

The area suggested for restoration in the lower Danube area includes relatively few settlements and very little infrastructure. Since the Danube serves as the border between Bulgaria and Romania, large areas in the 'Baltas' are still publicly owned, which should facilitate their restoration and further use for flood-mitigation purpos-es. Both the ecological and socio-economic analyses of the sites most affected in 2006 show clear advantages for restoration over polder management. The involvement and support of local people is particularly important when launching restoration activities. The combination of sustainable land use, river protection and restoration, and flood protection must be considered right from the beginning of the planning processes. This is crucial to generate both economic values and ecological benefits (Schwarz et al., 2006).

If the lessons learned from the flood events this century and pioneering work being carried out as part of the LDGC are properly acted upon, the Danube River may once again provide a vast array of benefits, including flood mitigation, for millions of people in Europe.

References

Alverson, K. (2005) 'Watching over the world's oceans', *Nature*, vol 434, pp19–20.

Badola, R. and Hussain, S. A. (2005) 'Valuing ecosystem functions: An empirical study on the storm protection function of Bhitarkanika mangrove ecosystem, India', *Environmental Conservation*, vol 32, no 1, pp85–92.

BBC (2006) news.bbc.co.uk/1/hi/world/europe/4951728.stm, accessed 1 August 2009.

Berthe, Y. (1997) *The Role of Forestry in Combating Desertification*, World Forestry Congress, Antalya.

Bosch, J. M. and Hewlett, J. D. (1982) 'A review of catchment experiments to determine the effect of vegetation changes on water yield and evapotranspiration', *Journal of Hydrology*, vol 55, pp3–23.

Bradshaw, C. J. A., Sodhi, N. S., Peh, K. S.- H. and Brooks, B. W. (2007) 'Global evidence that deforestation amplifies flood risk and severity in the developing world', *Global Change Biology*, vol 13, no 11, pp2379–95.

Brown, O., Crawford, A. and Hammill, A. (2006) *Natural Disasters and Resource Rights: Building Resilience, Rebuilding Lives*, International Institute for Sustainable Development, Manitoba.

Caldecott, J. and Wickremasinghe, W. R. M. S. (2005) *Sri Lanka: Post-Tsunami Environmental Assessment*, United Nations Environment Programme, Geneva.

Carpenter, S. R., Walker, B. H., Anderies, J. M. and Abel, N. (2001) 'From metaphor to measurement: Resilience of what to what?', *Ecosystems*, vol 4, pp765–81.

Christian Aid (2007) *Human Tide: The Real Migration Crisis*, Christian Aid, London.

Costanza, R., d'Arge, R., de Groot, R., Farberk, S., Grasso, M., Hannon, B., Limburg, K., Naeem, S., O'Neill, R., Paruelo, J., Raskin, R., Sutton P. and van den Belt, M. (1997) 'The value of the world's ecosystem services and natural capital', *Nature*, vol 387, pp253–60.

Danielsen, F., Sørensen, M. K., Olwig, M. F., Selvam, V., Parish, F., Burgess, N. D., Hiraishi, T., Karunagaran, V. M., Rasmussen, M. S., Hansen, L. B., Quarto, A. and Suryadiputra, N. (2005) 'The Asian tsunami: A protective role for coastal vegetation', *Science*, vol 310, no 5748, p643.

Department of Conservation (2007) *Economic Values of Whangamarino Wetland*, Department of Conservation, Auckland.

Dilley, M., Chen, R. S., Deichmann, U., Lerner-Lam, A. L. and Arnold, M. (2005) *Natural Disaster Hotspots: A Global Risk Analysis*, World Bank, Washington, DC.

FAO (2006) www.fao.org/forestry/coastalprotection/en/, accessed 4 July 2009.

Fernando, H. J. S., Mendis, S. G., McCulley, J. L. and Perera, K. (2005) 'Coral poaching worsens tsunami destruction in Sri Lanka', *Eos, Transactions (AGU)*, vol 86, no 33, pp301–304.

Field, C. D. (1999) 'Rehabilitation of mangrove ecosystems: an overview', *Marine Pollution Bulletin*, vol 37, nos 8–12, pp383–92.

Frihy, O. E., El Ganaini, M. A., El Sayed, W. R. and Iskander, M. M. (2004) 'The role of fringing coral reef in beach protection of Hurghada, Gulf of Suez, Red Sea of Egypt', *Ecological Engineering*, vol 22, no 1, pp17–25.

Harada, K. and Imamura, F. (2005) 'Effects of coastal forest on tsunami mitigation – a preliminary investigation', in K. Satake (ed.) *Tsunamis: Case Studies and Recent Developments*, Springer, The Netherlands, pp279–92.

HPN and ODI (2005) *Humanitarian Exchange*, no 32, Humanitarian Practice Network (HPN) and the Overseas Development Institute (ODI), London.

ICSU (2005) *Scoping Group on Natural and Human-induced Environmental Hazards*, Report to ICSU General Assembly, Suzhou, October 2005, International Council for Science, Paris.

IFRC (2007) *Defusing Disaster, Reducing the Risk: Calamity is Unnatural*, International Federation of Red Cross and Red Crescent Societies, Geneva.

ISDR (2004) *Living with Risk: A Global Review of Disaster Reduction Initiatives*, UN/ISDR, Geneva.

ISDR (2009) *Global Assessment Report on Disaster Risk Reduction*, United Nations, Geneva.

Jones, J. A. A. (2001) 'Human modification of flood producing processes: The evidence from catchment studies', in D. J. Parker (ed.) *Flood Hazards and Disasters*, Routledge, London.

Keating, B. H. and Helsley, C. (2005) '2004 Indian Ocean tsunami on the Maldives Islands: Initial observations', *Science of Tsunami Hazards*, vol 23, no 2, pp19–70.

Kramer, R. A., Richter, D. D., Pattanayak, S. and Sharma, N. P. (1997) 'Ecological and economic analysis of watershed protection in Eastern Madagascar', *Journal of Environmental Management*, vol 49, pp277–95.

Kunkel, K. M., Hallberg, R. W. and Oppenheimer, M. (2006) 'Coral reefs reduce tsunami impact in model simulations', *Geophysical Research Letters*, vol 33, no 23.

Lateltin, O., Haemmig, C., Raetzo, H. and Bonnard, C. (2005) 'Landslide risk management in Switzerland', *Landslides*, vol 2, pp313–20.

MacKinnon, K. S., Hatta, G., Halim, H. and Mangalik, A. (1997) *The Ecology of Kalimantan*, Oxford University Press, Oxford.

McShane, T. O. and McShane-Caluzi, E. (1997) 'Swiss forest use and biodiversity conservation', in C. H. Freese (ed.) *Harvesting Wild Species: Implications for Biodiversity conservation*, John Hopkins University Press, Baltimore and London.

Millennium Ecosystem Assessment (2005) *Ecosystems and Human Well-being: Synthesis*, Island Press, Washington, DC.

Mitchell, A. T. and Grau, H. R. (2004) 'Globalization, migration, and Latin American ecosystems', *Science*, 24 Sept 2004, pp1915.

Moberg, F. and Folke, C. (1999) 'Ecological goods and services of coral reef ecosystems', *Ecological Economics*, vol 29, no 2, pp215–33.

Mumba, M. (2008) 'Adapting to climate change and why it matters for local communities and biodiversity— the case of Lake Bogoria catchment in Kenya', *Policy Matters*, vol 16, pp157–62.

OCHA (2009) *Monitoring Disaster Displacement in the Context of Climate Change*, United Nations Office for the Coordination of Humanitarian Affairs and the Internal Displacement Monitoring Centre, Geneva.

Paul, B. K. (2009) 'Why relatively fewer people died? The case of Bangladesh's Cyclone Sidr', *Natural Hazards*, vol 50, pp289–304.

Pilon, P. J. (ed.) (1998) *Guidelines for Reducing Flood Losses*, ISDR, Geneva.

Revenga, C., Murray, S., Abramovitz, J. and Hammond, A. (1998) *Watersheds of the World: Ecological Value and Vulnerability*, World Resources Institute, Washington, DC.

Rice, R. M. (1977) 'Forest management to minimize landslide risk', in *Guidelines for Watershed Management*, FAO Conservation Guide, Rome, pp271–87.

Saenger, P. and Siddiqi, N. A. (1993) 'Land from the sea: The Mangrove Program of Bangladesh', *Ocean & Coastal Management*, vol 20, no 1, pp23–39.

Sathirathai, S. and Barbier, E. B. (2001) 'Valuing mangrove conservation in Southern Thailand', *Contemporary Economic Policy*, vol 19, pp109–22.

Schuyt, K. and Brander, L. (2004) *The Economic Values of the World's Wetlands*, WWF, Gland.

Seidl, A. F. and Steffens Moraes, A. (2000) 'Global valuation of ecosystem services: application to the Pantanal da Nhecolandia, Brazil', *Ecological Economics*, vol 33, no 1, pp1–6.

Shuto, N. (1987) 'The effectiveness and limit of tsunami control forests', *Coastal Engineering in Japan*, vol 30, no 1, pp143–53.

Simms, A., Magrath, J. and Reid, H. (2004) *Up in Smoke? Threats from, and Responses to, the Impact of Global Warming on Human Development*, New Economics Foundation, London.

Stolton, S., Dudley, N. and Randall, J. (2008) *Natural Security: Protected Areas and Hazard Mitigation*, WWF, Gland.

Schwarz, U., Bratrich, C., Hulea, O., Moroz, S., Pumputyte, N., Rast, G., Bern, M. R. and Siposs, V. (2006) *2006 Floods in the Danube River Basin: Flood Risk Mitigation for People Living Along the Danube and the Potential for Floodplain Protection and Restoration*, Working Paper, July 2006, WWF Danube Carpathian Programme, Vienna.

Swiss Re (2002) *Are Floods Insurable?*, Swiss Re, Zurich.

Tanaka, N., Sasaki, Y., Mowjood, M. I. M., Jinadasa, K. B. S. N. and Homchuen, S. (2007) 'Coastal vegetation structures and their functions in tsunami protection: Experience of the recent Indian Ocean tsunami', *Landscape and Ecological Engineering*, vol 3, no 1, pp33–45.

UNCCD (2006) *Ten African Experiences: Implementing the United Nations Convention to Combat Desertification in Africa*, Secretariat of the United Nations Convention to Combat Desertification, Bonn.

UNECE (2000) 'Sustainable flood prevention. Meeting of the parties to the Convention on the Protection and Use of Transboundary Watercourses and International Lakes', Economic and Social Council, UN Economic Commission for Europe, MP.WAT/2000/7.

UNEP (2002) *Global Environment Outlook 3*, United Nations Environment Programme, Nairobi.

UNEP (2005a) *Maldives, Post-Tsunami Environmental Assessment*, United Nations Environment Programme, Nairobi.

UNEP (2005b) www.gdrc.org/oceans/tsunami_coastal-guidelines.html, accessed 4 July 2009.

UNEP-WCMC (2006) *In the Front Line: Shoreline Protection and Other Ecosystem Services from Mangroves and Coral Reefs*, UNEP-WCMC, Cambridge.

UN/ISDR (2005) 'Disaster risk reduction is essential for sustainable development', Press Release, UN/ISDR 2005/13, 22 March.

Wilkinson, C., Souter, D. and Goldberg, J. (2006) *Status of Coral Reefs in Tsunami Affected Countries: 2005*, Australian Institute of Marine Science, Townsville, Queensland.

WWF (2000) *Declaration on the Cooperation for the Creation of a Lower Danube Green Corridor*, www.wwf.de/fileadmin/fm-wwf/pdf_neu/DanubeDeclaration2000.pdf, accessed 1 August 2009.

7

Safety Net: Protected Areas Contributing to Human Well-being

Liza Higgins-Zogib, Nigel Dudley, Stephanie Mansourian

and Surin Suksuwan

Around the biologically and culturally rich Kure Mountains National Park in Turkey are some 20,000–30,000 inhabitants, many of whom live on a per capita income of around 400 euros a year. The first question local inhabitants pose to park staff is: how will the protected area reduce poverty, contribute to rural development and stop outward migration? Responding to this question would be a tall order for anyone, not least in an underfunded protected area with a primary goal of biodiversity conservation. Yet the park authorities must respond and manage the resources of the protected area with the well-being of the local population in mind. And this is perfectly possible. Among many other real and potential benefits, the national park protects the region's main source of water, harbours major genetic materials and provides attractions for a growing number of international tourists.

Liza Higgins-Zogib

The Argument

The value: poverty reduction

> *In the 21st century, we will stand or fall on our ability to collectively eradicate poverty, guarantee human rights and ensure an environmentally sustainable future. Freedom from want, freedom from fear and sustaining our future are all part of the same equation.* (Klaus Töpfer, the former UNEP Executive Director, CBD, 2000)

Over the last decade, the challenge of reducing levels of global poverty has rocketed up the priorities of politicians, development organizations and the media, so that it now commands a dominant position among humanitarian aims for the new millennium. With good cause: despite the optimism of economists in the 1980s and 1990s, differences between rich and poor have in many respects continued to increase. Indeed, in 2000 world leaders gathered in New York at the UN Millennium Summit agreed that efforts to reduce poverty to date had not been satisfactory; 189 nations committed to renewed efforts to improve the lives of people on the planet by the year 2015, with the 8 'Millennium Development Goals' embodying this commitment (UN, 2006). The targets cover the different dimensions of human development, including income, education, gender equity, progress in combating infectious disease, environmental quality and access to clean water and sanitation.

The role that biodiversity can play in this global move to reduce poverty is not well understood and therefore often either overestimated or underestimated. As a first step it is important to have clarity on what we mean by 'poverty', 'poverty reduction' and 'well-being'. The understanding of what constitutes poverty has evolved over time. For many years it was assumed that if a nation's GDP grew, poverty levels would naturally drop (UNDP, 2000). Income, consumption and production measures provided an attractive way of putting figures on poverty. While for comparison purposes and for simplicity, the poverty threshold of 'one or two dollar(s) a day' retains its appeal, it is increasingly being replaced by multidimensional and more complex ways of defining and measuring poverty. In 1998, the Nobel Prize-winner for economics, Amartya Sen, stated that: 'Policy debates have indeed been distorted by overemphasis on income poverty and income inequality, to the neglect of deprivation that relates to other variables, such as unemployment, ill health, lack of education, and social exclusion' (Sen, 1999). A flurry of new definitions, frameworks and conceptual models has since emerged to try to counter this neglect.

To be able to discuss the role of protected areas in poverty alleviation we reviewed many of these definitions, including those from the World Bank, UK Department for International Development (DFID), WHO, OECD and World Summit on Sustainable Development (Dudley et al., 2008). Using the definitions from the OECD and DFID as a basis we recognize five fundamental dimensions of well-being – any improvement in which should contribute to reducing poverty:

1 *Subsistence*: non-economic benefits that contribute to well-being, i.e. health, nutrition, clean water and shelter .
2 *Economic*: benefits which provide the ability to earn an income, to consume and to have assets.
3 *Cultural and spiritual*: pride in community, confidence, living culture, spiritual freedom, education.
4 *Environmental services*: role in environmental stability and provision of natural resources.
5 *Political*: relating to issues of governance and thus influence in decision-making processes

Figure 7.1 *Several wells supplying local communities and Baka pygmies with drinking water have been created around Lobéké National Park, Cameroon funded by sport hunting fees*
Source: © Olivier van Bogaert/WWF-Canon

The benefit

Unlike some of the other benefits of protected areas discussed in this book, the role of protected areas in contributing to poverty reduction is complex. Protected areas have contributed in some cases to preventing further poverty, in others to reducing it and yet in others they may have exacerbated it (see Box 7.1).

The focus on ending poverty has to a certain extent moved international priorities, and often funding, away from conservation objectives. As a response many previously biodiversity-focused projects and organizations have tried to realign their activities to fit both conservation and development agendas. Such efforts have a mixed history; while some social programmes associated with protected areas have worked well there have also been plenty of failures. Meanwhile, the political pressure to show that conservation and poverty reduction can coexist is growing, particularly in the light of the Millennium Development Goals, and some governments are questioning commitments to protection in the face of economic or social pressures. As investors seek more guarantees or predictability of joint socio-economic and conservation success, implementing agencies are – rightly – being held more accountable for results.

Clearly, when discussing the relationship between protected areas and the often poor people who live in or near them, it is important to recognize that there have been both costs and benefits. In this book we consciously focus on the benefits which protected areas can provide and in this case it is important to distinguish between two types of benefit: compensatory and direct.

Compensatory mechanisms

These are mechanisms which give support to communities in and around protected areas to address problems of benefits foregone and in some cases to counter

Table 7.1 *Some of the potential compensatory mechanisms used in protected areas*

Compensatory mechanisms	Examples
Mitigating human–wildlife conflict	Protecting against elephant damage to farms: as in warning systems developed along the Kinabatangan River in Sabah, Malaysian Borneo
Insuring against human–wildlife conflict	Providing a flock of communally owned sheep to replace those lost to particular families as a result of predation from animals in protected areas in Pakistan
Modifying land management inside the protected area	Providing funds to compensate farmers for sympathetic management for wildlife: grants have helped to modify use of Alpine meadows in Hohe Tauen National Park, Austria
Modifying land management outside the protected area	Helping to develop sustainable agriculture near a protected area to compensate for loss of resources: as in Dja National Park, Cameroon
Supporting increased educational capacity	Providing funds for school buildings: tourists have funded schools around Bwindi Impenetrable Forest Reserve in Uganda
Supporting increased healthcare	Contributing to providing medical facilities: as in Djouj National Park in Senegal where a medical centre is included in the park headquarters
Building capacity for alternative livelihoods	Training local people as guides as in Keoladeo National Park, India, or in making local crafts to sell as around the Dana Reserve, Jordan
Providing alternative homeland	Resettlement of communities to other land: communities are being supported in moving from Cat Tien National Park in southern Vietnam.

Source: Dudley et al., 2008

additional problems created by the protection (e.g. crop raiding). They include: various management responses to reduce negative impacts; support for education and capacity-building; providing alternative livelihoods and homelands; and sometimes direct compensation or insurance schemes in cases of human wildlife conflict. They are largely independent of the particular mixture of species and ecosystems in the protected area except in the case of mitigation against problem animals. A range of examples of compensatory mechanisms is outlined in Table 7.1.

Direct benefits

These are potential or actual benefits from the protected area. They draw directly on the fact that the protected area is maintaining a natural or semi-natural ecosystem and can include: sustainability of resources; various forms of environmental benefits; a wider range of social and cultural attributes (see Chapter 9) and political considerations. These benefits are generally linked to the existence of a functioning ecosystem. Each of these can relate to poverty reduction in a number of different ways. In economic terms they can provide income for poor communities through direct sales or jobs and in some cases through newer mechanisms such as payments for environmental services (PES) schemes, whereby communities manage the ecosystem in a certain way that provides benefits (such as clean water or mitigating the impacts of climate change) to others who are willing to pay for this benefit.

If we take the broader definition of poverty to include the five elements described above, a matrix can identify the full range of possible direct benefits from protected areas (see Table 7.2).

It should also be noted that the size of the population living in and around a protected area as well as the amount of area protected may also have considerable influence on its ability to contribute to the people's well-being and provide the types of benefits outlined in Table 7.2. If only a relatively small population relies on the protected area's resources these could be sufficient to help to reduce poverty. On the other hand, when population pressure is too great or the protected area too small, individual protected areas may not be so successful in providing for the population; indeed, population pressure may also negatively affect the values of the protected area. There is a critical threshold beyond which human impact on the protected area would be too great to ever consider that poverty reduction and protected area objectives could co-exist (Grimble et al., 2002). Even initially successful protected area strategies that help address poverty may in time run into problems if they also lead to human migration to the protected area, thus stretching it beyond its carrying capacity.

Table 7.2 *Potential values from protected areas*

Values	Dimensions of poverty				
	Subsistence	Economic	Cultural/ spiritual	Environment services	Political
Food and drink					
Wild game	1	1	1	3	3
Wild food plants	1	1	2	3	3
Fisheries and spawning areas	1	1	2	2	3
Traditional agriculture	1	1	2	3	3
Livestock grazing and fodder	1	1	3	3	3
Non-commercial water use	1	3	3	2	3
Commercial water use	3	1	3	2	2
Cultural and spiritual values					
Cultural and historical values	2	1	1	3	2
Sacred natural sites/landscapes	2	1	1	3	2
Pilgrimage routes	3	1	1	3	2
Health and recreation					
Medicinal herbs for local use	1	2	2	3	3
Pharmaceuticals	3	1	3	3	3
Recreation and tourism	3	1	1	3	2

	Col 1	Col 2	Col 3	Col 4
Knowledge				
Research, traditional knowledge	2	1	3	2
Education	3	1	3	2
Genetic material	2	3	3	3
Environmental benefits				
Climate change mitigation	3	1	3	2
Soil stabilization	2	1	3	2
Coastal protection	2	1	3	2
Flood prevention	2	1	3	2
Water quality/quantity control	2	1	3	2
Materials				
Non-wood products	1	1	3	3
Management/removal of timber	1	1	3	3
Homeland, security of land tenure				
Home for local communities	1	2	3	1
Home for indigenous people	1	2	3	1
Peace Parks	2	2	3	1

Key: 1 = important value; 2 = usually only a minor value; 3 = not usually a value

Box 7.1 *The human costs of protection*

It is important to recognize that in some cases protected areas may also have exacerbated poverty, particularly if we understand poverty as being wider than mere income. The 20th century saw the creation of numerous protected areas, in an attempt to rescue our natural wealth in the wake of heavy industrialization, but, in some cases, this was done at a high human cost. One estimate suggests that over 10 million people have been displaced from protected areas by conservation projects (Schmidt-Soltau, 2003).

There are two main reasons why some protected areas may have enhanced poverty. Firstly, protected areas harbour resources that poor rural people depend upon. Fencing off such areas is like cutting off access to their bank account. For example, in the Democratic Republic of Congo, the Bambuti Batwa were evicted from their ancestral lands when the Kahuzi-Biega National Park was created in the 1970s. Given that their traditional way of life had been centred on hunting and gathering from within the forest, they subsequently suffered a dramatic decline in their welfare (Nelson and Hossack, 2003). In the Philippines, on Sibuyan island, the creation of Mount Guiting-Guiting Natural Park in 1996 and the consequent limitations on gathering products from the park affected 1687 individuals who considered this land their ancestral domain and who had until then collected honey, rattan, vines, medicinal plants and other non-timber forest products (NTFPs) central to their livelihoods (Tongson and Dino, 2004).

The second main reason that protected areas have sometimes enhanced poverty is that in times of difficulty, such as droughts or years of poor harvest, protected areas are often a back-up resource for poor people. Thus, while people may not use certain resources all year round, or even every year, they may need to turn to them in times of duress. This happened, for example, in Southeast Asia during the 1997–8 financial crisis when many urban dwellers affected by the economic downturn returned to their villages and to a more nature-based lifestyle (Steele et al., 2006). Should this option no longer be available to them because of a strict protection status, then their vulnerability may be further exacerbated.

However, the creation of a protected area need not be a cause for increased poverty. In many of these examples, it has often been the approach towards protected area establishment, management and governance that has been at the root of the problem. In fact, in many cases, attempts have subsequently been made to remedy the initial conflicts with rural people, with varying degrees of success.

Current Contribution of Protected Areas

Because for decades poverty has been interpreted as merely a financial issue, examples of protected areas' contributions to poverty reduction have been confined to the financial aspects of poverty and support packages reflect this. If, on the other hand, poverty is understood as about more than just dollars and we assume poverty is a state of 'non well-being', we can begin to see the different ways in which protected areas could potentially contribute to poverty reduction.

Subsistence

Protected areas can provide a range of non-economic benefits that are important for subsistence, such as health, nutrition, clean water and shelter. Protected areas conserve vital resources. These same resources have often been used by poor, rural communities in ways that are not always well understood by rich, western communities. One study on wildlife and poverty suggested that one-eighth of the world's poor (i.e. 150 million people) depend on wildlife for their livelihoods (DFID, 2002). These resources do not necessarily increase income, but provide many of the other elements of well-being. Many examples of important subsistence values from protected areas are included in other chapters of this book, including the contribution of protected areas to clean water, fisheries and health. However, subsistence needs and conservation and sustainability issues do need to be balanced.

Economic

Some protected areas can generate major economic gains (see Chapter 1). Analysis of costs and benefits for marine protected areas in Cape Province, South Africa, for example, found benefits outweighing costs (Turpie et al., 2006). Total added value of protected landscapes in the northeast of England was estimated at being US$446 million per year (Economic Development Consultants, 2004). The role that tourism in particular can play in providing economic benefits from protected areas is explored in Chapter 10.

Cultural and spiritual

Many protected areas have significant historical, cultural and/or spiritual values for local communities, nations or the global community as a whole (von Droste et al., 1998). Some protected areas, such as the Ecosystem and Relict Cultural Landscape of Lopé-Okanda, Gabon, which is recognized as a World Heritage site, have been designated at least in part because of their historical or cultural interest. Spiritual values are more complex, as is discussed in Chapter 8, but can include built places of worship or, much more commonly, sacred natural sites (sacred groves, mountains, waterfalls, etc.) or pilgrimage routes that pass through protected areas. Benefits can also include the cultural values that help to bind and shape societies (see Chapter 9). In some cases these values can also attract tourists, pilgrims and other visitors and thus provide direct economic benefits to local communities through ecotourism, guiding or provision of accommodation and other services. Examples include guided walks to bushmen rock painting in the Drakensberg National Park in South Africa; tourist venues based around historical slate-mining sites in the Snowdonia National Park, UK; and businesses linked around Mount Fuji, an extremely important sacred site in Japan. The existence of people living traditional lifestyles within protected areas can also be part of the attraction for visiting and providing local communities with cash opportunities through sale of crafts or home-stay, such as in the case of the Maasai in Ngorongoro Crater in Tanzania (Dudley et al., 2008).

Environmental services

Protected areas can supply numerous ecosystem services such as climate regulation, watershed protection, coastal protection, water purification, carbon sequestration and pollination – many of which are discussed in detail in other chapters in this book.

Political

Having access to land is ultimately a significant political matter. By having a say in the management of protected areas, poor rural people not only obtain the right to decide what happens to land that they and their children live on, but they also acquire an implicit role in society as managers of an important resource. For example, in 1980, the Kayan Mentarang National Park was created in East Kalimantan with 16,000 Dayak people living inside or near the park. Thanks to a participatory exercise involving community mapping the Dayak were able to establish their claims to the resources in the park and to continue to use and manage forest resources in the protected area (Ferrari, 2002). In Australia, Aboriginal and Torres Strait Islanders have been working with the government to declare protected areas within their territory, to increase levels of protection and gain other benefits (Gilligan, 2006).

Contribution to poverty alleviation

Table 7.3 provides just a few examples of protected areas which have contributed to poverty alleviation in a variety of ways. The countries are ranked by their place in the United Nations Human Development Index (HDI), a composite index that covers income, education and health (UNDP, 2008).

Table 7.3 *Examples of contributions of protected areas to poverty reduction*

Country, HDI ranking and GDP/capita (CIA, 2009)	Name of protected area and details	Contribution to economic dimension of poverty reduction
Low HDI ranking		
Zambia HDI rank: 163 GDP/cap: US$1500	Lupande Game Management Area, adjacent to the South Luangwa National Park (Forest Reserve, 5613ha, and Game Management Area, 484,000ha, category VI, established 1971)	Two hunting concessions earn annual revenues of US$230,000 for the 50,000 residents. The revenue is distributed both in cash to the local community and to village projects such as schools. Ultimately, a total of 80 per cent of revenue from hunting goes to the community.
Uganda HDI rank: 156 GDP/cap: US$1300	Bwindi Impenetrable Forest National Park (32,092ha, category II, established 1991)	A trust fund established to protect mountain gorilla habitat distributes 60 per cent of its funds to community projects promoting conservation and sustainable development activities (including schools, feeder roads, etc.). Two community campsites have been set up near the park. In 2004, Buhoma campsite earned US$70,628 (up from US$22,000 in 2001) and employed 11 local villagers on a permanent basis. The revenue is used in community infrastructure projects, such as provision of a water pump
Medium HDI ranking		
Tanzania HDI rank: 152 GDP/cap: US$1300	Selous Game Reserve (5,000,000ha, category IV, established 1922)	A retention fund holds 50 per cent of the revenue generated by the reserve. From 1999 to 2002, a total of US$890,000, or 11 per cent of the total retention fund, was committed to developing schools and infrastructure
	Serengeti National Park (1,476,300ha, category II, established 1951)	Serengeti generates 385 jobs. In the ten years between 1993 and 2003 the park contributed US$292,000 to local community projects (particularly in the field of education)

Country, HDI ranking and GDP/capita (CIA, 2009)	Name of protected area and details	Contribution to economic dimension of poverty reduction
Comoros HDI rank: 137 GDP/cap: US$1000	Moheli Marine Park (40,400ha, category II, established 2001)	Agreements signed with villagers to promote sustainable use of the resources have led to an increase in fish catch from 160kg/month to over 300kg/month. Revenues for 250 fishers working in the park have doubled. Thirty new jobs were created in ecotourism (the number is expected to increase)
Cambodia HDI rank: 136 GDP/cap: US$2423	Ream National Park (21,000ha, category II, established 1995)	About 30,000 people live in or around the park and up to 84 per cent of households depend on the park for their subsistence and income. The estimated net value of the park to households is US$1.24 million/year, an average of US$233/year per household
Lao PDR HDI rank: 133 GDP/cap: US$2100	Nam Et National Biodiversity Conservation Area (170,000ha, category VI, established 1993) and Phou Loei National Biodiversity Conservation Area (150,000ha, category VI, established 1993)	81 village communities depend on the area for NTFPs whose value is estimated at US$1.88 million/year. Of this amount about 30 per cent is cash income and the remainder is subsistence. In 2003, the sale of NTFPs accounted for between 41–76 per cent of average family income in the Nakai district. An assessment of NTFPs values them at US$250 per annum for each household living outside the conservation area, US$500 for those on the border and almost US$677 for those inside in the conservation area. These figures compare with a per capita GDP for Houaphan province of US$180

Country, HDI ranking and GDP/capita (CIA, 2009)	Name of protected area and details	Contribution to economic dimension of poverty reduction
	Xe Piane National Biodiversity Conservation Area (240,000ha, category VI, 1993)	In Kokpadek in southern Laos, before a co-management system was put in place, up to 60 per cent of working adults migrated to the Boloven Plateau in the dry season for jobs on plantations. Now reportedly less than 10 per cent of the work force migrates, an indicator that the population can obtain their daily needs from the protected area
Namibia HDI rank: 129 GDP/cap: US$6300	Caprivi Game Park (582,750ha, category VI, established 1968)	Good management and sustainable harvesting techniques of palms have enabled local women to supplement household incomes by selling woven palm baskets to tourists. Producers have grown from 70 in the 1980s to more than 650 by the end of 2001. This is one of the few sources of income for women
South Africa HDI rank: 125 GDP/cap: US$10,000	Kruger National Park (1,898,859ha, category II, established 1926)	Benefits from ecotourism mean that wildlife conservation is 18 times more profitable than using the same land for livestock and crops
Vietnam HDI rank: 114 GDP/cap: US$2800	Hon Mun Marine Protected Area (10,500ha, category unset, established 2002)	About 5300 people depend on the reserve, particularly for reef-related aquaculture and near-shore fishing; gross fisheries value is estimated at US$15,538 per km^2
Indonesia HDI rank: 109 GDP/cap: US$3900	Bunaken National Park (79,060ha, category II, established 1989)	30 per cent of the park entrance revenues are used for development programmes in local villages. 40,000 people benefit economically from the park and over 1000 jobs have been created for local people
China HDI rank: 94 GDP/cap: US$6000	Baimaxueshan Nature Reserve (281,640ha, category V, established 1988)	Mushroom harvesting in the park has spread to 70 villages and incomes have risen five- to tenfold. 1kg of matsutake mushrooms can earn a harvester more money than the average annual wage in Yunnan Province

Country, HDI ranking and GDP/capita (CIA, 2009)	Name of protected area and details	Contribution to economic dimension of poverty reduction
Jordan HDI rank: 90 GDP/cap: US$5100	Dana Wildlife Reserve (31,000ha, category IV, established 1989)	By 1997, income-generating activities in the Dana Reserve had raised US$260,000, created 38 new jobs and provided increased financial benefits to over 140 people

High HDI ranking

Brazil HDI rank: 70 GDP/cap: US$10,200	Mamirauá State Ecological Station (1,124,000ha, category Ia, established 1990)	An economic alternatives programme started in 1998 targeted 10,000 people living in 5 villages in the area. Subsequently incomes have increased by 50 per cent and in some areas by 99 per cent. Infant mortality has declined by 53 per cent with better health education and water quality
Ecuador HDI rank: 72 GDP/cap: US$7500	Awa Indigenous Protected Area (101,000ha, category VI, established 1988)	There are 4500 Awa living in 21 communities in the protected area. They manage the area for sustainable timber. While timber intermediaries paid only US$60 per m³ for sawn 'chanul', the Awa Forestry Programme sells its product for US$240 per m³. Of the US$240, US$60 goes to external costs, US$60 goes to community members who worked on the extraction and the remaining US$120 is a stumpage fee to the community (or family)
Costa Rica HDI rank: 50 GDP/cap: US$11,500	Tortuguero National Park (18,946ha, category II, established 1975)	In 2003, it was estimated that each local tour guide in Tortuguero earned on average US$1755–3510 during a 5-month period; 2 to 4 times the minimum wage. Overall it is e stimated that 359 jobs have been generated by ecotourism. In addition, a local high school, clinic and improved water and waste treatment were set up thanks to revenue from the park

Source: Dudley et al., 2008

Figure 7.2 *Students care for saplings at the Tibetan Community School in Baimaxueshan Nature Reserve, China*

Source: © Ramy Inocencio/WWF-Canon

Figure 7.3 *Learning about the plants in Bunaken Marine National Park, Indonesia*

Source: © Soh Koon Chng/WWF-Canon

Future Needs and Management Options: Recognizing the Role of Protected Areas

Managing protected areas to meet poverty reduction goals is a major challenge. Protected areas have not been created to reduce poverty. However, ignoring poor people living in and around protected areas is not a viable solution, either ethically or ultimately for the conservation aims of the protected area. Many protected areas actually represent an opportunity, given the right conditions, to reduce poverty levels because of their abundance of environmental goods and services – creating a so-called 'win–win' situation for poverty reduction and biodiversity conservation.

The term 'win–win' has been applied widely, and rather loosely, across different contexts, including conservation where often it is used to refer to the nature of the relationship between people and biodiversity. Thus, while the relationship between poverty and conservation is rarely a direct one of cause and effect (Fisher et al., 2005), given the many claims about protected areas' roles in poverty reduction (and poverty creation) a simple analysis to identify winners and losers, and cause and effect can help to disentangle myth from reality. Table 7.4 provides examples of different activities leading to different permutations of the 'win–win' relationship between poor people and biodiversity in protected areas.

Table 7.4 *Examples of the relationship between poverty reduction and biodiversity conservation in protected areas*

Activity	Impact on poor people (living in and around the protected area)	Impact on biodiversity (in the protected area)	Relationship between poor people and biodiversity conservation
Poor people are engaged as active managers of the protected area	Poor people are empowered	Biodiversity conservation is secured	Win–Win
Sustainable harvesting is allowed in the protected area	Poor people can meet their needs in non timber forest products (NTFPs) and other products	Biodiversity conservation is maintained (neither improved nor worsened)	Win–No change
Management plans are set up in the protected area, and capacity is in place to implement them, but there is little engagement with local people	People's poverty levels remain the same	Biodiversity conservation is improved	No change–Win

Activity	Impact on poor people (living in and around the protected area)	Impact on biodiversity (in the protected area)	Relationship between poor people and biodiversity conservation
Current situation is good enough that nothing worsens in the short term, but nothing improves	Status quo for people's poverty	Status quo for biodiversity conservation	No change–No change
Corruption leads to mismanagement in a protected area, reducing available resources for poor people and threatening their livelihoods as well as biodiversity	People's poverty levels are worsened	Biodiversity conservation is worsened	Lose–Lose
Unsustainable harvesting in the protected area	In the short term poor people can obtain NTFPs etc	Biodiversity conservation is negatively affected	Win–Lose
Poor people are banned from accessing a site that used to be an important burial ground for them	Poor people's cultural and spiritual needs are worsened	The status of biodiversity conservation remains the same	Lose–No change
Strict management plans are in place that forbid anyone from entering the protected area, including traditional people who used to depend on this land	People's poverty levels are increased	Biodiversity conservation is improved	Lose–Win
Uncontrolled tourism activities bring rapid economic change but profits are not equitably shared	People's poverty levels remain the same	Biodiversity conservation is threatened by degradation	No change–Lose

Although the 'win–win' result is obviously attractive, it is usually hard to achieve on the ground. Protected areas that are more flexible are more likely to provide a compromise solution. In fact, the 1990s saw a significant increase in protected areas in IUCN category VI, which seeks a better balance between biodiversity aims and human needs (Chomitz et al., 2007). In reality, while such approaches present an ideal situation, there are few concrete examples showing both measurable improvements in human welfare and biodiversity conservation, and there has not been a systematic comparison of the effectiveness of these different approaches in terms of biodiversity conservation. More often, trade-offs between conservation and development will be necessary (McShane and Wells, 2004). The relationship between poverty and biodiversity conservation is, however, far from static. Thus, while certain difficult trade-offs may be necessary at a given point in time, they may be more acceptable if viewed in a long-term context.

Given the complexities of the relationship between poverty and protection this chapter does not offer any easy solutions to the issues raised: in reality, there is no simple management solution that will ensure that protected areas are both effective at conserving biodiversity and successful at delivering poverty reduction in all circumstances. However, following a wide ranging review of the literature on the subject (Dudley et al., 2008) there are clearly some key points which should be considered by protected area managers:

- Poverty reduction policies connected to protected areas (or indeed any other poverty policies) have a far better chance of succeeding if they take place in a strong, transparent and non-corrupt political system.
- If poverty is understood as a multidimensional state rather than as just a question of income, then protected areas have more chances of contributing to well-being.
- Not only is the generation of benefits important, but their distribution is also key (benefits are only likely to be equitably distributed in situations where good governance is in place).
- Periods of transition when people are moving in and out of poverty are particularly sensitive; rapid ecological damage can occur at these times unless carefully managed. During these periods the immediate need for natural resources declines but often before a conservation ethic has developed.
- Land ownership/management agreements play a fundamental role.
- Monitoring is critical for effective conservation and development projects and it is important to be clear about what is being measured.
- The challenges involved in achieving a balance between conservation and poverty reduction must be acknowledged and managed.

Conclusions

Clearly the relationship between protected areas and poverty is both complex and multi-faceted. In some cases the creation of a protected area has undoubtedly contributed to poverty, while in other situations protected areas have played a positive role in its reduction. Protected area strategies are developing with far stronger social safeguards, as embodied in the CBD's Programme of Work on Protected Areas; in the future, by necessity, protected area establishment will be a more inclusive and thus altogether more complex procedure. When this is achieved the results are likely to be more positive, bringing conservation initiatives more fully into the mainstream and addressing what have clearly been inequalities in the past. However, the transition phase is proving a challenge.

There are no simple formulae for success. Mechanisms that have worked to reduce poverty in one protected area may have failed in another. Some approaches to reducing the impacts of establishing protected areas on poor people have succeeded in one place but failed in another. Some poor people may recognize the positive benefits of protected areas and welcome or even initiate their establishment, while others remain opposed to the whole concept. In some cases local people are the instigators of protected areas, whilst in other areas the people concerned in their creation are far removed from the land where protected areas are set up.

With respect to the types of benefits provided, our research has thrown up something of a mixed bag of results. On the one hand, protected areas can clearly provide important benefits that help to address issues of poverty. Sometimes these include direct economic benefits, although probably more often they are linked to other aspects of well-being such as the provision of food and pure water, maintenance of health and benefits linked to cultural and spiritual values. Sometimes they also play a direct role in poverty reduction, but more commonly they provide a safety net for some of the world's poorest people to stop them falling further into poverty and they afford them some of the prerequisites for improving their lifestyles.

Case Study 7.1:
Population–Health–Environment Approaches
in Kiunga Marine National Reserve, Kenya

Judy Oglethorpe, Ali Mwachui, Sam Weru and Cara Honzak

The Kiunga Marine National Reserve lies in the northern part of the Lamu Archipelago on the north Kenya coast. The archipelago is part of the East African Marine Ecoregion which stretches for 4600km along the coast of Kenya, Tanzania and Mozambique. Lamu's seascape of relatively undisturbed reefs, mangroves and seagrass beds supports the richest marine fishery in Kenya and important turtle nesting sites. The area is also important for a number of endangered marine species, including dugong (*Dugong dugon*) and five species of sea turtle. However, increasing population pressure and demand for fish are threatening the integrity of the archipelago's vital marine ecosystems.

In Kenya, fishing communities have the highest poverty levels in the country with over 60 per cent of the population in coastal areas living below the poverty line (Samoilys and Kanyange, 2008). The area around Kiunga is a case in point, with few opportunities for permanent employment for the 15,000 people living there.

Building community support through well-being

When the Kiunga Reserve was created in 1979, there was little local consultation and local communities resented the reserve. When WWF started working in Kiunga in 1995, the communities as well as the Kenya Wildlife Service and Fisheries Department found it very difficult to make headway with community conservation initiatives.

In 2003 a new model combining conservation and local people's well-being was introduced. The population–health–environment (PHE) approach integrates health and/or family planning with conservation activities, seeking synergies to produce greater conservation and human well-being results than if they were implemented in isolated single-sector approaches. Conservation projects working in remote areas of outstanding biodiversity in developing countries often partner with local communities, the key guardians of this biodiversity. Yet these people may suffer from ill health because they have poor access to modern health services, poor nutrition and little or no access to improved water supplies and sanitation (Oglethorpe et al., 2008). This case study illustrates how, through this approach, both compensatory mechanisms and direct benefits provided by the protected area can contribute to increased well-being and poverty reduction.

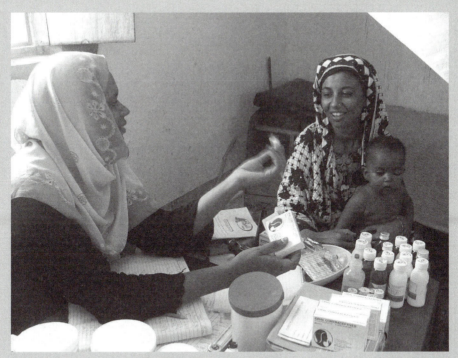

Figure 7.4 *A consultation at Mkokoni clinic*

Source: © Cara Honzak/WWF-US/Kiunga Project

The main health issues in Lamu District before the PHE project started were maternal and child health problems, malaria and HIV/AIDS, exacerbated by illiteracy, taboos and lack of information.

To improve access to health services and information the project established monthly mobile clinics by boat and vehicle to remote villages on the mainland and islands. Health professionals staff the clinics and WWF provides transport and logistics. The clinic provides general consultation, runs under-fives clinics, provides voluntary counselling and testing for HIV and makes referrals to medical facilities. An example of the clinic's impact is an increase, from 60 to 80 per cent, in immunization coverage for children's vaccinations.

The project supports the implementation of Kenya's second National Health Sector Strategic Plan, which at the local level aims to improve health services by establishing community units, each comprising 20 households that are served by a volunteer Community Health Worker (CHW). The CHWs are supported by government-employed Community Health Extension Workers. CHWs provide services such as awareness raising, training and support for home-care givers.

In Kiunga there is a shortage of good drinking water. Ground water is often saline and existing wells and rain water catchment tanks had been poorly managed, resulting in diarrhoeal infections – especially after heavy rain. The project has improved water supplies by building covers for wells, installing pumps and improving or building new rain-water catchment tanks. CHWs were trained to chlorinate water sources and local women were trained to treat water for children under five since they are most vulnerable. To date, there has been a 13 per cent decline in waterborne illness in villages which treat their water sources.

Before the project started, a health needs assessment found that, in remote villages, women's top health priority was better access to family-planning. The project established a system of Community Based Distributors (CBDs), who are volunteers who distribute pills and condoms and provide family-planning advice within their communities. Family planning and reproductive health discussion sessions are conducted for men, women and youths to reduce barriers and beliefs that discourage people from seeking relevant health-care services. Integrated messages that discuss trends in fish stocks, livelihoods and desired family size make it easier to broach the subject of family planning among men who have very traditional attitudes in this Muslim society. Higher use of family-planning is correlated with smaller family size and greater wealth per capita, particularly in areas like Kiunga where families are heavily dependent on natural resources. Since the project's inception, contraceptive use has increased by 10 per cent.

WWF also provides capacity-building support to the fishers' beach management units (BMUs) that are actively involved in resource use management and conflict resolution between fishers from different fishing villages. Health-care officials have worked with BMUs to maintain clean and healthy fish landing sites by securing clean watering points for migrant fishers and controlling waste disposal. At certain times of the year Indian Ocean currents deposit large amounts of garbage from Asia. It builds up, inconveniencing local communities, creating an eyesore for tourism and causing a hazard for turtle nestlings. The Kiunga project organizes beach clean ups involving BMUs, schools and other youth groups. A women's project turns trash to cash: women make handicrafts from washed up flip-flops, helping to generate income for household and school expenses.

Has PHE improved conservation success in Kiunga?

Community buy-in to conservation has been greatly catalyzed by provision of health-care, high-school scholarships to poorer families and women's income generating activities. Before these projects, communities were very suspicious of conservation activities, fearing their access to the fishery would be restricted.

Fishery management, and thus livelihoods, have been improved by promoting fishing-gear exchange, whereby fishers exchange their illegal, small-mesh fishing nets for legal larger-mesh nets, avoiding bycatch of young fish. Although there was resistance to this initially, fishers now like the new nets because without the bycatch, less work is needed to pull them in. BMUs have now taken charge of their fishery and have begun to establish saving and credit cooperative schemes for fishers, while communities are participating in the ecological monitoring of the reserve. Through the BMUs, fishers have also recently started setting aside no-take sanctuaries within the reserve where fish can breed and grow.

Attitudes have also changed to turtle conservation. Previously, the community harvested turtles for meat and eggs. As part of the education programme, students with scholarships attend environmental camps where they learn about conservation and help to tag hatchling turtles; they take environmental messages home to their families. Since 2006, 65 per cent of all monitored turtle nests have been reported by community members, compared to less than 30 per cent previously.

Building on these conservation and well-being successes, WWF and health partners are now expanding the PHE work by replicating successful approaches farther south to reach more people and benefit a larger part of the Lamu seascape.

References

CBD (2000) *Sustaining Life on Earth: How the Convention on Biological Diversity Promotes Nature and Human Well-being*, Secretariat of the Convention on Biological Diversity, Montreal.

Chomitz, K. P. with Buys, P., De Luca, G., Thomas, T. S. and Wertz-Kanounnikoff, S. (2007) *At Loggerheads? Agricultural Expansion, Poverty Reduction and Environment in the Tropical Forests*, World Bank, Washington, DC.

CIA (2009) *World Fact Book*, www.cia.gov/library/publications/the-world-factbook/rankorder/2004rank.html, accessed 2 September 2009.

DFID (2002) *Wildlife and Poverty Study*, Department for International Development, London.

Dudley, N., Mansourian, S., Stolton, S. and Suksuwan, S. (2008) *Safety Net: Protected Areas and Poverty Reduction*, WWF, Gland.

Economic Development Consultants (2004) *The Economic Value of Protected Landscapes in the North East of England: Report to ONE North East*, ONE North East, Leeds.

Ferrari, M. F. (2002) *Community Conserved Areas in South-East Asia: Synthesis of Lessons Learned in the Establishment and Management of Protected Areas by Indigenous and Local Communities in South-East Asia*, TILCEPA, IUCN, Gland.

Fisher, R. J., Maginnis, S., Jackson, W. J., Barrow, E. and Jeanrenaud, S. (2005) *Poverty and Conservation: Landscapes, People and Power*, IUCN, Gland and Cambridge.

Gilligan, B. (2006) *The National Reserve System Programme 2006 Evaluation*, Department of the Environment and Heritage, Canberra.

Grimble, R., Cardoso, C. and Omar-Chowdhury, S. (2002) *Poor People and the Environment: Issues And Linkages*, Livelihoods and Institutions Group, Natural Resources Institute, University of Greenwich, London.

McShane, T. O. and Wells, M. P. (eds) (2004) *Getting Biodiversity Projects to Work: Towards More Effective Conservation and Development*, Columbia University Press, New York, NY.

Nelson, J. and Hossack, L. (2003) *From Principles to Practice: Indigenous Peoples and Protected Areas*, Forest Peoples Programme, Moreton-in-Marsh.

Oglethorpe, J., Honzak, C. and Margoluis, C. (2008) *Healthy People, Healthy Ecosystems: A Manual for Integrating Health and Family Planning into Conservation Projects*, World Wildlife Fund, Washington, DC.

Samoilys, M.A. and Kanyange, N.W. (2008) *Natural Resource Dependence, Livelihoods and Development: Perceptions from Kiunga, Kenya*, IUCN ESARO, Nairobi.

Schmidt-Soltau, K. (2003) *Is Forced Displacement Acceptable in Conservation Projects?*, Id21 *Insights* no 57, Institute of Development Studies, University of Sussex, Brighton.

Sen, A. (1999) *Development and Freedom*, Oxford University Press, Oxford.

Steele, P., Oviedo, G. and McCauley, D. (eds) (2006) *Poverty, Health, and Ecosystems: Experience from Asia*, IUCN, Gland and Cambridge, and Asian Development Bank, Manila.

Tongson, E. and Dino, M. (2004) 'Indigenous peoples and protected areas: The case of the Sibuyan Mangyan Tagabukid, Philippines', in T. McShane and M. Wells (ed.) *Getting Biodiversity Projects to Work: Towards More Effective Conservation and Development*, Columbia University Press, New York, NY.

Turpie, J., Clark, B. and Hutchings, K. (2006) *The Economic Value of Marine Protected Areas along the Garden Route Coast, South Africa, and Implications of Changes in Size and Management*, WWF South Africa, Stellenbosch.

UN (2006) *The Millennium Development Goals Report*, United Nations, New York, NY.

UNDP (2000) *Overcoming Human Poverty*, United Nations Development Programme, New York, NY.

UNDP (2008) *Human Development Index, Statistical Update 2008*, United Nations Development Programme, hdrstats.undp.org/2008/countries/country_fact_sheets/cty_fs_ZMB.html, accessed 3 September 2009.

von Droste, B., Rössler, M. and Titchen, S. (1998) *Linking Nature and Culture, Report of the Global Strategy Natural and Cultural Heritage Expert Meeting 25–29 March 1998, Amsterdam, The Netherlands*, UNESCO, Paris.

8

Beyond Belief: Linking Faiths and Protected Areas to Support Biodiversity Conservation

Liza Higgins-Zogib, Nigel Dudley, Josep-Maria Mallarach
and Stephanie Mansourian

In 1778, a hundred years before Yellowstone National Park was established in the United States, the Emperor of Manchur passed the necessary resolutions to protect the sacred values of Bogd Khan mountain in Mongolia. This sacred natural site has, along with the other 15 sacred mountains in the country, been protected and revered for centuries. Ruins of the old Manzushiry monastery, dating from around 1750 and destroyed in the 1930s, are found in the south side of the protected area and monks have now rebuilt part of it to enable the spiritual traditions of the place to continue. Offerings to the mountain take place twice yearly. The Bogd Khan Uul 'strictly protected area' was established in 1995 and, in recognition of its ecological importance, it became a UNESCO Biosphere Reserve in 1997. These recent international conservation designations only continue an age-old tradition to protect the sacred elements of the landscape. Although this sacred natural site predates the first 'modern' protected area by a century, there are examples of other such sites receiving formal protection well before this. The sacred sites (haraam) around Mecca and Medina were formally established by the Prophet Muhammad during the 7th century with clear protection rules for all plants and animals included in them (O'Brien and Palmer, 2007).

Liza Higgins-Zogib

The Argument

The value

Vast numbers of sacred sites exist in officially protected areas. Indeed, it could be argued that a spiritual dimension exists in every protected area, given the sacred status that most faith traditions accord to the natural world. Yet how many protected area managers are actually aware of this or manage for it accordingly? Protected areas, if they are governed and managed appropriately, have an enormous potential to contribute to the safeguarding and enhancement of the cultural and spiritual diversity that makes the world wonderful and inspiring. Protected area status can also offer important advantages to some sacred sites, providing a valuable framework to help preserve their spiritual and religious values. This chapter considers the varied links between faiths and protected areas; provides some examples of how sacred nature, faith groups and protected areas interact; and offers some ideas for the future management of protected areas that contain sacred values.

Links between faiths and the conservation of land and water exist throughout the world and involve every belief system (Dudley et al., 2005). Faiths have been involved in some of the earliest forms of habitat protection in existence, both through the preservation of particular places as 'sacred natural sites' and through religious-based control systems such as the *hima* system in Islam, which protects areas of land to promote the sustainable use of resources. Sacred areas are probably the oldest form of habitat protection on the planet and still form a large and frequently unrecognized network of sanctuaries around the world (Dudley et al., 2009).

The very nature of sacred sites is that they evoke in people from many traditions, as well as from no specific tradition at all, a sense of awe, respect and reverence. Similar attitudes are experienced by many in areas protected for conservation, creating an immediate albeit intangible link between the two concepts.

Protected areas can help preserve a sense of 'special place' that is felt, often surprisingly strongly, in sacred areas. There is so much interplay between, for instance, a built place of worship and the land or water that surrounds it, that providing additional protection means in many cases retaining the very energy and spirit of the place that could otherwise be endangered by alternative land-use activities. Periyar Tiger Reserve in the southern Western Ghats of India is a good example. Sabarimala temple falls within the tiger reserve – where millions visit each year to pay homage to the tiger-riding deity, Lord Ayappa. Efforts by the reserve's administration have helped to keep infrastructure to a sustainable level and protected the forest to ensure that the sanctity of place is kept intact (Dudley et al., 2005).

The benefit

Most people in the world follow some kind of spiritual faith and in consequence faiths have enormous impacts on the way that we think and behave, including how we relate to the natural world. When considering protected areas, these links come in two major forms:

- *Sacred places* – which can include sacred natural sites, sacred buildings or monuments existing in natural or semi-natural areas and also places set aside to protect particular species that are considered to be sacred. These can contribute very directly to global conservation efforts because they are often themselves well-conserved through traditions that sometimes stretch back for thousands of years.
- *Influence of faiths* – through their philosophy, cosmology and moral or sacred laws, faiths can have a major influence on the way their followers view nature and hence their attitudes towards nature conservation. This includes more direct links

through ownership and/or management of land, investment and considerable political and social influence.

The interplay between belief systems and nature is complex and deeply rooted. Recognition of this link has grown enormously in the last few years, with statements of support for environmental concerns from all 11 of the world's so-called 'mainstream religions'[1] as well as from innumerable smaller and more localized belief systems (Palmer with Findlay, 2003).

Conversely, the practice of biodiversity conservation itself, deeply rooted in western science with its associated secular and materialistic worldview, can sometimes jeopardize sacred spaces if spiritual, cultural and religious values are not taken into consideration adequately when planning conservation management. Imposing an 'official' protected area status on to a sacred site in a way that prevents its traditional use is likely to cause cultural disruption and resentment, and can paradoxically lead to exactly the type of degradation that the site's sacred nature had until then prevented.

However, sacred natural sites are increasingly threatened in many parts of the world. Threats come from the external forces that jeopardize the natural world in general, but also from breakdown of traditions and belief systems that have hitherto ensured the protection and management of sacred sites. Because of these threats, sensitive use of the modern concept of protected areas can provide added security to these traditional conservation methods. And this security is vital for conservation; a review of over a hundred scientific papers on how well sacred natural sites contribute

Figure 8.1 *Sacred grove in Maharashtra, India, kept from destruction to protect the Gods living there*

Source: © Mauri Rautkari/WWF-Canon

to biodiversity conservation suggests that these areas are often under a stricter regime of conservation management than many official protected areas (Dudley et al., forthcoming). Such areas need to be supported and conserved.

Current Contribution of Protected Areas

Faith groups interact with protected areas and the concept of protection in several ways, and different traditions within a single faith have varying attitudes towards nature. Examples include the following:

- Sacred sites or built structures of spiritual importance may lie within protected areas.
- Faiths may protect land themselves for a variety of reasons, often completely apart from any official protected area network (and often preceding it by hundreds or even thousands of years). Indigenous and other traditional peoples play a key role here as custodians of land and water that they consider to be sacred; many areas of outstanding natural beauty and ecological value have been preserved from interference solely because of their sacredness.
- Pilgrimage ways or routes, either from mainstream faiths or local spiritual traditions, may provide conservation for significant corridors or landscape linkages between protected areas.
- The mainstream faiths are often important owners of land and major investors, who by their management and investment decisions have the opportunity to play an influential role in conservation.

These links present tremendous opportunities. If managed correctly, protected areas that encompass sacred sites can offer benefits for both faiths and biodiversity. However, they can also create some important challenges as well, such as when the sometimes very different priorities of conservationists and faith groups impact on one small area of land or water. It is important to explore how faith groups and protected area managers and agencies might gain a better understanding of each others' points of view and thus coordinate their actions more effectively. We also need to know the conditions in which protected areas might provide benefits to faith groups and vice versa.

In Table 8.1 we give some examples of sacred sites within protected areas; we indicate the faith initially identified with each site but in many cases the site is also important to other religions in that region. For example, in Mexico, the Huichol pilgrimage route ends at a sacred mountain which is sacred also to Catholics – which today includes many Huichol – and is dedicated to St Francis. The plurality of sacred sites in terms of the different groups they appeal to can also be seen in Mount Sinai, which is holy for Jews, Christians and Muslims. In Sri Lanka, as another example, Sri Pada or Adam's Peak is of great religious significance for Buddhists, Hindus, Muslims and Christians. Likewise, many ancient sites appeal deeply to people from a wide range of mainstream religions and to people with no specific faith, while in some cases they have even become the focal point of new religions (Dudley et al., 2005).

Table 8.1 *Examples of sacred elements in 'official' protected areas*

Country, protected area and data	Interaction of spirit and protected areas
Australia: Kakadu National Park. Declared 1991; size 1,980,400ha; IUCN category II and World Heritage site.	Kakadu National Park is in the Northern Territory heartland of the Aboriginal 'Dreamtime', the origin of the creator beings who sanctified the earth with its landforms and people, and who are now immortalized in some of the most prolific rock art on the continent. There are over 200 sacred sites within the lease area, including burial sites, creation sites, living areas and art sites (Gillespie, 1983).
China: Autonomous Region of Tibet, Parsa Wildlife Reserve (specifically Mt Kailash). Declared 1984; size 49,900ha; IUCN category II.	Mount Kailash is an important pilgrimage site for followers of many faiths, including Buddhism, Bön, Jainism and Hinduism. Most pilgrims walk a holy '*kora*' or circuit of the mountain, a distance of 56km which ascends to over 5700 metres above sea-level (Dudley et al., 2005).
Indonesia, West Timor: Gunung Mutis Nature Reserve (Cagar Alam Gunung Mutis). Declared 1983; size 90,000ha.	For the Meto, the indigenous people of Gunung Mutis, the spiritual relationship with nature is of great significance to daily life. Nature is believed to be reflected in humans and vice versa. Rituals are centred on ancestor worship. In Meto beliefs soil is considered the 'source of life'. This means that agricultural crops are the embodiment of ancestors and ceremonies are held throughout different cultivation phases. The concept of *le'u*, which means holy or sacred, is a force that can be either dangerous or favourable. Anything can transform to *le'u* as a result of a ceremony (Asian Development Bank, 2002).
Japan: Sacred Forest of Kashima. Declared 1956; size 1500ha.	Important for the Shinto faith, Kashima (Deer Island) in Lake Kitakata, near the mouth of southern Ishikawa's Daishoji River, is joined to the mainland by only a thin neck of land. At 30m high and 600m around, this gently rounded oval area of land is covered with a remnant of the original primeval forest that, like the sacred shrubbery of the nearby Shrine of Hachiman, remains comparatively well preserved. Kashima Jingu has 800 species of trees and an exceptionally rich bird life; one grove is designated as a Natural Monument (Anon, 2005).

Country, protected area and data	Interaction of spirit and protected areas
South Korea: Jirisan National Park. Declared 1967; size 417,758km^2, incorporating 3 provinces, 5 cities and counties, and 15 towns; IUCN category II.	In Jirisan National Park there are 8 Buddhist temples: Chilbulsa, Ssanggyesa, Daewonsa, Naewonsa, Beopgyesa, Silsangsa, Yeongwonsa and Hwaeomsa. The latter is possibly the most famous and sits in the middle of Nogodan peak. Yeongidaesa, a Buddhist priest, built this temple during the reign of King Jinheung, in the 5th year of Silla (544). Destroyed during the Japanese invasion, it was subsequently restored by Byeokamseonsa, another esteemed priest, during the reign of King Injo, in the 8th year of Silla (1630). Many cultural treasures are housed here, including four national treasures, e.g. Gakhwangjeon, a three-storey stone pagoda propping up four lions, and the remarkable Gakhwhangjjeon seokdeung, one of the largest existing stone lights (KNPS, 2008). The temples are still being expanded today.
Nepal: Shivapuri National Park. Declared 1958; size 15,600ha; IUCN category II.	The protected area is spiritually significant for the popular shrines and meditation centres nestled in natural surroundings. It includes several religious and cultural heritage sites for Hindus and Buddhists. They include the peaks of Shivapuri, Manichur and Tarkeswor, and the source of the Bagmati and Bishnumati rivers. The Budhanilkantha and Sundarimai shrines and the Nagi monastery attract thousands of pilgrims during festive seasons (Dudley et al., 2005).
Argentina: Lanin National Park. Declared 1937; size 379,000ha (Park 194,600ha, Reserve 184,400ha); IUCN category II (National Park) and IV (Managed Reserve).	This is the land of the Mapuche Indians or the 'Earth people' (*Mapu* means 'Earth' and *Che* means 'people'). The name *Lanin* in Mapuche means 'dead rock'. It is famous for its Chilean pine trees (*Araucaria araucana*) which are sacred to the Mapuche. Lanin contains a dormant volcano. Its legend, according to the Mapuche, relates to Pillán, the evil god, who is also the god of nature (Dudley et al., 2005).
Bolivia: RB-EB del Beni (Beni Biosphere Reserve and Biological Station). Declared 1896; size 135,000 ha.	The Reserve is home to the Chimane people, who keep and practise their ancestral rites and customs. The Chimane live principally along the shores of the Maniqui River. Their economy is based on agriculture and they cultivate more than 80 species of plants, including perennials and medical plants. In addition, they hunt, fish, gather and produce crafts. About 30,000ha of the station are part of the Chimane Indigenous Territory (Miranda, 1995).

Country, protected area and data	Interaction of spirit and protected areas
Ecuador: Cayapas Mataje (mangroves). Declared 1995; size 51,300ha; IUCN category VI.	Local mythology believes that: 'Animas' are the guardians of natural resources and bad spirits; 'Tunda' protects the mangrove and has the power to convert itself into a human; the 'Riviel' is a being from the water who travels between the estuaries, canals and the sea; the mermaid attracts sailors and takes them to the waters' depths. All of these figures have survived new beliefs brought in by the Catholic faith and are still worshipped. A number of different rituals and feasts are celebrated around them (Briones, 2002).
Spain: Muntanya de Montserrat. Declared Picturesque Landscape 1950 and a Natural Park and a Nature Reserve were established in 1987; size 9259 ha. IUCN categories V and III.	Since the beginning of history Montserrat ('serrated mountain' in Catalan), situated near Barcelona, has been considered a holy mountain. Nestled in the rocky mountain, there are around 12 hermitages and 2 Catholic monasteries, one of which includes a sanctuary devoted to the Holy Virgin Mary that has been a continuous pilgrimage centre since the 14th century. Over the centuries the Benedictine community has had a significant spiritual and cultural influence. Currently, the Natural Park receives almost 3 million visitors per year; the vast majority visit the area of the monastery of Saint Mary. Because of its many spiritual, cultural and natural values, the mountain of Montserrat has become an outstanding identity symbol of Catalonia (Mallarach and Papayannis, 2007).
Ghana: Boabeng Fiema-Monkey sanctuary, size196ha.	The Boabeng Fiema-Monkey sanctuary in Ghana provides an example of a sacred grove that has not only been protected by customary law, but also by modern legislation under District Council by-laws and is managed as a wildlife sanctuary (Ntiamoa-Baidu, 1987). The grove is considered sacred because it supports populations of black and white colobus monkeys (*Colobus vellerosus*) and mona monkeys (*Cercopithecus mona*), both of which are revered and strictly protected as sons of the gods of the people of Boabeng and Fiema villages (Akowuah et al., 1975). So strong is the belief surrounding these monkeys that in the past, when a monkey died, the corpse was given the same respect and funeral rites as would be accorded to a human being (Fargay, undated). Because of the effectiveness of the protection, this small forest supports the highest density of the two species of monkeys anywhere in Ghana (163 black and white, 347 mona) according to a 1997 census (Kankam, 1997).

Country, protected area and data	Interaction of spirit and protected areas
Mali: Cliffs of Bandiagara (Land of the Dogons). Declared 1969; size 400,000ha; IUCN category III.	The region is one of the main centres for the Dogon culture, rich in ancient traditions and rituals, art, culture and folklore. Village communities are divided into the *inneomo* and *innepuru*, living men and dead men respectively, which exist in symbiotic union with each other. Symbolic relationships also exist with respect to the environment, such as with the pale fox (*Vulpes pallida*) and jackal (*Canis aureus*). Semi-domestic crocodiles are kept as sacred protectors of Bandiagara Village and its ancient founder, Nangabanou Tembèly. They are also revered in ritual rain dances (Cissé, 2004).

The scattering of examples above show some of the ways in which faith groups, sacred sites and protected areas meet and interact. If managed in a positive and sensitive way, the interaction between faiths and nature has the potential to impact positively on the protection of biodiversity and increase the support that local communities and others can bring to bear for protected area management. At the same time, protected areas can provide important additional safeguards to sacred sites that are otherwise increasingly under pressure of degradation or destruction.

Bringing Sacred Natural Sites into the Global Protected Areas Network

Sacred sites have in many cases already been in existence for hundreds or even thousands of years, often cases carrying out a useful conservation function alongside their spiritual role. Now there is increasing discussion about bringing them more formally into the protected areas network. Governments are often interested because they can help to increase protected area coverage with little effort. Conservation organizations tend to be enthusiastic because of the new and highly secure additions to national protected area systems. But what is in it for the faiths themselves? Are there any advantages in gaining 'official' protected area status or would they be better off in keeping things as they are? Protected area status for sacred sites offers the possibility of a number of benefits but also carries some potential costs.

Potential benefits to faith groups of gaining protected area status for sacred sites

- Strengthening protection: becoming an officially recognized part of a national protected area network gains valuable recognition for the significance of a site and the importance of maintaining its integrity. It means in most cases that the sacred site will then also be protected by both policy and legislation. This can be critically important at a time when cultural conditions are changing fast and global pressures are increasing; for instance, several communities in Madagascar are currently discussing options for gaining protected area status for their sacred sites to help protect them from degradation, following the example of Ankodika, the first community conserved area officially established in the country, which includes a sacred forest (Gardner et al, 2008).

• Strengthening management capacity: integration also usually brings additional resources to a site for management, including new partners such as the national protected area agency and sometimes also national or international NGOs, plus access to other forms of capacity building and support. In Xishuangbanna, China, for example, protected area status has enabled local communities to attract additional resources for managing holy hills that they have been protecting without reward for centuries (Sochaczewski, 1999).

• Attracting funds and support: being a protected area also increases options for developing fundraising activities such as ecotourism; in many countries it may also allow the traditional managers of sacred sites to access local, national or regional conservation funding or to attract foreign donors. Access to support has been an important factor in the involvement of the Baka people in management within Lobéké National Park in Cameroon.

• Increasing recognition: gaining additional status and recognition for the site and for the people revering it may help to protect it in more subtle ways than simply through government regulations, e.g. by drawing international attention to the importance of the site's faith values, which may help to reinvigorate weakened local traditions.

Figure 8.2 *Anosiarivo sacred forest, Madagascar, is protected by local belief and respect*
Source: © John E. Newby/WWF-Canon

Potential costs of bringing sacred sites into protected area systems

- *Loss of sacred values*: protected area status also attracts greater attention to many sacred sites including increased visitors, many of whom may not share the same cultural views of the site's values and importance. Some communities believe that their sites have suffered loss of intangible and spiritual values as a result. A proportion of visitors to Uluru (Ayers Rock) in Central Australia continue to climb over it, despite the presence of signs requesting that this is unsuitable for a sacred site (James, 2007).
- *Loss of sovereignty*: if being a protected area means direct control by a governmental agency, custodians and local communities risk losing control over their own sacred site. Even in cases where they retain a management or co-management role, the fact that there are more stakeholders involved can lead to a more subtle loss of control.

Management strategies

None of these advantages or disadvantages is inevitable and the costs and benefits will depend largely on how issues of management and governance are approached. IUCN recognizes a number of different management objectives and governance strategies within protected areas and sacred sites can be totally protected from visitation and/ or continue to be managed by their traditional owners within 'official' protected area networks. Conversely, unless carefully planned, the supposed advantages of being within a protected area system may never materialize.

Whether or not protected area status is likely to be good for sacred sites will depend on individual conditions, including the needs, aspirations and strengths of the traditional owners or custodians, the nature of the site, and what protected area status can offer. An assessment of current and anticipated pressures will also help determine the value of turning a site into a protected area. This will also depend on whether the site fits the IUCN definition of a protected area (see Chapter 1) and whether the government agrees to include the site within the official network. In some cases it may be more effective to maintain a more traditional form of management or control.

However, conservation strategies are increasingly moving away from the traditional, rather ad hoc, practice of protecting land and instead are focusing on the careful planning of protected area networks, using a variety of protected area types and governance models, integrated with other forms of land use (Groves, 2003). Sacred sites are, by their nature, in places where faiths acknowledge them to be, sometimes being located using traditional sciences like feng-shui in China or Korea, rather than selected through some western conservation planning exercise; on the other hand, they are also often highly diverse sites that are likely to feature among the priority areas in any conservation planning exercise. Sacred sites can therefore contribute to regional conservation in a number of ways, either 'officially' as part of a protected area network or 'unofficially'. As we have discussed, there are arguments for and against both strategies and different approaches are required for different situations. We discuss five of these approaches:

Inside protected areas

By far the commonest way in which sacred sites and protected areas overlap is through particular sacred sites being contained within protected areas. This situation has in the past often arisen by accident, although today it is also being applied as part of collaborative exercises between local communities or faiths and conservation organizations. In some countries, such as Australia, the density of areas considered to be of spiritual importance is so great that virtually all protected areas will be in this position. Inclusion of sacred sites within protected areas offers both opportunities and challenges to managers. Sacred sites can in some circumstances provide highly protected core zones within protected areas, and additional justification for closing off sensitive habitats: this can be seen in the case of sacred mountains in protected areas in New Zealand, Nepal and elsewhere. Conversely, sacred sites can also increase pressures on biodiversity if, for instance, they become the object of mass pilgrimage or if sacred rituals themselves involve hunting or other forms of resource use that impact upon vulnerable elements.

As entire protected areas

There is increasing interest among both faith and conservation communities in the concept of converting an entire sacred site into a protected area, and managing it for its dual spiritual and biodiversity values. The IUCN World Commission on Protected Areas is currently considering how the IUCN protected area management category III, currently aimed at natural monuments, could be applied increasingly to sacred sites as well, although in practice sacred natural sites occur in all IUCN categories (Verschuuren et al., 2007). For the most strictly protected sacred sites, IUCN category Ia, which effectively prohibits most visitation, can be ideal. In this case, protected area status would be conferring additional protection on to a site of spiritual value to a faith, which could help to prevent degradation by people from other cultures. From a conservation perspective, such sites will often, although not invariably, be small. Small sites generally have more limited value (for example, generally being unable to conserve whole ecosystems or large mammals) but can be extremely valuable in terms of protecting particular components, such as rare plant species and nesting colonies of birds. In a landscape or seascape approach to conservation, small, discrete protected areas should generally be integrated with other natural habitats through the use of buffer zones, biological corridors, etc.

Within broader conservation networks

We have already concluded that conferring protected area status on to sacred sites may not always be appropriate or useful. This does not prevent such sites being effective vehicles for conservation nor necessarily stop them from being included in widescale conservation strategies. It may suit certain faiths or indigenous peoples better to keep their sacred sites outside the official protected area network, for reasons discussed above, but the fact that they are there can still play an important role in landscape-scale conservation strategies and can sometimes be factored into planning as buffer zones, landscape linkages or unofficially protected sites. Long pilgrimage trails, like the Ways of Saint James (Spain, France and Portugal) may also play a significant role in articulating protected areas, as happened in the main complex of Reserves of Biosphere of Spain, linked to this World Heritage site pilgrimage route.

Protected areas around built sacred sites

Sacred buildings are often surrounded by land and sometimes this can be in a very natural state; in other cases faiths are willing to manage land specifically for its biodiversity values. In Bulgaria, the monks of Rila monastery manage a nature reserve in the heart of the Rila National Park. In the UK, the sacred lands project run by the Alliance of Religions and Conservation is working with over a thousand churchyards to increase their value to biodiversity, in effect creating tiny reserves in what are often otherwise very altered landscapes. Many older sacred sites are now surrounded by native vegetation that may be almost indistinguishable from completely natural habitat and in these cases management of the site can cover both its natural and its built environment.

Through land owned and/or managed by faith organizations

Some faith groups own both large and small amounts of land and even slight changes in policy towards the management of this land can have major implications for its conservation value. Organic agriculture practised on most monastic managed lands in Europe is an example of good practice. This is a very important and frequently overlooked way in which faiths and protected area agencies can collaborate.

Management Options

Attempts to work with custodians of sacred sites (local communities or indigenous peoples) in the context of protected areas will always be flawed unless conservationists start to view the land or seascape as the local populations or custodians do. In practical terms this means that such protected areas must be viewed as more than simply safe places for biodiversity. They also have a role to play in upholding cultural and spiritual values that, like biodiversity, are at risk from a number of diverse external pressures and threats. Many times these are places where people live and worship and, where this is the case, it is critical that sacred elements be treated with the utmost care and respect. Failing to do so can often be cause for conflict. Below we list some ways in which conflict can arise (Higgins-Zogib, 2007), if:

- there is no common understanding of sacred places. This may be because these special areas are kept so strictly secret that even protected area staff do not know where they are, e.g. Bwindi Impenetrable Forest, Uganda;
- there is no common understanding of protected area objectives. This may be due to a lack of suitable communications and outreach on the part of protected area administration, e.g. the illegal building of a monastery within the special conservation area of Ceahlau National Park in Eastern Romania;

- there is no respect for the sacred elements of a site. This may be because of a general lack of understanding or willingness to understand, or due to differences in religious beliefs and tendencies, e.g. Kata Tjuta National Park, Australia;
- the effects of one place-view[2] are damaging to the objectives of the other. This can work both ways. The effects of pilgrimage, for example, can sometimes prove detrimental to the biodiversity values of a protected area, e.g. Periyar, India, or the effects of tourism can be detrimental to sacred places or offensive to the spiritual values of the place, e.g. Devil's Tower National Monument, US.

Managing for natural and spiritual heritage conservation thus clearly needs a sensitive approach and can seem to be a complicated matter, but it is far from impossible. The often elusive 'win–win' situation (results positive for both faith groups and for nature conservation) can emerge when the right governance and management elements are in place. More detailed guidance is beginning to be developed and disseminated. For example, in 2008 the IUCN World Commission on Protected Areas Task Force (now Specialist Group) on the Cultural and Spiritual Values of Protected Areas, in collaboration with UNESCO's Man and the Biosphere Programme, produced guidelines for protected area managers on best practices for managing for sacred values focusing on indigenous peoples (Wild and McLeod, 2008). The Delos Initiative, which belongs to the same Specialist Group, is preparing guidelines for sacred sites related to mainstream religeons (Papayannis and Mallarach, 2010).

Conclusions

Sacred natural sites occur in many official protected areas around the world and they are revered by the vast majority of the world's people. This presents an as yet untapped potential for building further support for protected areas. Many 'unofficial' areas protected traditionally because of their sacredness are coming under threat and in these cases bringing them into official networks can provide the further protection that they need. The coming together of sacred natural sites and official protection requires careful consideration. Decisions about individual sites need to be taken by all the key stakeholders if they are to be effective, i.e. by faith groups depending on their own assessment of what impacts will affect the sacred nature of the site and by conservation specialists regarding the question of whether the site will be a useful addition to protected area systems.

More generally, conservation organizations need to work much more closely with faith groups, given the potential and actual influence of faith communities over aspects of the environment, to identify more effective ways of collaboration. And clearly protected area managers and conservation organizations need to recognize the significance and legitimacy of spiritual values of nature, to improve training in these issues and to work cooperatively with faith organizations in ensuring that relevant spiritual and cultural values are also effectively preserved within protected areas. At the same time, faith leaders might look carefully at options to increase their contributions to the historic aim of completing an ecologically representative system of protected areas, for example, by committing a proportion of the land and water that they own or control to this purpose.

Finally, sacred natural sites are undoubtedly coming under increasing threat both from external sources and from the breakdown of traditional beliefs and practices. In this developing crisis for some faith groups, protected areas could have a critical role to play in ensuring additional protection for these places of reverence and hence the maintenance of the cultures for whom they are sacred.

Case Study 8.1:
The Ancient Sacred Natural Sites in al Hoceima National Park, Morocco

Josep-Maria Mallarach

Established in 2004 after a disastrous earthquake, the al Hoceima National Park, an IUCN category V protected landscape, is the main protected area in the Rif region of north Morocco. Its total area is over 48,000ha, of which 18,000ha are marine areas. The Mediterranean cliffs are spectacular, reaching an altitude of 700m. Altitudinal variations create quite diverse landscapes, therefore biodiversity is high, particularly in the coastal and marine parts of the park.

A stronghold of the Amazig (berber) culture, in particular the Bokkoya tribe, the terrestrial zone is quite densely populated with some 15,000 people living there in 36 *douars* (traditional villages), in addition to some 33,000 people in the peripheral zone. The park includes some of the highest concentrations of sacred natural sites of North Africa and the area has a long history of community conserved areas. Although the national park is underfunded and has limited planning and management resources, it provides much needed additional protection for these sacred areas.

A sacred landscape

The sacred sites have many different names: *murabitun* or *klalwa* in Arabic, *amrabd* in Amazig (the ancient regional language) and *site marabutique* in French. Although *murabitun* usually refers to a shrine where a holy person was buried, it also includes, by extension, the natural area around it. The natural area itself is called *hurm* which has the same root as *haraam*, meaning reserved or forbidden, because of its holiness. *Khalwa*, spelled *khaloa* in the region, refers to a place of spiritual retreat. The custodians of these sacred sites, usually people from nearby villages or farms, are called *lamkaddam*, which comes from *al-muqaddam*, i.e. the representative. All these Arabic names are used in Tarifit, the Amazig dialect of the region.

The *murabitun/amrabd* of al Hoceima are outstanding: ecologically they protect the best relicts of the original vegetal communities, which have been severely deteriorated almost everywhere else in the region. Culturally, they are important sites of history, memory and identity for the local population over the ages. Most important decisions have been taken around them. Spiritually, they normally include tombs of holy people, often in small shrines, sometimes together with small mosques. A variety of rituals and ceremonies are still enacted there, such as annual pilgrimages or festivals (*mussem*) and sacrifice of young animals, usually goats or sheep. Most *douars* have one or several sacred natural sites nearby. The origin of these sacred sites seems very ancient, pre-Christian in many cases, perhaps Phoenician, although all of them have been 'Islamized'. Therefore, it is likely that many of them have been actively conserved for over 30 centuries.

A striking fact is that the sacred natural sites are found within mountain landscapes that have been seriously degraded due to deforestation and overgrazing, and stand out as relatively pristine patches of vegetation, without any physical walls. For generations the high respect that the local population, including the shepherd boys and girls, has had for the sites has been the most effective safeguard against any misuse or exploitation. In fact, for centuries the strength and resilience of the beliefs supported the conservation of these sacred natural sites more effectively than any legislation or official surveillance. However, under current circumstances, additional conservation measures are required.

Conservation areas

From a conservation point of view, these sacred sites have a particular value as reference plant communities for mountain landscape restoration and also to monitor the responses and resilience of slightly altered natural vegetation patches to climate change impacts. These relict forests contain unique gene pools, which have allowed them to overcome multiple changes over the centuries. From a cultural and spiritual point of view, they are significant places of tribal and local memory and identity. Moreover, these sites are the result of an open interpretation of the Islamic tradition, concerning the 'friends of God' (*awliyyah*) role and influence, which has deep roots in the region.

The main features of these sacred natural sites include patches of forests, sometimes less than 1ha in size, other times a few hectares, often with a particular sacred tree, preserving a considerable array of plant and animal species. Very old specimens of cypress tree (*Tetraclinis articulate*), olive tree (*Olea europea*), pistachio (*Pistacia lentiscus*), European fan palm (*Chamaerops humilis*), carob tree (*Ceratonia siliqu*), Kermes oak (*Quercus coccifera*) and lotus (*Zyziphus lotus*) are common. They often include a water spring, well or small stream, and a small mosque which hosts a tomb of a holy person, a spiritual leader or a high political or military authority. The physical distribution of the sacred natural sites is complex. The largest sites seem related to strategic lines, such as the borders of tribal lands, defensive lines against the invaders from the north, and also some key passage points, located from the coast or over cliffs, to hilltops or slopes over 1500m in altitude.

As Regato and Salman (2008) point out, these sacred natural sites are very valuable areas for conservation and their species populations may have an important role to play in adaptive management strategies against the changing climatic conditions of mountain biodiversity hotspot areas. This role could be very significant in places undergoing accelerated ecological degradation where social resistance to nature conservation arguments alone may be high, as is the case in North Africa.

Figure 8.3 *An extraordinary ancient mastic tree (Pistacia lentiscus) protected in the area around the tomb of Sidi Hajj Musa, al Hoceima National Park*

Source: © Josep-Maria Mallarach

Conserving traditions

The main threats to the integrity of the murabitun/amrabd are a consequence of the erosion or weakening of the traditional cultural values in younger generations, including the spread of the Islamic fundamentalism. Therefore, recovering or strengthening the cultural values and knowledge is one of the main challenges that the national park is facing.

The opportunities to conserve the entire heritage of these sacred sites are very significant:

- Most sacred natural sites are the property of the Ministry of Islamic Affairs and Habous which is very much interested in their conservation and restoration.
- Several local and regional NGOs are involved in safeguarding and restoring the sacred sites and their spiritual, cultural and natural heritage, as well as other significant related projects like the nursery of Tafnasa.
- Some local NGOs are interested in promoting ecotourism routes, which could allow visits to some of the less fragile sacred sites, adding value, providing resources to local populations and thus helping to conserve them.

- Selected plant species from these sites are critically important for ecological restoration, which should be done by local organizations
- There is a growing interest in recovering traditional knowledge and management practices related to these sacred sites.
- Future inclusion of those sacred sites in local and regional educational programmes will help in strengthening cultural identity and values related to them.
- Last but not least, future planning and management of the national park should have as a priority conserving and restoring the full spectrum of values of these outstanding sacred natural sites.

Acknowledgements

In December 2008 a seminar was organized by the Azir NGO and its Spanish counterpart, Ecodesarrollo, at the town of al Hoceima. Attended by some 50 people, including the managers of the national park and representatives of the main local authorities and several active local and regional NGOs, most of the debates focused on the significance, threats and opportunities for conserving the heritage of the sacred natural sites included in the national park and around it. This paper includes the author's summary of the seminar. Four people deserve special recognition: Soussan Fikrt, regional delegate of the Ministry of Islamic Affairs and Habous, Monhamed Al-Andalousi, President of the Azir Association, al Hoceima; Anissa El Kahttabi, Associación Rif para el Desarrollo del Turismo Rural, and Miriam Zaitegui, former environmental consultant of Ecodesarrollo.

Notes

1. In alphabetical order: Bahá´i, Buddhism, Christianity, Daoism, Hinduism, Islam, Jainism, Judaism, Shinto, Sikhism and Zoroastrianism.
2. A place-view is defined as a consistent (to a varying degree) and integral sense of existence in a place, which provides a framework for generating, sustaining and applying knowledge or wisdom.

References

Akowuah, D. K., Rice, K., Merz, A. and Sackey, V. A. (1975) 'The children of the gods', *Journal of the Ghana Wildlife Society*, vol 1, no 2, pp19–22.
Anon (2005) 'The ten most exquisite sacred forests in Japan', *Kateigaho International Edition*, Spring 2005, Tokyo.
Asian Development Bank (2002) *Indigenous Peoples/Ethnic Minorities and Poverty Reduction, Indonesia*, Asian Development Bank, Manila.

Briones, E. E. (2002) 'Valores sociales y culturales', article prepared for the Ramsar Bureau for World Wetlands Day, www.ramsar.org.

Cissé, L. (2004) 'La participation communautaire à la gestion du site de la falaise de Bandiagara: "Ecotourisme en pays Dogon"', in *Linking Universal and Local Values: Managing a Sustainable Future for World Heritage*, UNESCO, Paris.

Dudley, N., Higgins-Zogib, L. and Mansourian, S. (2005) *Beyond Belief, Linking Faiths and Protected Areas to Support Biodiversity Conservation*, WWF, Gland, and Alliance for Religion and Conservation, Bath.

Dudley, N., Higgins-Zogib, l. and Mansourian, S. (2009) 'The links between protected areas, faiths, and sacred natural sites', *Conservation Biology*, vol 23, no 3, pp568–77.

Dudley, N., Bhagwat, S. Higgins-Zogib, L. Lassen, B., Verschuren, B. and Wild, R. (forthcoming) 'Conservation of biodiversity in sacred natural sites in Asia and Africa: a review of the scientific literature' in *Precious Earth*, Verschuren, B. and Wild, R. (eds), Earthscan, London.

Fargey, P. J. (undated) *Assessment of the Conservation Status of the Boabeng-Fiema Monkey Sanctuary*, Final Report to the Flora and Fauna Preservation Society: University of Science and Technology, Kumasi.

Gardner, C., Ferguson, B., Rebara, F. and Ratsifandrihamanana, N. (2008) 'Integrating traditional values and management regimes into Madagascar's expanded protected area system: the case of Ankodida', in Josep-Maria Mallarach (ed.) Protected Landscapes and Cultural and Spiritual Values, Values of Protected Landscapes and Seascapes, volume 2, IUCN, GTZ and Obra Social de Caixa Catalunya/Kasparek Verlag, Heidelberg, pp92–103.

Gillespie, D. (ed.) (1983) *The Rock Art Sites of Kakadu National Park*, Special Publication 10, Australia National Parks and Wildlife Service, Canberra.

Gray, M. (1993) *Sacred Earth*, Sterling Publishing, New York, NY.

Groves, C. R. (2003) *Drafting a Conservation Blueprint*, Earth Island Press, Covelo, CA, and Washington, DC.

Higgins-Zogib, L. (2007) 'Sacred sites and protected areas: An interplay of place-views', in B. Haverkort and S. Rist (eds) *Endogenous Development and Bio-cultural Diversity*, Compas series on Worldviews and Sciences 6, Leusden, pp287–98.

James, S. (2007) 'Constructing the climb: Visitor decision-making at Uluru', *Geographical Research*, vol 45, pp398–407.

Kankam, B. O. (1997) 'The population of black-and-white colobus (*Colobus polykomos*) and the mona monkeys (*Cercopithecus mona*) at the Boabeng-Fiema Monkey Sanctuary and surrounding villages', B.Sc. Thesis, University of Science and Technology, Kumasi.

KNPS (2008) *National Parks of Korea*, Korea National Parks Service, Seoul.

Mallarach, J.- M. and Papayannis, T. (eds) (2007) *Proceedings of the First Workshop of The Delos Initiative, Montserrat 2006*, IUCN, Gland, and Publicacions de l'Abadia de Montserrrat, Montserrat.

Miranda, C. (1995) *Beni Biosphere Reserve*, UNESCO Working Paper no 9, UNESCO, Paris.

Nasr, S. H. (1989) *Knowledge and the Sacred*, State University of New York Press, New York, NY.

Ntiamoa-Baidu, Y. (1987) West African wildlife; A resource in jeopardy, *Unasylva*, vol 39, no 2, pp27–35.

O'Brien, J. and Palmer, M. (2007) *The Atlas of Religion*, Earthscan, London.

Palmer, M. with Finlay, V. (2003) *Faith in Conservation*, World Bank, Washington, DC.

Papayannis, T. and Mallarach, J.-M. (2010) The Sacred Dimension of Protected Areas, Proceedings of the Second Workshop of The Delos Initiative, Ouranoupolis, 2007, Athens, Greece, IUCN and Med-INA

Regato, P. and Salman, R. (2008) *Mediterranean Mountains in a Changing World: Guidelines for Developing Action Plans*, IUCN Centre for Mediterranean Cooperation, Malaga.

Sochaczewski, P. (1999) 'Life reserves, opportunities to use spiritual values and partnerships in forest conservation', in S. Stolton and N. Dudley (eds) *Partnerships for Protection*, Earthscan, London.

Taiqui, L., Seva, E., Roman, J. L. and R'Ha, A. (2005) 'Los bosquetes de los *khaloa* (morabitos) del Rif, Atlas Medio y región del Sur de Marruecos', *Ecosistemas*, no 2005/3, www.revistaecosistemas.net/articulo.asp?Id=173&Id_Categoria=2&tipo=portada, accessed 27 September 2009.

Verschuuren, B., Mallarach, J. M. and Oviedo, G. (2007) 'Sacred sites and protected areas', in N. Dudley and S. Stolton (eds.) *IUCN Categories of Protected Areas Summit, Almeria, Spain*, IUCN, Gland.

Wild, R. and McLeod, C. (eds.) (2008) *Sacred Natural Sites, Guidelines for Protected Area Managers*, Task Force on the Cultural and Spiritual Values of Protected Areas in collaboration with UNESCO's Man and the Biosphere Programme, World Commission on Protected Areas, Best Practice Protected Area Guidelines Series no 16, IUCN, Gland.

9

Living Traditions:
Protected Areas and Cultural Diversity

Liza Higgins-Zogib, Nigel Dudley and Ashish Kothari

In 1992, an article in the Hindu newspaper inspired a remarkable community conservation effort in Iringal village in Kerala, India. The newspaper carried a story on the Olive Ridley turtle (Lepidochelys olivacea); it explained that although globally endangered, the turtle was still a regular visitor to the village's local beach. When some of the young people in the village realized that the turtle nesting sites were so special and in need of protection they formed a small committee and started to learn about the turtle's lifestyle and, as a consequence, the benefits of the coastal ecosystem as a whole. Today an 8km seashore community-conserved area stretches along the common land of the village. Conservation activities are focused on the turtle nesting season and mangrove restoration.

Although no scientific studies have been carried out in the area, local people report many positive benefits from their efforts. Ecologically these include increased fish-catch and better quality drinking water in the restored mangrove areas, as well as higher numbers of nesting turtles and better hatching success on the beach. Socially, the benefits range from the empowerment of young people to better relationships and interactions with the local forestry department. Culturally, the traditional activities carried out in the village were dying out due to declining fish-take and people's aspirations going beyond the lifestyle offered in a small fishing community (Kutty, 2009).

Although the links between species protection and the wider defence of human cultural values can appear to be tenuous, and are rarely investigated by researchers from a traditional scientific background, they can be critical in gaining acceptance for both conservation activities and the ideas of protected areas. The activities in Iringal, which link the protection of species and ecosystem services with the development of strong community action, governance and empowerment, are leading to the kind of social cohesion needed to ensure both ecological and cultural survival.

Liza Higgins-Zogib

Figure 9.1 *Himba traditional village, Puros Conservancy, Namibia*

Source: ©WWF-Canon/Edward Parker

The Argument

The value

'Culture' is a particularly value-laden word, sometimes simplified into a synonym for the arts but in reality a broad-ranging concept that includes aspects of history, anthropology, spiritual values, aesthetic appreciation and personal perception. UNESCO has attempted to pin it down in the Universal Declaration on Cultural Diversity:

> *Culture takes diverse forms across time and space. This diversity is embodied in the uniqueness and plurality of the identities of the groups and societies making up humankind. As a source of exchange, innovation and creativity, cultural diversity is as necessary for humankind as biodiversity is for nature. In this sense, it is the common heritage of humanity and should be recognized and affirmed for the benefit of present and future generations.* (UNESCO, 2001)

The UNESCO Convention for the Safeguarding of the Intangible Cultural Heritage goes further: '"intangible cultural heritage" means the practices, representations, expressions, knowledge, skills – as well as the instruments, objects, artefacts and cultural spaces associated therewith – that communities, groups and, in some cases, individuals recognize as part of their cultural heritage' (UNESCO, 2003).

These values occur in all countries and all places. The 'Bwrlwm Eryri' project of the Snowdonia National Park Authority in Wales in the UK states the issue very clearly:

> *Cultural heritage can mean our visual heritage: the landscape, traditional architecture, historical places and valuable habitats for wild life. But there is a need to delve deeper and give due respect to the invisible heritage: people's feelings of belonging to this truly amazing and incredible area through their language, literature, art, music, sayings, place names, history, recollections, legends, folk customs and also the wealth of oral wisdoms and information on all sorts of craft.* (Stolton et al., 2008)

The definition of a protected area, which includes 'associated ... cultural values' (Dudley, 2008), reflects that such areas also have at least the potential, if not the mandate, to maintain the cultural heritage and diversity related to a particular place. Indeed, in many places 'biodiversity' and 'culture' remain closely entwined. Traditional methods and ways of governing territories have been effective in the conservation of biocultural diversity for millennia, but there are growing threats both to many places of traditional importance (e.g. sacred sites) and to the very traditions that have conserved them over time. In such cases recognition and designation as a 'protected area' may provide the needed support to counter emerging threats. In other cases such recognition might be neither desirable nor effective. This chapter provides an outline of how protected areas can help to protect cultural values (note that those cultural values that relate more explicitly to religious or sacred values are discussed separately in Chapter 8).

Before delving further into the subject matter at hand, a brief discussion on what actually constitutes a 'protected area' in this context is necessary. The complexity comes from a gradually shifting protected area paradigm to one that is slowly beginning to embrace what is broadly termed as Indigenous and Community Conserved Areas (ICCAs) – whether they are formally recognized by state legislation or not. Protected areas in the form of ICCAs have integrated conservation and culture in seamless ways since time immemorial. Indeed, conservation is an outcome of the specific and complex cultures that these people have developed in response to their natural surrounds. However, the paradigm shift is far from being fully realized and the conservation community has some way to go before a full adoption of these ideals is achieved. Until that time, we must be specific about the different governance types, which in the end makes a world of difference to how the 'other dimensions' of protected areas (specifically cultural and spiritual) are provided for.

It is in government-designated and managed protected areas that the relationship is often more difficult and therefore there must be an additional note of caution. While this book is primarily looking at the benefits of protected areas, it is clear that many government-run protected areas have not considered local cultures and livelihoods in their management practices. A growing body of literature exists criticizing governments and large conservation organizations in relation to the impact that protected areas are having on the lives and rights of local communities and, in particular, indigenous peoples (Colchester, 2003; Chapin, 2004). The term 'conservation refugees' has emerged to describe people who have been displaced to make way for protected areas, adding weight to the voices calling for the full recognition of rights, tenure and participatory governance processes in existing and new protected areas (Dowie, 2009). A number of indigenous peoples have even demanded a halt to the creation of new protected areas in their territories until these issues are resolved.

Most conservationists would argue that the conservation of biodiversity is worth some sacrifices by people; indeed, that today's 'sacrifices' are necessary for future generations. However, such choices become morally unacceptable when a few people (or the same kind of people) shoulder most of the costs. As it is often the least powerful who are expected to meet the costs, conservation through protected areas can, at its worst, exacerbate existing social inequalities, in effect putting the needs of wildlife before the needs of the marginalized.

Indigenous people have been expelled from protected areas throughout their history; the Shoshone people were expelled from Yellowstone National Park at the very start of the modern protected areas development in 1872. Other examples include the Ik from Kidepo National Park in colonial Uganda, the Vedda from the Madura Oya National Park in Sri Lanka and the Batwa of Rwanda, Uganda and DR Congo from mountain gorilla reserves. The results have been disastrous for some indigenous groups, leading to their near extinction (Colchester, 2003; Dowie, 2009). Such clashes have, apart from their serious humanitarian impacts, done little for conservation. Many problems have been created or intensified because local human populations oppose the protected area. Loss of traditional rights can reduce peoples' interest in long-term stewardship of the land and therefore the creation of a protected area can, in some cases, paradoxically increase the rate of damage.

However, protected areas do not have to be culturally oppressive mechanisms. They can offer unique opportunities to continue traditional lifestyles, especially in the new 'governance' types that are now recognized in global policy (see more on this below). In parts of the world where land-use change is taking place most quickly, some indigenous peoples are now virtually confined to protected areas. In the most innovative cases, indigenous communities are heavily involved with or even leading the process of management. For example, Colombia has moved towards much greater participation of indigenous peoples, peasant communities and others. It also encouraged the creation and incorporation of a complex set of regional and local reserves, collaboratively managed protected areas, indigenous territories, private protected areas and community conserved areas (see Case Study 2.1 on Colombia).

These examples are spreading. Under a project linked with the CBD Programme of Work on Protected Areas, 19 countries (Afghanistan, Antigua Barbuda, Armenia, Benin, Burundi, Cambodia, Comoros, DR Congo, Guatemala, Guinea, Honduras, Kiribati, Maldives, Mali, Mauritania, Micronesia Federated states, Samoa, The Gambia and Uganda) are assessing and diversifying protected area governance types (see below). Although bad practice undoubtedly continues, there are many cases where protected areas can and do have a positive role to play in the maintenance of cultures and related cultural values – when they are governed and managed appropriately. We will concentrate on these examples here.

The benefit

We pastoral peoples have always considered our land what you call a 'protected area'. We have always embraced 'conservation' not as a professional activity but as intimate duty and pride of every member of our tribes, as the heart of our livelihood, because our very subsistence depends on it. I hear you talk of ecosystems, landscapes, and connectivity. We have always known about this without using your terms. Our migration patterns transfer seeds. Our grazing patterns shape the landscape. We subsist on our lands; we know and care for its diversity of plants and animals. We pray on this land, and we guard its many sacred places. For the land provides us also with spiritual well-being. But we can no longer do it alone. In the world of today, we need the concurrence of our governments and all the support that brothers can give. (The late Sayyaad Soltani, Council of Elders of the Kuhi subtribe of the Qashqai Confederation, Iran, excerpt from the address to the Plenary of the World Parks Congress, Durban 2003, translated by Aghaghia Rahimzadeh, quoted in Dowie, 2009)

Because protected areas usually aim to maintain ecosystems as they are or restore them to resemble what they were, protected areas can in theory fulfil a dual function of protecting both biodiversity and human culture in the many places where humans have interacted with natural ecosystems over long periods of time. Such a win–win situation assumes that the human culture will remain the same or will change in ways that do not then undermine natural ecology. A large factor in the success of such approaches will be in providing recognition to and supporting indigenous peoples or local communities in their traditional and ongoing conservation practices (in the form of ICCAs) or, in the case of government managed protected areas, bringing local or resident communities within the process of management (collaboratively managed protected areas or CMPAs).

In addition to the six management categories of IUCN there are four broad areas of governance type (Dudley, 2008) – the latter now recognized internationally as equally important as the former. These are:

- areas governed by states;
- areas governed by a variety of different actors – co-management;
- areas governed by a private entity (e.g. a company or other private owner);
- areas governed by local communities and indigenous peoples – indigenous and community conserved areas (ICCA).

Although important cultural values can and are maintained in all protected area governance types (and under all available management models), it is within the realm of the last governance type that there is the widest scope for protected areas to contribute substantially to the enhancement and maintenance of cultures and cultural values, although co-management also offers important possibilities. An ICCA is described as 'natural and modified ecosystems including significant biodiversity, ecological services and cultural values voluntarily conserved by indigenous and local communities through customary laws or other effective means' (Pathak et al., 2004; Borrini-Feyerabend and Kothari, 2008).

ICCAs are both some of the oldest and newest forms of protection. Management systems that fit the above description have existed for hundreds or thousands of years and are now often being 'recognized' by the outside world. They are also increasingly being incorporated within national conservation plans and protected area systems. For example, Brazil has 65 indigenous lands in the community-conserved areas, of which 38 are demarcated and 28 are legally established; Australia has established 22 indigenous-protected areas covering 14 million hectares and implementing new forms of conservation and covenanting programmes (CBD, 2009). All of these and others are consciously mixing protection of culture with protection of biodiversity.

While the notion of governance is not necessarily synonymous with protecting cultures, most self-generated areas are predicated on the idea that they are also run by or at least with, the communities concerned. Table 9.1 shows some positive examples of protected areas with a variety of management and governance types providing valuable support to communities, helping to maintain chosen lifestyles and protecting cultural values from increasing threats.

Current Contribution of Protected Areas

Four aspects of cultural values can be seen as related to protected areas:

1   particular features in a landscape or seascape, either natural or constructed;
2   management techniques or other behavioural characteristics;
3   entire lifestyles of particular peoples or communities linked with the area in question;
4   traditional ecological knowledge and knowledge related to the wider values of lands and waters.

Features of cultural value

All natural landscapes/seascapes which are inhabited by or used by people are also 'cultural-scapes'. In this sense almost all protected areas are also cultural landscapes, with cultural significance for one people or another. Indeed, if one thinks of modern conservation also as a 'culture' in that it embodies certain values and ethics, all protected areas are cultural sites/scapes.

However, particularly special features of land or seascapes can be identified and have been protected by people for millennia. They can range in size from massive landscapes like the Grand Canyon to small but special elements of an area such as waterfalls, fish pools or individual trees. Examples exist of such important cultural features in many protected areas; these are often but not invariably associated with spiritual values. Conservation of individual features valued for cultural or spiritual reasons by society is probably the oldest reason for establishing some kind of protection regime.

IUCN category III designates areas managed 'to protect specific outstanding natural features and their associated biodiversity and habitats' (Dudley, 2008). These natural or natural/cultural features are of outstanding or unique value because of their inherent rarity, representativeness, aesthetic qualities or cultural significance. Many category III sites are relatively small. The category has been used particularly in North America through the National Monument system and examples from there illustrate the range of cultural features that might be included. Most of these are natural features although in some cases they also have important historical or cultural associations and modifications:

- Garden of the Gods in southern Illinois, important for its unusual rock formations;
- Amboy Crater in the Mojave Desert, protecting an extinct volcano crater and lava field;
- John Day Fossil Beds in Oregon, important because of the high density of fossils;
- Giant Sequoia in California, maintaining habitat for some of the world's largest trees;
- Head Smashed In Buffalo Jump in Alberta, the site of an unusual cliff feature that was used to trap buffalo by First Nations groups;
- Petroglyph National Monument in New Mexico, protecting both an extinct volcano and also important rock paintings; in this case the link between natural and cultural features becomes even more blurred.

Management techniques or other behavioural characteristics

Much less common than the above, but increasingly important in a world where agricultural/forestry/fishing/pastoral techniques and lifestyles are becoming less diverse, is the conservation of culturally important uses of the ecosystem. These include the variety of forest-management techniques, traditional agriculture/pastoralism/fishing and organizational systems to manage lands and waters. Such an approach only works in the protected areas' framework if the particular use also encourages or supports biodiversity (in theory biodiversity elements that have become adapted to, or are immune to, human intervention); this situation is less common than often assumed, at least in government-run protected areas. Examples might include European nature reserves where traditional wood-coppicing and pollarding are maintained to protect associated biodiversity or the reintroduction of traditional grazing patterns to prevent scrub encroachment on flower-rich meadows or hillsides.

IUCN category V protected areas are managed mainly 'to protect and sustain important landscapes/seascapes and the associated nature conservation and other values created by interaction with humans through traditional management practices' (Dudley, 2008). Safeguarding the integrity of this traditional interaction is vital to the area's protection, maintenance and evolution. Such approaches have traditionally been used particularly in Europe, where over half the amount of protected areas is in category V, mainly areas of traditional, non-intensive agriculture and forestry where biodiversity conservation and recreational uses exist alongside traditional management. Examples include the Camargue Regional Park in France, where conservation of rare birds and other species takes place alongside unique agricultural systems; and Dolomiti d'Ampezzo in Italy, an area of mountains and traditional agriculture.

Figure 9.2 *The Camargue, France*

A large number of ICCAs are explicitly oriented towards maintaining traditional management practices, with or without modern adaptations, which help sustain biodiversity. This is true, for instance, of the Locally Managed Marine Areas of the Southern Pacific (Govan et al., 2008).

Protection of peoples and lifestyles

The concept of using protected areas as a tool to protect whole peoples and their lifestyles is relatively new as a conscious strategy and is still controversial, both among indigenous and traditional peoples, some of whom reject the whole idea, and also among some conservationists who see this as a dilution of biodiversity conservation aims. However, there is a growing number of cases where indigenous peoples' groups and other local communities have used the protected areas concept strategically in their quest to secure land rights, which also works effectively to maintain biodiversity. Some communities are also seeking recognition of their ICCAs, within or outside the protected area system, to obtain an additional buffer against external threats from logging, mining, dams or political take-over. While conflicts still exist in many parts of the world between protected area authorities and indigenous people there are beginning to be examples of how protected areas can help to sustain the cultures of the marginalized societies around the world.

Traditional ecological knowledge

Linked to the survival of cultures in the point above is the understanding and appreciation of traditional knowledge, and specifically ecological knowledge. Local knowledge (also variously referred to as traditional, indigenous, community, customary or practical knowledge) refers to the long-standing information, wisdom, traditions and practices of certain indigenous peoples or local communities. In many cases, traditional knowledge has been orally passed for generations from person to person. Some forms of local knowledge are expressed through stories, legends, folklore, rituals, songs, art and even laws. One distinction that is often made between local knowledge and modern or 'western' knowledge is that unlike the latter, it does not separate 'secular' or 'rational' knowledge from spiritual knowledge, intuitions and wisdom. It is often embedded in a cosmology, and the distinction between 'intangible' knowledge and physical things is often blurred. Indeed, holders of local knowledge often claim that their knowledge cannot be divorced from the natural and cultural context within which it has arisen, including their traditional lands and resources, and their kinship and community relations.

Although there has been a tendency among modern societies (and, learning from them, among traditional ones too) to consider such knowledge as 'primitive' and outmoded, it is increasingly clear that it has tremendous contemporary relevance. Traditional knowledge is one of the fulcrums of survival of traditional societies; it is a part of their life and it is impossible to separate it from all other aspects of living. It is what gives them the ability to make sense of nature, to find their place and meaning within nature and in relation to each other, to derive physical, material and cultural sustenance from nature, and to devise means by which nature can be sustained along with sustaining society. Protected management has often been imposed on top of these long developed knowledge systems and has, in several cases, undermined traditional knowledge-based management which had developed and adapted for hundreds if not thousands of years.

However, it is not only for the holders of traditional knowledge that it remains relevant. Traditional knowledge has a significant contribution to make in a range of contemporary issues faced by all of humanity, including sustainable livelihoods and economies, governance, climate change and, not least of all, conservation (Kothari, 2009).

For traditional ecological knowledge to survive in protected areas there needs to be support and acknowledgement for the continuation of the social, cultural, economic and political contexts within which such knowledge thrives. This means the full recognition of the territorial, cultural and political rights and responsibilities of indigenous peoples and local communities, and increasing use of various governance types of protected areas including, in particular, ICCAs.

Table 9.1 below provides some examples of where protected areas have been developed or where management has acknowledged the value and benefit of preserving cultural heritage.

Table 9.1 *Use of the protected areas concept to maintain traditional human societies*

Best practice	Details
Protected areas managed and declared by indigenous people to preserve cultural heritage	Kayapò Center for Ecological Studies was set up in 1992 in an 8000ha mahogany forest reserve, established by the Kayapò people for the conservation of biodiversity. The reserve is managed jointly by A'Ukre villagers and the environmental NGO Conservation International, Brazil. Entry fees and obligatory donations of medicine (primarily for malaria) paid by scientists and other visitors provide economic benefit to the entire community without disrupting the Kayapò culture (Daniels, 2002)
Land claim settlements aiding protected area establishment and guiding management to focus on conserving indigenous cultural heritage	The 3000km² Kusawa Park in the Yukon Territory, Canada, was established through a cooperative effort by a number of First Nations and the Yukon Government. The guiding objectives for management are from the Carcross/Tagish and Kwanlin Dun First Nation settlement agreements. A management plan being prepared (by the founding partners) will recognize and protect the traditional use and sharing of the area by Carcross/Tagish, Kwanlin Dun and Champagne and Aishihik People and recognize and honour their history, heritage and culture through the establishment and operation of the park (Kusawa Park Steering Committee, 2009)
Network of national parks and indigenous reserves protecting against development and colonization	50,000 Ashaninka inhabit the Peruvian Amazonian rainforests, representing the largest ethnic group in the region. In the early 20th century the area was colonized by rubber tappers; in the 1970s and 1980s the Ashaninka lands were usurped for farming and forestry, by gold prospectors and by a new wave of colonists. Some 700,000ha of forest was also lost to coca production. Such threats, combined with the lack of indigenous land titles, led to many conflicts between Ashaninka communities, colonists, international corporations and state authorities, as well as irreversible ecological damage. However, NGOs became involved in the Ashaninkas' protest campaign and helped secure important advances, such as the establishment of a large new protected area, the Otishi National Park, along with two indigenous communal reserves, the Ashaninka and Machiguenga Community Reserve (Minority Rights Group International, 2008)

Best practice	Details
Protection for groups who wish to live in isolation from the rest of society	In 2006, the government of Bolivia declared 'an exclusively reserved, inviolable and fully protected area' inside the huge Madidi National Park in the Amazonian highlands (Administrative Decision No 48/2006). The area aims to protect the home of the last peoples living in isolation in Bolivia and perhaps the world: the presumed descendants of the Toromona people, one of several ethnic groups or segments of ethnic groups which may still be living in isolation in Bolivia. Decision No 48 sets a strategic precedent for the protection of isolated indigenous peoples in Bolivia and the wider world. It includes the prohibition of any settlement other than that of the peoples living inside the inviolable area, unwanted contact with the Toromona people and activity related to prospecting for or exploiting the area's natural resources (WRM, 2009; UN, 2009)
Capturing cultural information to inform protected area management and consolidating autonomy of resource use and management	The Toro people of Indonesia, who traditionally inhabited the area in Sulawesi now known as the Lore Lindu National Park, implemented a project between 1993 and 2000 to document customary law and map their territories. The resulting plan served as a basis for the negotiation of a formal agreement with the park authorities and led to the recognition of the Toro indigenous territory alongside the system of national parks. The benefits include the prevention of illegal logging, which used to be widespread in the park, and the strengthening of the system of traditional authorities and the customary system of national resource use and protection (UN, 2007)
Protected area management by local communities	Cuochi (known locally as 'mtsho 'khri') Community Conserved Area in Qinghai Province, China, is a Tibetan village entirely within the Suojia-Qumahe Core Protection Zone of the Sanjiangyuan (Three River Source) National Nature Reserve. Since October 2006, the management office of the nature reserve has signed an incentive agreement with Cuochi village and given stewardship of an area of 2440km^2 to the village. The agreement is the first of its kind in China. The overall management objectives for the reserve relate to biodiversity, ecosystem security and watershed protection. In addition, in Cuochi the objectives also include cultural, spiritual and self-education. The Cuochi CCA is managed by the village, represented by the village committee (Bo et al., 2008)

Best practice	Details
A new vision for protected areas managed by communities to safeguard their territory and livelihoods	In 2005 the Mursi tribe of Ethiopia were campaigning against protected areas. The legal establishment of boundaries of two protected areas, Omo and Mago National Parks, were threatening to deny them access to land for cultivation and cattle herding (Hurd, 2005). Although the problems faced by the Mursi are not solved, in 2009 the people of Buruba province, Mursiland, were developing plans to establish their own protected area to help influence land and resource policies to their advantage. Following a visit to a number of community conservancies in Kenya representatives from Buruba were starting a process to map traditional practices and values and conservation assets. Discussion centred on the challenge of balancing protected core areas and sustainable use areas, managing coexistence between domestic and wild animals, the limits of traditional regulation based on compliance, sources of conservation revenues, community institutions for allocating revenues and the capacities needed by the Mursi to capitalize upon these opportunities (Muchemi, 2009). Such an initiative will take time and much support to realize, but it does show how indigenous people are beginning to see afresh the role of protected areas in their cultural survival

Figure 9.3 *Kayapò girl, Brazil*

Source: © Mauri Rautkari/WWF-Canon

Future Needs and Management Options

Of the four options described above, the third – the use of protected areas to protect traditional cultures – is by far the most significant, but also the most complex. The split that has arisen between indigenous peoples or local communities and protected area managers in some places is a tragedy that threatens, over time, to undermine the aims of both cultural and ecological conservation. These groups should all be natural allies in resisting large-scale environmental degradation, and contemporary attempts to build partnerships are to be welcomed. The concept of self-generated indigenous protected areas, which is one important result of taking a fresh view at this issue, has developed particularly in Australia, Canada and Latin America.

In fact, there is strong evidence that cultural diversity and biological diversity often go hand in hand. For example, there are marked overlaps between biological megadiversity and areas of high linguistic diversity (Harmon and Maffi, 2002), meaning that twin approaches to conservation and culture need to become the norm in many of the places where conservation is most urgently required. In addition to approaches such as the ICCA concept described above, this may involve, for example, working with or building on traditional laws (such as taboos) rather than introducing altogether 'new' conservation laws in places where there is low opportunity for enforcement, as has been proposed in Madagascar (Jones et al., 2008).

Protected area agencies should take a critical look at their role in contributing to any country's cultural diversity and robustness. Countries with poor records on governance and human rights are generally unlikely to have very good conservation records, and protected areas are sometimes used as an excuse to dispossess people of their land for other purposes, such as mining. Conservation organizations need to be extremely careful about the partnerships they form in repressive or undemocratic countries to ensure that well-meaning conservation projects are not a smokescreen for economic and political activities that are undermining human rights and equity. Some of the existing guidelines and principles can and do help, although there are still many instances in which they are not applied. There are no underlying reasons why the concepts of biodiversity conservation through protected areas and of maintaining cultural integrity should be in conflict.

Such changes assume a shift away from old ideas of protected areas always being equivalent to exclusion to a new more inclusive approach, including principles of free prior informed consent and the use of a full range of governance types within protected areas. Protected area staff need to be trained not just for their biological skills but also for awareness of how to manage appropriately for different cultures and cultural values and to be able to communicate the full range of protected area values to a variety of audiences. Combining a good variety of management and governance types in any protected area system will help to ensure that coverage and representativeness are enhanced. It will start to address gaps in the system and also connectivity. Additionally, and perhaps most importantly for sustainability, it will certainly improve public support for conservation (see Case Study 9.2 from Canada).

A crucial factor in the success of such culture-specific and human rights-based experiences is capacity-building for the indigenous peoples and local communities concerned, which facilitates their administrative participation and institutional reform at the local level (UN, 2007). Successful conservation depends also on communities retaining a feeling of self-esteem and self-respect and being fully aware of the signifi-cance of their traditional cultural and spiritual values within the protected area; they should be able to maintain their core values while adapting to new circumstances (Mallarach, 2008). This does not preclude changes that may be needed in socie-ties and communities that have practices of inequity and exploitation, traditional or newly generated; indeed, conservation programmes themselves could become a catalyst for such changes, if sensitively introduced by either the community itself or by external agents.

Conclusions

The hybrid role of protected areas in both conserving 'nature' and protecting 'culture' is clearly of growing importance and for some people there is no distinction between the two concepts anyway. However, it is still sometimes an uncomfortable mixture for a proportion of the stakeholders involved, especially in the context of government-managed protected areas.

The role that existing protected areas play in maintaining cultural diversity and entire cultures is also still poorly understood. There is, for example, no agreed meth-odology for cost-benefit analysis of protected areas or methods for assessing the equity of distribution of any costs and benefits. More research and best-practice examples are urgently needed. It is also a major challenge to formal conservation organizations to look at 'natural' landscapes/seascapes as 'cultural' scapes, which is how indigenous peoples and local communities view them. A converse challenge is for communities to understand the value of the full range of biodiversity that the formal conservation world stresses. What this calls for, clearly, is more mutually respectful, collaborative partnerships than have been witnessed so far in dominant conservation practice.

Such research and practices need to consider the dilemma of protecting the local values of ecosystems versus the need to conserve the so-called public goods values that accrue to society at large, either within a country or even on a global basis. In 1810, the poet William Wordsworth wrote in his introduction to John Wilkinson's *Select Views of the Lakes* (about the English Lake District) that he saw the region as a 'sort of national property, in which every man has a right and interest who has an eye to perceive and a heart to enjoy' – a strikingly democratic and inclusive view of conservation (Stolton et al., 2008). The challenge in its application is ensuring that the costs of such an approach do not fall entirely or predominantly on the people living there or traditionally using the region's resources. The beneficiaries of the ecosystem services and other values from protected areas have long regarded them as 'free goods' but maintaining them is often not cost-free for those living nearby. And society is just starting to wrestle with the question of restitution.

Whether or not rural communities wish to link the sustenance of their own cultural traditions with recognized protected areas, of any governance type, will be a matter of judgement. It will be influenced by the other alternatives on offer, the openness of official protected area agencies, the feelings of the people involved, and the more general economic and political context. There are times and places where protected areas appear to offer real benefits as tools for cultural survival but there are certainly other possibilities, which in some cases may be more effective or more attractive. However, it is likely that the role of protected areas in maintaining cultural values will gain a much higher profile in the future.

Case Study 9.1:
Angkor Wat Protected Landscape –
Where Culture, Nature and Spirit Meet

Liza Higgins-Zogib

Angkor Wat Protected Landscape is a prime example of a protected area whose role is not only to protect biological diversity but also, and perhaps even more importantly, the cultural heritage of an entire nation. As this ancient place of living culture and worship moves into the 21st century, the practical challenges involved in managing the site without losing any of its cultural or spiritual integrity are intensifying. This case study outlines the cultural and spiritual elements of Angkor's increasingly threatened 'protected landscape', considers the growing challenge posed by tourism and 'development' and concludes with some recommendations for how to improve the management of the protected area in order to take into full consideration its cultural and spiritual dimensions.

The diverse values of Angkor Wat

In December 1992, Angkor's 42,000ha of natural, cultural and spiritual opulence was designated as a World Heritage site. It is located in northwestern Cambodia, south of the Kulen Hills and north of Tonle Sap, the Great Lake. Known as Angkor Archaeological Park, its 50 or so kilometres from east to west comprise a landscape of forests, rice paddies, lakes, waterways, towns and villages, among which are scattered hundreds of temples and other buildings (Freeman and Jacques, 2003). These range from small piles of rubble to the most magnificent specimens of Khmer architecture, including the internationally celebrated Angkor Wat. Reputed to be the world's largest single religious monument, Angkor Wat is undoubtedly the main attraction of this landscape and Cambodia's most valuable landmark, drawing between 1 and 2 million visitors to the country each year. In 1993 the area surrounding Angkor Wat was designated a 'Protected Landscape' (category V protected area).

It is safe to say that the Archaeological Park and, in particular, the Angkor Wat landscape, provides more national and local economic benefits than any other site in Cambodia. Indeed, it would be difficult to find many other category V protected landscapes in the world of such economic importance.

In addition to its significant economic importance, the larger Angkor landscape is critical from an ecological point of view. Despite increasing fragmentation, the area still contains extensive and predominantly mature natural forests (Dudley et al., 2005). The forests of Angkor are intricately entwined with the site's spiritual heritage, having protected it for centuries after the decline of the ancient city, Yasodharapura. This is perfectly illustrated in temples such as Ta Prohm and Ta Som, where the trees and temples seem to spring from the very same source and it is difficult to say whether the trees hold the temples up or vice versa (Coe, 2003). As such, the natural elements of the protected area contribute quite dramatically to the cultural heritage, helping to maintain a certain energetic dimension that would certainly be lost were the surrounding and intertwining environment spoiled.

Architecturally, Angkor is the most important site in Southeast Asia, having fascinated the world since its 'rediscovery' in 1863 by French naturalist, Henri Mouhot. The Khmers themselves never forgot the existence of the Angkor monuments and, although many fell into disrepair, Angkor Wat, for example, was continually used for worship (Freeman and Jacques, 2003). There are a variety of architectural styles in the landscape reflecting the differing religious tendencies and royal reigns of the time. These range from the Preah Ko Style (AD 877–86), through the classical or Angkor Wat Style (1080–1175), to the Post Bayon Style (1243–1431) (Coedès, 1943; 1968).

The conservation challenge

Culturally and spiritually, Angkor is of undeniable importance to Cambodia as a whole. An image of Angkor Wat appears proudly on the country's flag and its spirit underpins the dance, drama, music and art of the nation. It is a sacred landscape that exudes spiritual value and demands reverence from even the most hardened of visitor. Unfortunately, however, its sacred status is often neglected.

Figure 9.4 *Plants and architecture combine at the Angkor Wat complex of temples*
Source: © Nigel Dudley

Tourism figures vary from source to source but, on average, Angkor has seen a shift from 7600 tourists in 1993 to well over 1 million in 2007. Admittedly, this huge rise in paying visitors brings economic benefits for the country as a whole, but who is really benefiting? Who will end up footing the bill? For one, the temples themselves are suffering and the Phnom Bakheng hilltop temple has to bear the weight of around 3000 tourists on its steps every evening, as enthusiasts make their way up to watch the sun set over Angkor Wat. Busloads of tourists queue at the temple entries and many inevitably do not follow the rules of conduct during their visits (Uchida et al., 2007; Higgins-Zogib, 2008).

Where does all this leave the sacredness and cultural significance of the landscape? At Angkor the will to grow and develop at any cost currently outweighs any intentions to manage the landscape appropriately for all the different values it possesses. But all is not lost. If the right management response is put into place, one that takes into consideration the landscape's cultural and spiritual values as well as its needs for development, then a much better balance will be established.

Conclusions

The mounting threats touched on above are clearly a real challenge for protected area management – but they make the additional layer of protection afforded by its status of 'protected landscape' all the more important. The many integrated values of this place are what make it special and the protected area has a critical role to play if the biological and associated cultural and spiritual values are to survive. Several steps could help the current authorities and decision-makers to maintain and enhance Angkor's cultural landscape, including:

- formally recognizing the entire landscape as a 'sacred landscape' with important religious and spiritual values for millions of Buddhists and Hindus the world over;
- recognizing that the religious and spiritual values also need to be managed appropriately;
- increasing the capacity of management staff to incorporate cultural/spiritual considerations into decision-making;
- ensuring that appropriate visitor guidelines are in place and fully implemented;
- further involving local communities and religious groups in decision-making and management of the landscape;
- encouraging and supporting cultural and spiritual traditions, including dance and theatre, and sustainable development in the Siem Reap region;
- encouraging and supporting cultural exchange events with other countries (such as the International Ramayana Festival).

Case Study 9.2:
Inuit Partnerships in the
Torngat Mountains National Park, Canada

Judy Rowell

The park will help us protect our land and our memories and our stories.
(John Jararuse, Inuk from Saglek, Labrador)

The Torngat Mountains National Park Reserve is situated within Nunatsiavut (northern Labrador), the homeland and settlement area of the Labrador Inuit. The history of the efforts to establish the national park reserve is one that has taken place within the context of an evolving vision of what a national park should be and of changing attitudes as to how we should go about the process of national-park establishment. It is a story that includes the hard-learned lessons of the importance of working with Inuit as equal partners, of the need to achieve mutual respect and trust, of lengthy setbacks and of tough negotiations and compromise among diverse parties that were nevertheless dedicated to the vision of protecting this magnificent area in perpetuity.

Whereas a true partnership was entered into between Parks Canada, the Labrador Inuit Association and the government of Newfoundland and Labrador to undertake the national-park feasibility study, a very different and strained relationship with Nunavik Inuit, represented by the Makivik Corporation, led to a challenge to the park-establishment process in the federal court of Canada in 1997. However, today both Nunavik Inuit and Labrador Inuit support the creation of the park, and both have achieved full equality through such measures as participation in the park's cooperative management board and in sharing potential economic benefits associated with the park.

Separate Park Impacts and Benefits Agreements were negotiated between Parks Canada and the Labrador Inuit Association and the Makivik Corporation. The agreements confirm the creation of the park, and that it will be operated and managed through a cooperative management regime that recognizes Inuit as partners and recognizes and honours Inuit knowledge and the special historical and cultural relationship between Inuit and the land. The agreements provide for a seven-member cooperative management board to advise the federal minister of environment on all matters related to park management. Parks Canada, Makivik Corporation and the Nunatsiavut government each appoint two members and an independent chair is jointly appointed by all three parties. The cooperative management board members act in the public interest rather than as a representative of the appointing party. In that spirit Parks Canada appointed two Inuit as its representatives on the cooperative management board – an Inuk from Nunavik and an Inuk from Labrador. The Nunatsiavut government and Makivik Corporation each appointed two Inuit and the three parties jointly appointed a Labrador Inuk as independent chair. This makes the cooperative management board for the Torngat Mountains National Park Reserve the first all Inuit cooperative management board in the history of Parks Canada.

Figure 9.5 *The Inuit of Torngat Mountains*

Source: © H.Wittorn

Initiative

I would like to take this opportunity to express my support for the approach taken by the Parks Canada Agency to create an all-Inuit board. It is a forward-looking step and signals great progress in the relationship between your Agency and the Inuit of the Region. (Letter to Parks Canada from Pita Aatami, President, Makivik Corporation, 5 September 2006)

It was in this spirit and context that Parks Canada planned its base camp in the park as an opportunity to bring together Inuit from Nunatsiavut and Nunavik and Parks Canada managers to connect with each other and reinforce the shared objectives and commitments.

Torngat Mountains is a remote park and not easily accessible to Parks Canada staff, Inuit or visitors. The area has always been an Inuit homeland but over the past few decades Inuit have shifted from a nomadic life to community-based life, which has meant that they had to move further south away from the park. A trip by boat or skidoo into the mountains for an Inuk to hunt or fish is costly and sometimes challenging. Parks Canada believes that establishing a national park in the Torngat Mountains provides an opportunity to facilitate ways for Inuit to get to this area, for elders to reconnect with their homeland and for youth to experience it for the first time. Establishing a base camp in the park as a pilot project allowed Parks Canada to scope out the feasibility of this initiative as a way to bring Inuit into the park and make vital connections.

The base camp ran from 24 July–10 August 2006. Parks Canada contracted local Inuit from Nain to organize and manage the camp and used the services of local Inuit-owned and operated long liner boats for logistical support. The first week of the camp was dedicated to supporting the Nunatsiavut government's Youth Division's summer youth camp. It was an opportunity for Inuit youth to learn traditional skills and spend time with Inuit elders who are from this area.

The second week was dedicated to bringing Inuit elders from Nunavik and Nunatsiavut back to their traditional homeland. It was a time for rediscovery and sharing stories. For park managers and Inuit it was an opportunity to get to know each other, to travel on the land and, more importantly, for park managers it was an opportunity to see the park through Inuit eyes. So began the first discussions about a shared vision for the future management of the park.

Lessons learned

> *The Torngat Mountains National Park Reserve is a fitting symbol of the overlapping values that bind us together as Canadians. We have created a lasting legacy for all Canadians, made possible through trust, mutual respect and a deep understanding of Labrador Inuit values and traditions. It is truly a gift to us all.*
> (William Andersen III, President, Labrador Inuit Association, 22 January 2005)

The participants in the camp and the Inuit who managed the camp clearly endorsed the initiative as one that Parks Canada should continue each year. It allowed all participants and particularly Parks Canada staff to see the Torngat Mountains National Park Reserve as not just a spectacular wilderness but as an Inuit homeland and a cultural landscape. The camp experience allowed participants to 'blur' the border between Nunavik and Labrador. Nunavik Inuit shared their stories of their travel routes through the Torngat Mountains and of special places and memories of their land-use in this area. The experience that they had in the park, through the base camp, paved the way for later meetings in Kangiqsualujjuaq in Nunavik to talk about the park and the role that Nunavik Inuit will play in its cooperative management. Including Nunavik Inuit in the first base camp provided them with an understanding of how cooperative management would be implemented and how Inuit knowledge would be celebrated and honoured, while also establishing important connections with Parks Canada. The Nunatsiavut government and Makivik have both endorsed the base-camp initiative as a way to facilitate opportunities for Inuit to get back to the Torngat Mountains and are interested in becoming partners in the operation of future camps.

Conclusions

Establishing a new park through constitutionally protected land-claim agreements provides a vital foundation for the partnerships that are necessary for cooperative management and a shared vision. It is important that Parks Canada's role in park establishment and management respects and reflects the commitments made to Inuit in their agreements and ensures that the relationships built with Inuit are reinforced as partners. The base-camp initiative and the appointment of Inuit to the cooperative management board provide a clear signal to Inuit that Parks Canada believes in the cooperative management relationship that it negotiated with Inuit and intends to honour the spirit in which this arrangement was negotiated (Canadian Parks Council, Aboriginal Peoples and Canada's Parks and Protected Areas, 2008).

References

Bo, L., Fangyi, Y. Suo, M. Zhongyun, Z. Shan, S. Xiaoli, S. and Zhi, L. (2008) *Review of CCA Studies in South-West China*, ICCA regional review for CENESTA/TILCEPA/TGER/IUCN/GEF-SGP,   http://cmsdata.iucn.org/downloads/sw_china_cca_study.pdf, accessed 28 September 2009.

Borrini-Feyerabend, G. and Kothari, A. (2008). 'Recognizing and supporting indigenous and community conservation – Ideas and experience from the grassroots', CEESP/WCPA briefing note 9, September 2008, http://cmsdata.iucn.org/downloads/ceesp_briefing_note_9_iccas.pdf, accessed 1 October 2009.

Canadian Parks Council, Aboriginal Peoples and Canada's Parks and Protected Areas (2008) *AkKutiliuk – Making a Path. Torngat Mountains National Park Reserve of Canada*, www.parks-parcs.ca/english/cpc/aboriginal.php, accessed 1 September 2009.

CBD (2009) *Progress Towards Achieving Targets of the Programme of Work*, UNEP/CBD/SBSTTA/14/5, Convention on Biological Diversity, Montreal.

Chapin, M. (2004) 'A challenge to conservationists', *Worldwatch Magazine,* November/December.

Coe, M. D. (2003) *Angkor and the Khmer Civilization*, Thames and Hudson, London.

Coedès, G. (1943) *Pour mieux comprendre Angkor*, Imprimerie d'Extrême Orient, Hanoi.

Coedès, G. (1968) *The Indianized States of Southeast Asia*, East West Center Press, Honolulu.

Colchester, M. (2003) *Salvaging Nature: Indigenous Peoples, Protected Areas and Biodiversity Conservation*, World Rainforest Movement and Forest Peoples Programme, Montevideo and Moreton-in-Marsh.

Daniels, A. E. (2002) 'Indigenous peoples and neotropical forest conservation:

Impacts of protected area systems on traditional cultures', *Macalester Environmental Review*, 23 September 2002.

Dowie, M. (2009) *Conservation Refugees*, MIT Press, Cambridge, MA, and London.

Dudley, N. (ed.) (2008) *Guidelines for Protected Area Management Categories*, IUCN, Gland.

Dudley, N., Higgins-Zogib, L. and Mansourian, S. (2005) *Beyond Belief, Linking Faiths and Protected Areas to Support Biodiversity Conservation*, WWF, Gland, and Alliance for Religion and Conservation, Bath.

Freeman, M. and Jacques, C. (2006) *Ancient Angkor*, River Books Press, Bangkok.

Govan, H., Aalbersberg, W., Tawake, A. and Parks, J. (2008) *Locally-Managed Marine Areas: A Guide for Practitioners*, Locally-Managed Marine Area Network, Lami.

Harmon, D. and Maffi, L. (2002) 'Are linguistic and biological diversity linked?', *Conservation Biology in Practice*, vol 3, no 1, pp26–7.

Higgins-Zogib, L. (2008) 'Dancing the Ramayana in Angkor, Cambodia', in J.- M. Mallarach (ed.), *Protected Landscapes and Cultural and Spiritual Values*, IUCN, Gland.

Hurd, W. (2005) 'Mursi land threatened by government', www.survival-international.org/news/943, 8 August 2005, accessed 1 September 2009.

Jones, J. P. G., Andriamarovololona, M. M. and Hockley, N. (2002) 'The importance of taboos and social norms to conservation in Madagascar', *Conservation Biology*, vol 22, no 4, pp976–86.

Kothari, A. (2009) *Role of Local Knowledge in Science-Policy Interface Relevant to Biodiversity*, Contribution to UNEP-WCMC gap analysis for the proposed Intergovernmental Platform on Biodiversity and Ecosystem Services, www.ipbes.net, accessed 1 October 2009.

Kusawa Park Steering Committee (2009) www.kusawapark.ca, accessed 1 September 2009.

Kutty, R. (2009) 'Kolavipaalam beach, Iringal village, Kozhikode', in N. Pathak (ed.) *Community Conserved Areas in India – A Directory*, Kalpavriksh, Pune, Delhi.

Mallarach, J. M. (ed.) (2008) *Protected Landscapes and Cultural and Spiritual Values*, IUCN, Gland.

Minority Rights Group International (2008) *World Directory of Minorities and Indigenous Peoples – Peru: Ashaninka*, www.unhcr.org/refworld/docid/49749ccb37.html, accessed 31 August 2009.

Muchemi, J. (2009) *Community Conservancy Kenyan Pastoral Areas: A Lesson for Ethiopian Mursi Pastoralist*, International Land Coalition (ILC), Rome.

Pathak, N., Bhatt, S., Balasinorwala, T., Kothari, A. and Borrini-Feyerabend, G. (2004) 'Community conserved areas: a bold frontier for conservation', www.iucn.org/themes/ceesp/Wkg_grp/TILCEPA/CCA%20Briefing%20Note.pdf, accessed 31 August 2009.

Stolton, S., Hourahane, S., Falzon, C. and Dudley, N. (2008) 'Landscape, aesthetics and changing cultural values in the British National Parks', in J. M. Mallarach (2008) *Protected Landscapes and Cultural and Spiritual Values*, IUCN, Gland.

Uchida, E., Cunin, O., Suda, C., Ueno, A. and Nakagawa, T. (2007) 'Consideration on the construction process and the sandstone quarries during the Angkor period based on the magnetic susceptibility', *Journal of Archaeological Science*, vol 34, pp924–35.

UN (2007) *Report of the Special Rapporteur on the Situation of Human Rights and Fundamental Freedoms of Indigenous People*, Human Rights Council 6th Session, A/HRC/6/15, 15 November 2007, United Nations, Geneva.

UN (2009) *Mission to Bolivia*, Human Rights Council 11th Session, A/HRC/11/11, 18 February 2009, United Nations, Geneva.

UNESCO (2001) *UNESCO Universal Declaration on Cultural Diversity*, portal.unesco.org/en/ev.php-URL_ID=13179&URL_DO=DO_TOPIC&URL_SECTION=201.html, accessed 5 September 2009.

UNESCO (2003) *Convention for the Safeguarding of the Intangible Cultural Heritage*, www.unesco.org/culture/ich/index.php?pg=00022&art=art2#art2, accessed 5 September 2009.

WRM (2009) 'Bolivia: For the protection of the last isolated indigenous peoples', *World Rainforest Movement Bulletin*, vol 141, April.

10

Diverting Places:
Linking Travel, Pleasure and Protection

Sue Stolton, Nigel Dudley and Zoltan Kun

Once we leave the main river, our guides paddle slowly along the tributary, pointing out kingfishers and herons darting ahead of the canoe and capuchin monkeys in the trees overhead. Our destination is an eco-lodge by a small lake. Rather a luxurious lodge as it turns out; a village of smart, thatched cabins running down to the water, a watch tower and a dining hall that serves excellent food. Each afternoon a caiman swims slowly across the surface of the lake and after dark the shores are bright with fireflies. Guests are taken on forest walks, to birdwatching hides and on leisurely boat trips.

We are also taken to the village of the local indigenous community. But unlike most 'native village experiences' offered to tourists, this one doesn't make us cringe with embarrassment, because we are in a very real sense guests of the community. The Napo Wildlife Center in the Ecuadorian Amazon is owned and run by the Anangu Quichua Community, who own a stretch of rainforest within the Yasuni National Park. The region has experienced conflict for decades, as companies jostle for oil rights inside and outside the park. Indigenous peoples are caught in the middle, with decisions affecting their lives often made in boardrooms thousands of miles away. However, unlike many of their neighbours, who have either been coerced into selling land for oil or rented cheap space to tourism companies, the owners of Napo control their own destiny, selling a unique experience to tourists and ploughing the profits back into the community. Many community members work directly as guides, boatmen or cooks. Tourists give the natural forest an economic value along with the spiritual and subsistence value that the Quichua have recognized for millennia. No wonder their approach to tourism was honoured as the Community Sustainable Standard-Setter of 2009 by the Rainforest Alliance.

Sue Stolton

Figure 10.1 *Napo Wildlife Center on Anangucocha Lake in Yasuni National Park*
Source: © Nigel Dudley

The Argument

The value

Today tourism is often described as the world's 'biggest' industry. Global tourism was estimated to have generated US$7 trillion in 2007, rising to US$13 trillion in the following decade (WTTC, 2007), reflecting the sector's rapid growth. The term 'tourism' defines an ever wider range of leisure and travel experiences, from going a few miles to spend a day on a crowded beach to a once-in-a-lifetime trip to the Arctic. The links between protected areas and tourism go back to the first 'modern' protected areas, declared over a hundred years ago. For example, US Congress mandated from the beginning that US parks should serve as 'pleasure grounds' for visitors and travellers (Ceballos-Lascuráin, 1996).

Tourism in protected areas is generally nature-based; that is, directly dependent on the use of natural resources in a relatively undeveloped state, including scenery, topography, water features, vegetation and wildlife. However, the term nature or nature-based tourism involves no indication of how nature is used – and can thus include destructive practices (Ceballos-Lascuráin, 1996).

To denote and encourage a more responsible and sustainable type of tourism a new phrase was coined in the 1980s: 'ecotourism' (or ecological tourism). Ecotourism was defined by IUCN in the 1990s as: environmentally responsible travel and visitation to relatively undisturbed natural areas, in order to enjoy and appreciate nature (and any accompanying cultural features – both past and present) that promotes conservation, has low visitor impact, and provides for beneficially active socio-economic involvement of local populations (Ceballos-Lascuráin, 1996). For a relatively new phenomena, ecotourism was considered one of conservation biology's hottest 'buzzwords' by the 1990s (Krüger, 2005), as it helped to identify some sustainability principles around the rapidly growing nature-based tourism developments. It seemed to present a much hoped for 'win–win' solution for the ever increasing challenge of financing conservation and was included in many conservation development strategies. In reality, however, ecotourism could not always deliver the expected benefits and values as ecotourism developers and protected area managers had principally different primary goals: developing tourism or protecting habitats or species (biodiversity). In the end ecotourism was sometimes only used as a buzzword and not as a real tool to help solve conservation problems or conflicts.

Even so, the term spawned a new industry and in 2002 the United Nations declared the International Year of Ecotourism. By 2004, ecotourism/nature tourism was growing globally three times faster than the tourism industry as a whole and it was predicted that by 2024 ecotourism could represent 5 per cent of the global holiday market (Sharpley, 2006) –although as noted below quite what is meant by ecotourism in this context is not always clear.

We do not need to be tourists to exist, in the same way as we do need potable water or food. Critics blame tourism for many of the problems facing the world, from global warming caused by air travel, to the cultural hegemony that rich western society is imposing on a diverse world through its desire to experience new places coupled with its expectations of culturally familiar food and accommodation standards (Cater, 2006; Duffy, 2006). Yet it also has many positive aspects, for tourists themselves in terms of enhancing life experiences, in promoting better health (see Chapter 2) and for the possibilities it creates to build positive links between people in different societies, faith groups and political systems.

Multiple definitions of ecotourism exist (Weaver and Lawton, 2007), but most suggest that it encompasses social objectives, such as: helping educate travellers; funding conservation; benefiting economic development and political empowerment of local communities; and fostering respect for different cultures and for human rights (Honey, 2008). Other commonly cited objectives include: influencing the tourism industry, public institutions and donors to integrate the principles of ecotourism into their operations and policies (ITES); and making sure that experience and product management follow the principles and practices associated with ecological, socio-cultural and economic sustainability (Weaver and Lawton, 2007). Two further aims, which might be considered to ensure a truly sustainable and ethical tourism trade (a kind of 'gold standard, perhaps) are: linking tourism with the overall effectiveness of park management (as has been achieved with PAN Parks, see Weening, 2007); and including ethical criteria (although this can pose many challenges, for instance the difficulty of finding common values and clear standards when trying to address ethical concerns relating to endangered species when they are in conflict with the cultural norms of indigenous or impoverished people) (Buckley, 2005).

A major review of ecotourism literature in 2007 found that virtually all ecotourism case studies involving protected area venues are predominately from the less developed countries, in particular Latin America, Africa and Southeast Asia, and overwhelmingly occur in public protected areas (although it was noted that private protected areas were emerging as an increasingly popular venue) (Weaver and Lawton, 2007). Europe and North America were already well-developed tourism 'destinations' when the word ecotourism evolved and thus ecotourism projects have often been retro-fitted on to existing situations.

The benefit

Protected areas are often set up in remote, rural areas because politicians (local and national) hope to use them as tools for regional development. However, such plans are frequently not backed up with any strategy or real understanding of what is required to develop successful tourism. Indeed, the many efforts to define types of tourism which can happily coexist with the objectives of conservation and the needs of local communities are an indication of the fact that tourism and protected areas have not always had a relationship that has resulted in mutual benefit.

However, the sort of ecotourism defined above, if implemented carefully, can clearly have many benefits: from broadening the understanding of visitors about both ecology and culture to empowering local communities. Tourism can provide important additional income for protected areas from a variety of sources, including donations, entrance and user fees, levies, concession fees and licences, taxes on purchases by visitors and increased general tax revenues from economic activity associated with tourism (see Box 10.1). This financial contribution can be considerable; across southern Africa nature-based tourism reportedly now generates roughly the same revenue as farming, forestry and fisheries combined (Balmford et al., 2009).

Unfortunately, potential or actual increases in revenue can sometimes lead to increased and uncontrolled tourism, which ends up putting extra pressure on the protected area (Bushell, 2005). The result is that tourism is now seen as a major threat to many protected areas. A global study of protected area management effectiveness assessment evaluations in over 7000 sites found recreational activities (mainly unregulated tourism) as equal third among all threats to protected areas (Leverington et al., 2008). As tourism numbers increase, the failure of countries to manage and budget adequately for tourism management in protected areas could threaten the very values that visitors have travelled to see. What makes a destination attractive to tourists has many variables including: overall biodiversity, spectacular landscapes, access, lodging facilities, charismatic species, effectiveness of protected area management, relations with local communities, etc. The challenge is to derive economic benefit through ecotourism, without unacceptable degradation of both social and environmental values.

For local people, working in the tourism business has many benefits; it is comparatively labour intensive, with proportionately high opportunities for women, low barriers to entry and high multipliers into the local economy, and it can be available in areas with low agricultural potential. However, it is also relatively high-risk and susceptible to rapid changes due to internal and external costs (Elliott et

Box 10.1 *Financing conservation through tourism*

A survey conducted in the early 1990s suggests that about half the world's protected areas charged entrance fees (Lindberg, 2001) and this proportion has increased since. The arguments in favour of charging a user-fee include: funds for conservation, local development and maintenance of tourist facilities; employment (in relation to collecting and administering fees); and as a method of controlling visitor numbers. The arguments against a fee include: an exclusive rather than inclusive approach to biodiversity and conservation; and reducing local tourist-orientated business opportunities by either reducing visitor numbers or reducing cash for purchases when high fees are charged.

For many parks agencies, charging is vital, with some earning up to 80 per cent of total revenue by charging individual visitors directly (Buckley, 2009). It helps fund investments that are vital to maintaining tourism. In Bolivia, the Ministry of Planning and Development estimates US$1.22 of indirect benefits for every US$1 spent on cultural and natural tourism (Flek et al., 2006) and in Costa Rica while about US$12 million is spent annually to maintain the national parks, the foreign exchange generated by parks in the 1990s was more than US$330 million from some 500,000 overseas visitors (WCPA, 1998). However, in other countries collection of fees is not allowed; none of the large national parks in Europe, for example, collect fees.

Determining the right level of fee can be a challenge. After conducting over 800 surveys at Entebbe airport, one research project concluded that considerably more revenue could be gained from Uganda's protected areas. The study calculated that an entrance fee of US$47 (at 2001 values) to visit the Mabira Forest Reserve, famous for its number of bird species, would maximize tourism revenues. International tourists and foreign residents of Uganda were currently charged US$5.00 (Naidoo and Adamowicz, 2005). Similarly, a meta-review of 18 studies reviewing fees in relation to marine protected areas found overwhelming support for paying for entry to marine parks, with all studies indicating an acceptance of introducing fees or increasing fees where charges exist. Factors that positively influenced these decisions include visitors' income, level of education, environmental awareness, residency and desire to provide a legacy to future generations. Factors which can negatively impact willingness to pay included lack of trust in the fee collection agency and openness in how the money is spent (Howard and Hawkins, 2009). Many countries charge different rates for international tourists and for local visitors.

However, relying on foreign tourism can be a dangerous policy. The conflicts that arose after the Kenyan election in 2007 provide a sobering illustration of what happens when tourism declines. Tourism numbers dropped by some 90 per cent in 2008, 25,000 people directly employed in tourism related industries and countless more indirectly employed were laid off and revenues to protected areas plummeted, putting at risk countless conservation initiatives carried out by the Kenya Wildlife Service and others (UNEP, 2008).

al., 2002). The growing popularity of a tourist area can also bring problems for local communities such as increasing prices for land, food and other products. For instance, in Tonga, tourism-driven inflation has reportedly caused shortages of arable land (Vanasselt, 2000).

For some communities the ability to use protected areas as a source of tourism income that helps them simultaneously to preserve traditional lifestyles is itself a clear benefit. In other cases, critiques of ecotourism have suggested that linking a community's development prospects with a preexisting, and thus static, relationship with their immediate natural environment limits economic development opportunities which might otherwise change this relationship (Butcher, 2005).

Protected Areas and Tourism – A Vital Link

The majority of global protected areas permit public access, with the exceptions being a few strict scientific reserves and some sacred sites that are also protected areas. Access to some of the more popular wilderness areas is restricted; it can take years to get a permit to raft down the Grand Canyon, for example. Most protected area systems in Europe, North America and Australia operate under a dual mandate to provide recreational opportunities while conserving natural resources (Reed and Merenlender, 2008). However, it is worth mentioning that such a dual mandate is not always reflected in the skills of protected area management authorities. While it is understood that management authorities focus mainly on conserving natural resources, they too often miss any expertise on tourism development. Such a lack of expertise might be a major factor of tourism turning to be a threat in several protected areas instead of being an opportunity.

Nearly all protected areas receive some tourists although numbers vary from just a handful to millions. Bukhansan National Park outside Seoul, South Korea, currently receives over 10 million visitors a year (KNPS, 2009) and the protected areas in the state of Victoria, Australia, received 28.6 million visitors in 2004–05 (Parks Victoria, 2008). At the other end of the spectrum, some protected areas in Iceland only receive a few hundred visitors every year.

A recent review of visitors to 280 protected areas in 20 countries between 1992 and 2006 confirmed the popularity of visiting protected areas (Balmford et al., 2009). The study found that overall visitor numbers are increasing, although numbers are static or declining in some of the wealthier countries – possibly due to tourists seeking overseas travel experiences rather than those on offer in their home countries. More specific links between tourism, protected areas and conservation include the following:

- In Peru, the government reports that over 70 per cent of international tourists in 2007 came to visit a protected area (Drumm, 2008).
- In many countries, such as Belize, Brazil, Costa Rica, Kenya, Madagascar, Mexico, South Africa and Tanzania, biodiversity represents the primary tourism attraction (Christ et al., 2003).
- Tourism is the largest foreign exchange generator in New Zealand, where at least 65 per cent of tourists visit at least one park; 10 per cent say their stay would be

shorter if no park was visited and 12 per cent travel to the country exclusively to visit parks (SCBD, 2008).

- Protected areas represent one of the greatest tourism assets in Australia with over 40 per cent of all international visits including a visit to a national park (Parks Forum, 2008).
- Biodiversity hotspots in the global south are experiencing very rapid tourism growth: 23 countries record over 100 per cent growth in tourism over the last 10 years (Christ et al., 2003).
- In China, tourism has been developed in about 80 per cent of the nature reserves since the early 1990s and is growing rapidly. During the development phase in the 1990s visitors to nature reserves rose by 87.8 per cent in three years (Li, 2004).
- It is only within national parks that humans can get near to our closest living relatives, the mountain gorillas (*Gorilla beringei beringei*), whose tiny remaining populations live within four national parks in central Africa (AWF, 2009).
- Profits from ecotourism are not confined to the poorest countries; for example, it is calculated that the presence of nesting ospreys (*Pandion haliaetus*) in Scotland brings an addition US$7 million per year into the area as a result of nature tourism (Dickie et al., 2006).
- In the Caribbean and the Pacific coast of Central America, 50 per cent of recreational dives, approximately 7.5 million annually, take place within MPAs (Howard and Hawkins, 2009).

Figure 10.2 *Ecotourism guesthouse, Baima hilltribe village near Wanglang Panda Reserve, China*
Source: © WWF-Canon/Bernard de Wetter

Figure 10.3 *Tourists at Okaukuejo water hole, Etosha National Park, Namibia*
Source: © WWF-Canon/Martin Harvey

Future Needs

The most fundamental question here is: can tourism and protected areas be mutually beneficial? It is clear from the discussion above that tourism, and in this context particularly nature-based and ecotourism, can provide multiple benefits to both the user and the provider in terms of economic benefits and, in ideal circumstances, related governance issues and cultural understanding.

But is tourism good for biodiversity conservation? Understanding the impacts of tourism on biodiversity remains a challenge and little has been done to investigate how they can be monitored and managed. Research has tended to focus on two areas: the 'tourism experience' such as visitor satisfaction, visitor characteristics, carrying capacity and impacts on the natural environment and associated trade-off analyses (Rodger and Moore, 2004) and 'habitat impacts' such as eroded tracks, damaged trees, fire scars, trampled vegetation and the proliferation of weeds (Hadwen et al., 2007).

Research to date shows that the relationship between tourism and biodiversity has not always been beneficial. In the US, for example, recreational hiking is seen as one of the least intrusive tourism pursuits in protected areas, but has still been shown to correlate with decreases in abundances and activity levels in North American wood turtles (*Clemmys insculpta*) in Connecticut; caused desert bighorn sheep (*Ovis canadensis nelsoni*) in Canyonlands National Park, Utah, to flee; resulted in some 7 per cent of the Antelope Island State Park, also in Utah, being unsuitable for wildlife; and led to a five-fold decline in the density of native carnivores and an increase in non-native species in 28 parks and preserves in northern California (Reed and Merenlender, 2008). There is also a major lack of research into the actual socio-economic impact of ecotourism on local communities and protected areas, which again makes it hard to make conclusions about its success as a strategy for local development.

As a result ecotourism is facing a minor crisis of credibility. The perceived value of the word itself has led to many tourism products that do not fulfil the widely recognized elements of ecotourism described at the start of this chapter (Fennell and Weaver, 2005). Even those ecotourism ventures that follow best practices may not find it easy to balance the many demands of biodiversity and habitat conservation with the needs of local people and visitor expectations. As a result various national and international certification systems are now being developed to try to set some basic standards for sustainable tourism, such as the European Charter for Sustainable Tourism in Protected Areas coordinated by the EUROPARC Federation and the PAN Parks certification system (Vancura, 2008).

Many of these systems are underpinned by the Global Sustainable Tourism Criteria (GSTC), the product of a coalition of over 40 organizations working to increase sustainable tourism practices. The partnership was initiated by the Rainforest Alliance, the United Nations Environment Programme (UNEP), the United Nations Foundation, and the United Nations World Tourism Organization (UNWTO). The GSTC have four main elements: to demonstrate effective sustainable management; to maximize social and economic benefits to the local community and minimize negative impacts; to maximize benefits to cultural heritage and minimize negative impacts; and to maximize benefits to the environment and minimize negative impacts (GSTC, 2008). Many 'ecotourism' enterprises still fall far short of these ideals.

Management Options

Although principles, guidelines and standards are being developed, tourism in protected areas is still often failing to achieve its potential. An analysis of over 180 worldwide ecotourism case studies in 2005 reported both good and bad practices. Of the 180 case studies, 70 were classified as unsustainable, with negative impacts falling into the 4 major categories highlighted in Table 10.1. When assessing these impacts from a habitat perspective the studies indicated that ecotourism was less sustainable in mountain regions and on islands, probably due to the higher fragility of these ecosystems and hence their lower carrying-capacity for tourists. Lack of effective control and management of tourist numbers and distribution were the most important reasons for lack of sustainability (Krüger, 2005).

For those ecotourism projects which were regarded as having positive effects, the key success factor seemed to be the presence of viewable flagship species, e.g. charismatic birds or mammals. The other key success factor was the participation of the local community in the project. One of the benefits of ecotourism development is the fact that it forces people with different interests to plan together and develop common goals and objectives. Overall, ecotourism is most likely to benefit protected areas and the surrounding local communities if it is small-scale and locally

Table 10.1 *Negative and positive effects of ecotourism projects and perceived reasons for success or failure*

Effect	Impacts	Causes
Negative	Habitat alteration, soil erosion, pollution; Local community not involved, leads to consumptive land-use; Flagship species affected, population decline, serious behaviour alteration; Not enough revenue creation for conservation and consumptive use practised	Too many tourists; Local community not involved; Not enough control and management; Not enough local revenue creation; Protected area has priority over local people; Locals do not get environmental education
Positive	More conservation: new areas, more effective management; Revenue creation increased for local communities, non-consumptive use; Increased revenue creation, regionally and nationally; Conservation attitude of local communities changed	Flagship species; Local community involved at most stages; Effective planning and management; Ecotourism an economic advantage, locally and regionally; Differential pricing of entry fees

Source: Adapted from Krüger, 2005

operated or owned (Krüger, 2005). Recommendations for developing ecotourism, rather than simply nature-based tourism, at the Ngorongoro Conservation Area in Tanzania, for example, note that opportunities for local communities to capture the economic benefits of tourism must be structured in a way that is culturally appropriate and therefore accessible to the target population. Communities can also usually only benefit from ecotourism if they have secure land tenure over the area in which tourism takes place, as well as the ability to make land-use decisions for that area (Charnley, 2005).

WWF has produced guidelines on community-based ecotourism (WWF, 2001), which are divided into four parts, each with specific guidelines, which suggest:

1   Considering whether ecotourism is an appropriate option: before beginning a community-based ecotourism project it is important to ensure that the conditions are appropriate.
2   Planning ecotourism with communities and other stakeholders: it is important to consider the necessary structures and processes that should be in place to deliver the required social and environmental benefits.

3   Developing viable community-based ecotourism projects: an appropriate business plan is very important to ensure the viability of an ecotourism venture.
4   Strengthening benefits to the community and the environment: specific measures can be optimized to ensure the required delivery of social and environmental benefits.

Guidelines for tourism and biodiversity have also been developed by the CBD (Tapper, 2007). The authors note that where tourism is established in protected areas the key management options are to find ways to minimize the damage caused by existing tourism to sensitive sites and to direct new tourism (and if possible to redirect existing tourism) to less sensitive sites.

Conclusions

Human populations are growing, but the area of parks is not keeping pace. The area of land and water available for conservation outside protected areas is continually shrinking, so parks themselves are increasingly critical. Parks are assets for tourism, but they are not tourism assets. (Buckley, 2009)

For many people the whole concept of ecotourism is a contradiction in terms, with the environmental costs of travel outweighing any gains. However, as long as people are travelling to look at nature, it is important that they do so in the most responsible way possible, both from an environmental and a social perspective. In the future, we can expect a reduction in mass foreign travel, due to both rising fuel prices and the growing awareness of the environmental costs of air travel. For the rich countries, where the concept of nature tourism is well developed, this could result in an increase in visits to their own protected areas. For developing countries, where the incentive for protection is bound up closely with the need for foreign exchange, the future is less certain. Yet it may not be entirely bleak either. Thirty years ago, South Korea had a GDP around the same as many African states; now its average wages are around the same as Australia. With this prosperity and an urbanizing society has come new interest in nature in the space of a single generation. Thirty-eight million people visited South Korea's national parks in 2007 (KNPS, 2009), around 99 per cent of which were domestic (see Case Study 10.1). Domestic tourism is increasing quickly with development all around the world.

Unless we can find some less polluting way of travelling quickly, ecotourism in the future may well be confined to those who live relatively locally or are prepared to travel for a long time. However, this does not eliminate the possibilities of protected areas playing a role in tourism, but rather that the types of tourists are likely to be slightly different from those who visit today.

Case Study 10.1:
Managing Tourism in
South Korea's Protected Area System

Nigel Dudley, Hyun Kim and Won Woo Shin

South Korea provides an interesting example of a successful and popular protected area system running in a recently developed country, where visitation is overwhelmingly domestic. Many visitors are themselves only one generation removed from a poor and primarily agrarian lifestyle and represent a newly wealthy, urbanized society seeking recreation in the countryside. The Korean experience shows that with government determination, interest in and support for protected areas can develop very quickly when conditions are right.

Restoration and protection

Korea is a peninsula with 64 per cent of its area mountainous, around 3000 offshore islands and 63 important freshwater wetlands. The ecology has been transformed through long habitation and overexploitation during the latter part of the Japanese occupation and the civil war. Today only an estimated 0.4 per cent of vegetation is in a fully natural state, mainly as forest and alpine meadows. Virtually all the lowland has been transformed for agriculture or infrastructure and mountain areas are recovering from deforestation. The protected area system protects the best of what remains but also includes areas that have been restored, so that many forests are a similar.

South Korea's entire protected area system has developed in little over 40 years. Hongdo Island and Mount Sorak were designated as the country's first natural reserves in 1965. The national park system was adopted in March 1967 and the first national park, Mount Jirisan, was designated in the same year. Today there are around 1300 protected areas in a variety of designations and management types, including 20 national parks covering 6580 km^2, which are managed by the Korea National Park Service (KNPS). Most of these are category II national parks along with a few protected landscapes (category V).

A Korean-based industry

Tourism is afforded a high priority, at least within the national park system where almost 30 per cent of the budget is allocated to visitor management and associated infrastructure. National parks and nature areas are extremely popular, with a high and apparently stable demand. In 2007 there were 38 million visitors to national parks, a sharp increase caused in part by the government abandoning entrance fees. Unusually, visitation is almost entirely domestic, with only 1 per cent coming from abroad (KNPS, 2009).

Figure 10.4 *Bukhansan National Park in South Korea receives up to 10 million visitors every year*
Source: © Nigel Dudley

National parks have a high level of visitor infrastructure, with 75 offices, 8 visitor centres, 75 guide posts, 29 shelters and 47 camp sites. There are 265 walking trails covering a total of 1222km. Korean visitors have high expectations for infrastructure in protected areas and expect, for instance, trail quality to be high and shops and restaurants in or around the park. There are visitor programmes available such as guided walks: in 2007 KNPS ran 284 programmes attended by 225,000 people (KNPS, 2009).

In some protected areas over-visitation is considered to be a problem, particularly in Bukhansan National Park where the abolition of gate fees doubled visitor numbers to over 10 million people a year; an extraordinary density in an area of only 80km². The weight of visitors is undoubtedly having side-effects in terms of path erosion and the proliferation of unofficial walking paths, although there is little evidence that visitor numbers are undermining the protected area's core biodiversity values. Most people walk up the trail to the mountain top and back, but new trails around the base of the mountain are being introduced to try to lessen visitor pressure on the peak.

Interest in nature, landscape and physical exercise are probably the primary motivations for people to visit. For many people reaching the top of a mountain is a major attraction, in some cases this also has spiritual significance if the mountain is considered sacred. There are also more than 300 temples within national parks and a proportion of visitors come specifically to visit these; others stop and visit in passing. In Gyeongju National Park many visitors are primarily interested in the cultural sites relating to the Silla dynasty. Efforts are also being made to widen the experience of visitors; for instance, there has been a programme of poetry readings in national parks, displaying poems on banners and providing poetry books inspired by nature.

Surveys are undertaken both of people visiting protected areas and, less frequently, of the general public: these show that visitor satisfaction is high and continuing to increase.

Educational and interpretive facilities are provided, particularly in visitor centres but also through nature trails with signs and increasingly through programmes involving trained rangers. Rangers have worked overseas to learn from other park agencies. An accreditation scheme has been introduced for visitor programmes. Services for disabled people and socially alienated people have been upgraded and a joint environmental education programme with local groups, including schools, was started in 2007, involving over 25,000 people in its first year. Visitor safety management is given high priority, with 119 rescue teams, detailed weather forecasting, safety classes for walkers and climbers, and information on visitor centres (KNPS, 2009).

References

AWF (2009) www.awf.org/content/wildlife/detail/mountaingorilla, African Wildlife Foundation, accessed 11 August 2009.

Balmford, A., Beresford, J., Green, J., Naidoo, R., Walpole, M. and Manica, A. (2009) 'A global perspective on trends in nature-based tourism', *PLoS Biology*, vol 7, no 6.

Buckley, R. (2005) 'In search of the narwhal: Ethical dilemmas in ecotourism', *Journal of Ecotourism*, vol 4, pp129–34.

Buckley, R. (2009) 'Parks and tourism', *PLoS Biology*, vol 7, no 6.

Bushell, R. (2005) 'Building support for protected areas through tourism', in J. A. McNeely (ed.) *Friends for Life: New Partners in Support of Protected Areas*, IUCN, Gland and Cambridge.

Butcher, J. (2005) 'The moral authority of ecotourism: A critique', *Current Issues in Tourism*, vol 8, pp114–24.

Cater, E. (2006) 'Ecotourism as a Western construct', *Journal of Ecotourism*, vol 5, pp23–39.

Ceballos-Lascuráin, H. (1996) *Tourism, Ecotourism, and Protected Areas*, IUCN, Gland and Cambridge.

Charnley, S. (2005) 'From nature tourism to ecotourism? The case of the Ngorongoro Conservation Area, Tanzania', *Human Organization*, vol 64, no 1, pp75–88.

Christ, C., Hillel, O., Matus, S. and Sweeting, J. (2003) *Tourism and Biodiversity: Mapping Tourism's Global Footprint*, Conservation International, Washington, DC.

Dickie, I., Hughes, J. and Esteban, A. (2006) *Watched Like Never Before: The Local Economic Benefits of Spectacular Bird Species*, Royal Society for the Protection of Birds, Sandy.

Drumm, A. (2008) 'The threshold of sustainability for protected areas', *BioScience*, vol 58, no 9, pp782–3.

Duffy, R. (2006) 'Global environmental governance and the politics of ecotourism in Madagascar', *Journal of Ecotourism*, vol 5, pp128–44.

Elliott, J., Grahn, R., Sriskanthan, G. and Arnold, C. (2002) *Wildlife and Poverty Study*, Department for Environmental Development, London.

Fennell, D. and Weaver, D. (2005) 'The ecotourism concept and tourism conservation symbiosis', *Journal of Sustainable Tourism*, vol 13, pp373–90.

Ferraro, P. J. (2002) *The Local Costs of Establishing Protected Areas in Low-Income Nations: Ranomafana National Park, Madagascar,* Environmental Policy Working Paper Series no 2001-006, Department of Economics, Georgia State University, Atlanta, GA.

Flek, L., Amend, M., Painter, L. and Reid, J. (2006) *Regional Economic Benefits from Conservation: The Case of Madidi*, Conservation Strategy Fund, La Paz.

GSTC (2008) 'Global Sustainable Tourism Criteria, Version 5, October 2008', www. sustainabletourismcriteria.org/index.php?option=com_content&task=view&id=192&It emid=373, accessed 13 August 2008.

Hadwen, W. L., Hill, W. and Pickering, C. M. (2007) 'Icons under threat: Why monitoring visitors and their ecological impacts in protected areas matters', *Ecological Management & Restoration*, vol 8. no 3, pp177–81.

Honey, M. (2008) *Ecotourism and Sustainable Development: Who Owns Paradise?* (Second ed.), Island Press, Washington, DC.

Howard, P. and Hawkins, J. P. (2009) 'Access to marine parks: A comparative study in willingness to pay', *Ocean & Coastal Management*, vol 52, pp219–28.

ITES www.ecotourism.org/site/c.orLQKXPCLmF/b.4835251/k.FF11/Our_Mission__The_ International_Ecotourism_Society.htm, accessed 6 August 2009.

KNPS (Korea National Park Service) (2009) *Korea's Protected Areas: Assessing the Effectiveness of South Korea's Protected Areas System*, KNPS, Jeju Island and IUCN, Seoul.

Krüger, O. (2005) 'The role of ecotourism in conservation: panacea or Pandora's box?', *Biodiversity and Conservation*, vol 14, pp579–600.

Leverington, F., Hockings, M. and Lemos Costa, K. (2008) *Management Effectiveness Evaluation in Protected Areas: Report for the Project 'Global Study into Management Effectiveness Evaluation of Protected Areas'*, University of Queensland, IUCN WCPA, TNC and WWF, Gatton.

Li, W. (2004) 'Environmental management indicators for ecotourism in China's nature reserves: A case study in Tianmushan Nature Reserve', *Tourism Management*, vol 25, pp559–64.

Lindberg, K. (2001) 'Tourist "consumption" of biodiversity: Market characteristics and effect on conservation and local development', Paper presented at the World Bank/OECD Workshop on Market Creation for Biodiversity Products and Services, Paris.

Naidoo, R. and Adamowicz, W. L. (2005) 'Economic benefits of biodiversity exceed costs of conservation at an African rainforest reserve', *Proceedings of the National Academy of Sciences*, vol 102, no 46, pp16712–16.

Parks Forum (2008) *The Value of Parks*, Parks Forum, Victoria.

Parks Victoria (2008) www.tourism.vic.gov.au/strategies-and-plans/strategies-and-plans/ nature%11based-tourism-%11-key-facts/, accessed 11 August 2009.

Reed, S. E. and Merenlender, A. M. (2008) 'Quiet, nonconsumptive recreation reduces protected area effectiveness', *Conservation Letters*, vol 1, pp146–54.

Rodger, K. and Moore, S. (2004) 'Bringing science to wildlife tourism: The influence of managers' and scientists' perceptions', *Journal of Ecotourism*, vol 3, pp1–19.

SCBD (2008) *Protected Areas in Today's World: Their Values and Benefits for the Welfare of the Planet*, Technical Series no 36, Secretariat of the Convention on Biological Diversity, Montreal.

Sharpley, R. (2006) 'Ecotourism: A consumption perspective', *Journal of Ecotourism*, vol 5, pp7–22.

Tapper, R. (ed.) (2007) *Managing Tourism and Biodiversity: User's Manual on the CBD Guidelines on Biodiversity and Tourism Development*, Secretariat of the Convention on Biological Diversity, Quebec.

UNEP (2008) 'Early recovery of nature-based tourism good for Kenya and good for biodiversity says UNEP head', www.unep.org/Documents.Multilingual/Default.asp?DocumentID=528&ArticleID=5756&l=en, accessed 14 August 2009.

Vanasselt, W. (2000) *Ecotourism and Conservation: Are They Compatible?* Earthtrends, World Resources Institute, Washington, DC.

Vancura, V. (2008) *Conducting Independent Audits*, PAN Parks Lessons Learned Series no 8, Pan Parks Foundation, Györ.

WCPA (1998) *Economic Values of Protected Areas: Guidelines for Protected Area Managers,* Task Force on Economic Benefits of Protected Areas of the World Commission on Protected Areas (WCPA) of IUCN, in collaboration with the Economics Service Unit of IUCN, Gland and Cambridge.

Weaver, D. B. and L. J. Lawton (2007) 'Twenty years on: The state of contemporary ecotourism research', *Tourism Management*, vol 28, pp1168–79.

Weening, G. (2007) *Combining Business with Conservation*, PAN Parks Lessons Learned Series no 3, Pan Parks Foundation, Györ.

WTTC (2007) *Progress and Priorities 2007/2008*, World Tourism and Travel Council, London.

WWF (2001) *Guidelines for Community-based Ecotourism Development*, WWF International, Gland.

11

Climate Change: The Role of Protected Areas in Mitigating and Adapting to Change

Nigel Dudley, Trevor Sandwith and Alexander Belokurov

Britain's peat ecosystems have long been regarded as little more than wastelands: not much good for agriculture, until recently a source of poor quality fuel for crofters in Scotland and often simply set aside for hunting. It is no coincidence that Britain's first national park, the Peak District, is made up largely of unwanted peat; an ecosystem further battered by soot and acid-rain pollution from surrounding industrial cities, which has eliminated many native plant species (Dudley, 1987). Solitary walks across Kinder Scout and the aptly named Bleaklow and Black Hill gave me both my first taste of the concept of wilderness and my first real understanding of how badly we have undermined our ecology. Yet all this could change. Peat is recognized as the ecosystem that stores more carbon than any other and is thus a potentially critical tool in mitigating climate change. It also plays a fundamental role in storing and releasing water, and therefore mediating seasonal groundwater and surface flows, but only if it is managed properly: the balance of greenhouse gas emissions and sequestration in peat is delicate and easily upset so that inappropriately managed peat can quickly become a net carbon emitter, which is probably the case in the Peak District. New projects are springing up around the country to improve management of peat, which invariably means introducing a form of management involving a great deal of protection. The economic value of the Peak District's uplands may be on the rise again.

Nigel Dudley

Figure 11.1 *Upland peat in the UK*

Source: © Nigel Dudley

The value

There is now increasing consensus on the high probability that climate change is already affecting terrestrial and marine ecosystems and that these changes will increase in rate and severity during the 21st century. Generally negative impacts can be expected on food and water availability, frequency of natural disasters, human health and the survival of natural species and ecosystems.

The Fourth Assessment Report of the Intergovernmental Panel on Climate Change (IPCC), published in 2007, draws on more than 29,000 observational data series from 75 studies (Pachauri and Reisinger, 2007). The results show significant changes in many physical and biological systems, more than 89 per cent of which are consistent with the direction of change expected as a response to global warming. Overall the analysis of this research led the IPCC to conclude: 'Observational evidence from all continents and most oceans shows that many natural systems are being affected by regional climate changes, particularly temperature increases.'

In the face of such an unprecedented rate of change and disruption, local communities and governments alike will have to respond by changing patterns of resource use, settlement and investments in measures to cope with disasters and increased risk. Many strategy and policy interventions will be needed. Addressing climate change requires major and fundamental changes in the way that we live, do business and interact with each other. In addressing climate change the overwhelming priority is to reduce emissions of greenhouse gases and to increase rates of carbon sequestration and thereby to halt and even reverse the rate of global climate change, but while these measures are being put in place there remains a need to address the very real challenges facing life on the planet through adaptation strategies.

Although in no way a complete solution, or one that should replace or undermine efforts to reduce emissions at source, protected areas should be included in climate change response strategies. In particular, they can be used as a tool to manage natural and semi-natural systems, both to store and capture carbon from the atmosphere and to help humanity adapt to current and future stresses being created by climate change (Dudley et al., 2009).

The benefit

The IPCC has carried out the most authoritative assessment of climate change. Its 2007 report covers a wide range of adaptation and mitigation recommendations, including: 'Synergies between mitigation and adaptation can exist, for example properly designed biomass production, *formation of protected areas*, land management, energy use in buildings and forestry' (IPCC, 2007) (our italics). As with the Kyoto Protocol, the IPCC report focused in particular on the role of forestry in terms of limiting climate impacts, stating that: 'About 65 per cent of the total mitigation potential (up to 100 US\$/tCO$_2$-eq) is located in the tropics and about 50 per cent of the total could be achieved by reducing emissions from deforestation, suggesting that tools for controlling tropical deforestation should play a key role in mitigation strategies.' (IPCC, 2007). The expert findings also noted that: 'While regrowth of trees due to effective protection will lead to carbon sequestration, adaptive management of protected areas also leads to conservation of biodiversity and reduced vulnerability to climate change.' (Nabuurs et al., 2007)

The UN Framework Convention on Climate Change (UNFCCC) has not yet referred specifically to protected areas. However, its 2007 'Bali Action Plan' set the roadmap for the further negotiations and specifically called for more action on mitigation and adaptation strategies – a call that is beginning to be answered by many countries (see Table 11.1). In June 2009, UNEP released a report urging the UNFCCC and others to take greater account of the role of natural ecosystems in carbon sequestration (Trumper et al., 2009). The CBD has recognized the role of protected areas in addressing climate change in its Programme of Work on Protected Areas (PoWPA) and it is likely that the review of the PoWPA scheduled for late 2010 will increase the emphasis on climate change mitigation and adaptation within protected area policies and practice. Building on this recognition, an increasing number of governments are drawing on protected areas as tools for combating climate change. Table 11.1 outlines some examples of national policy initiatives.

Table 11.1 *National climate change responses using protected areas*

National initiative	Details
Australia National Biodiversity and Climate Change Action Plan 2004–2007 (www.environment.gov.au/biodiversity/publications/nbccap/pubs/nbccap.pdf)	The plan includes strategies and actions directly related to protected areas including the development of new reserves incorporating assessment of climate change impacts (Strategy 5.2 and related actions) specifically in relation to marine areas (Strategy 4.2 and 4.5)
Brazil National Plan on Climate Change 2008 (www.mma.gov.br/estruturas/208/_arquivos/national_plan_208.pdf)	A major objective of the plan is to reduce deforestation, including by: 'identification of public forests to be protected, preserved and managed'.
China National Climate Change Program 2007 (www.ccchina.gov.cn/WebSite/CCChina/UpFile/File188.pdf)	Natural resource conservation is mentioned twice in the programme; to 'strengthen forest and wetland conservation' in order to enhance adaptation and capacities for carbon sequestration (Section 2.3.4) and to enhance adaptation by ensuring: 'By 2010, 90% of typical forest ecosystems and national key wildlife are effectively protected and nature reserve area accounts for 16% of the total territory.' (Section 3.3.2)
India National Action Plan on Climate Change 2008 (http://pmindia.nic.in/Pg01-52.pdf)	The plan identifies eight core national missions running through to 2017; the National Mission for Sustaining the Himalayan Ecosystem includes: 'aims to conserve biodiversity, forest cover, and other ecological values in the Himalayan region, where glaciers that are a major source of India's water supply are projected to recede as a result of global warming'.
South Africa National Climate Change Response Strategy 2004 (unfccc.int/files/meetings/seminar/application/pdf/sem_sup3_south_africa.pdf)	The strategy concludes with 22 key actions on a range of issues, including to 'Develop protection plans for plant, animal and marine biodiversity.'

Current Contribution of Protected Areas

Although any natural ecosystem can help to mitigate or adapt to climate change, protected areas offer several unique advantages: recognition (often legal); agreed management and governance approaches; and management planning and capacity. They are often the most cost-effective option and in any case not infrequently represent the only natural habitats remaining in large areas. Protected areas can serve to both mitigate and adapt to climate change (see Figure 11.2).

Much of the rest of this book looks at the wider role of protected areas in ecosystem services and the provision of basic human needs. Maintaining these services in the face of climate change, and especially through the adaptive design and management of protected area systems, is growing in importance as part of national response strategies. However, the more urgent task is to address the underlying causes; therefore this chapter focuses on how protected areas will contribute to climate change mitigation through carbon storage and further carbon sequestration in forests, inland and marine waters, grasslands and within agricultural systems, as outlined below.

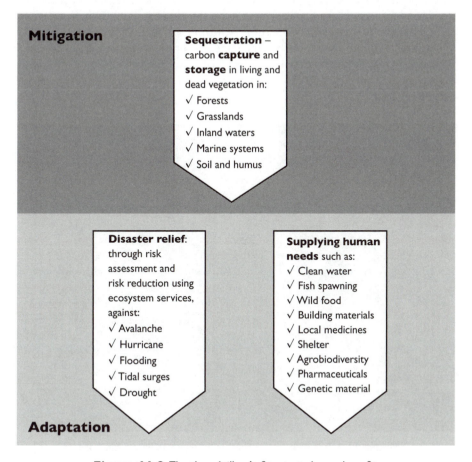

Figure 11.2 *The three 'pillars' of protected area benefits*

Forests

It is widely recognized that protected areas could and should have a key role in reducing forest loss and degradation (Noss, 2001). Forests contain the largest terrestrial stock of carbon, and deforestation and forest degradation are seen as key drivers of climate change. The IPCC estimates that forest loss and degradation are together responsible for 17 per cent of global carbon emissions, making this the third largest source of greenhouse gas emissions, outstripping the entire global transport sector (Nabuurs et al., 2007). Protected areas can provide an important delivery mechanism for maintaining and enhancing carbon stores in forests, although they need careful management if they are to be successful. Expanding protected area systems to include carbon-rich habitats could markedly increase their role in the future.

Tropical moist forests are the largest terrestrial carbon stores and are still active sinks; recent research has provided strong evidence that tropical forests continue to sequester carbon once they reach old-growth stage, both in the Amazon (Baker et al., 2004) and in tropical forests in Africa (Lewis et al., 2009), adding to the arguments for retaining natural forests. Old-growth boreal forests can also continue to sequester carbon (Luyssaert et al., 2008); however, fire is likely to increase dramatically in Russia and Canada due to higher temperatures (Stocks et al., 1998), thus increasing carbon loss (Bond-Lamberty et al., 2007), which means that the boreal region could switch from a sink to a source of carbon without appropriate management strategies in place. Finally, although temperate forests have undergone an enormous historical retraction, they are currently expanding in many areas and actively building carbon

Figure 11.3 *Tropical moist rainforest in the western Congo Basin, Gabon*

Source: © Martin Harvey/WWF-Canon

stores. In Europe, for example, forests are currently sequestering 7–12 per cent of European carbon emissions (Janssens et al., 2003).

Inland waters and peat

Wetlands, particularly peatlands, tend to be sinks for carbon and nitrogen but sources for methane and sulphur (Ramsar Secretariat, 2002); the balance between these various interactions determines whether the wetland system as a whole is a net source or sink of carbon. However, peat in particular is currently a very important carbon store. Although only covering about 3 per cent of the land surface, peat is believed to contain the planet's largest store of carbon; the same in total as all terrestrial biomes, with twice the carbon stored in forests (Parish et al., 2007). However, mismanagement of wetlands, and particularly of peat, can result in substantial carbon losses (Ramsar, 2007), making effective protection and management strategies critical elements in reducing emissions in peat-rich countries such as Russia, Canada and Indonesia.

Marine ecosystems

Marine areas also store huge amounts of carbon, particularly in coastal zones where capture is equivalent to 0.2 Gigatonnes per year. Salt marshes, mangroves and seagrass all have important potential to sequester carbon, although our understanding of mechanisms remains incomplete. All these systems are currently under pressure, to the extent that without better protection they could switch from sinks to sources. Extensive areas of salt marsh continue to be lost through drainage, with nutrient enrichment and sea-level rise adding threats to their survival and integrity. Restoration of tidal salt marshes could help to increase the world's natural carbon sinks. For example, it has been estimated that if all of Bay of Fundy marshes that have been 'reclaimed' for agriculture could be restored, the rate of CO_2 sequestered each year would be equivalent to 4–6 per cent of Canada's targeted reduction of 1990-level emissions under the Kyoto Protocol (Connor et al., 2001).

Natural grasslands

Grasslands contain large stores of carbon, mainly but not entirely within soils. Although historical changes, including particularly conversion to agriculture, have released large amounts of carbon, estimates suggest that grazing lands alone could hold 10–30 per cent of the world's soil carbon (Schuman et al., 2002). Grassland is the least protected terrestrial biome and conversion continues at a rapid pace, as a result of intensive grazing and replacement with agricultural crops, biofuels and pulp plantations.

Soil

Soils are thought to hold more carbon than the atmosphere and vegetation combined (Lal, 2004), although estimates vary widely. Relatively small changes in soil-carbon flux can be significant on a global scale, yet soil carbon has often been ignored as a mitigation strategy in intergovernmental climate-change initiatives (Scherr and Sthapit, 2009). Many protected areas, particularly IUCN category V protected landscapes, contain farms, including the 52 per cent (by area) of protected areas in Europe that are in that category (Gambino, 2008). Carbon is sequestered into agricultural soils by transferring CO_2 from the atmosphere through crop residues and other organic solids, in a form that is not immediately re-emitted. Soil carbon sequestration is therefore increased by management systems that add biomass to the soil, reduce soil disturbance, conserve soil and water, improve soil structure and enhance soil fauna activity. Conversely, stored soil carbon may be vulnerable to loss through both land management change and climate change (Easterling et al., 2007).

Although the amounts of carbon stored and sequestered vary between biomes, and in addition there are still large gaps in our knowledge, some common trends emerge:

- All biomes store important reservoirs of carbon.
- Current changes in land and water use frequently result in the loss of this carbon, often at an accelerating rate.
- All biomes also sequester carbon, although there is uncertainty about the amounts.
- In most cases ecosystems can switch between being sinks of carbon to becoming net sources depending on a variety of factors including management.
- Climate change may create a negative feedback: as climate change progresses it could further undermine the sequestration potential of natural ecosystems.

In a worst-case scenario, many natural ecosystems could continue to lose carbon and also lose some or all of their ability to sequester carbon, changing them from sinks to sources, thus rapidly increasing the rate and severity of climate change. Protected areas provide one of the most effective tools for maximizing and retaining the carbon sequestration and climate change adaptation functions of natural ecosystems. In many cases, well-managed protected areas are likely also to ensure that the ecosystems they contain continue to be net carbon sinks rather than becoming carbon sources.

A growing number of protected area authorities have started to view carbon storage and capture as key functions of many of their protected areas, which should be recognized in assessments of their overall worth and political importance. Carbon sequestration is being promoted as a way of financing protected areas (see Box 11.1) and of persuading governments that avoiding deforestation is a legitimate and important political priority. As part of this process, protected area practitioners are calculating the value of carbon sequestration and storage; some early results are summarized in Table 11.2 (Stolton et al., 2008).

Table 11.2 *Examples of carbon sequestration by protected areas*

Country	Amount of carbon sequestered
Argentina	Sustainable forest management of 70,000ha, including Baritu and Calilegua National Parks, is expected to sequester 4.5 million tonnes of carbon over 30 years
Belize	The Rio Bravo Conservation project aims to protect 61,917ha of forest, thus mitigating 8.8 million tonnes of CO_2 over 40 years
Bolivia	Over 800,000ha has been added to Noel Kempf National Park, estimated to sequester 7 million tonnes of carbon over 30 years
Canada	4.43 gigatonnes of carbon in 39 national parks, at a value of US$72–78 billion (although figures range from $11 billion to $2.2 trillion depending on valuation of carbon sequestration)
Czech Republic	Replacement of monocultures with mixtures of indigenous species in the Kroknose and Sumava National Parks, are expected to sequester 1.6 million tonnes over 15 years
Ecuador	Purchase of an additional 2000ha of the Bilsa Biological Reserve, are expected to sequester 1.2 million tonnes over 30 years
Madagascar	A project to reduce forest loss in 350,000ha of the Makira Forest to the same rate as in nearby national parks is expected to sequester 9.5 million tonnes of CO_2 over the next 30 years
Philippines	Protection and restoration of 12,500ha in the Sierra Madre Quirino Protected Landscape is expected to sequester 126,000 tonnes of CO_2 over 25 years
Uganda	Calculation of carbon sequestration in the national park system estimates that it is worth US$17.4 million a year. Reforestation of 27,000ha in Mount Elgon and Kibale National Parks is expected to sequester 7.1 million tonnes
US	The 16,000 culturally and ecologically significant trees in |Washington, DC, managed by the National Parks Service, store 4000 tonnes of carbon and sequester 90 tonnes each year

Future Needs:
Recognizing the Role of Protected Areas

Modelling exercises, backed by field observations, provide the basis for assessment of climate change impact on ecosystems. It might be expected that protected areas, which have fixed locations and are often isolated, will be particularly vulnerable to these changes. In fact, modelling and field observations show mixed responses. Many individual protected areas are likely to lose habitats and species, but there is evidence that well-designed protected area networks may be able to withstand climate change reasonably well (Hole et al., 2009; Araújo et al., 2004). However, as things stand, climate change may have even greater impacts for protected areas than for the wider landscape or seascape as most protected area systems at the moment are not fully representative and furthermore there is a northerly bias to protected areas where more extreme climate change is predicted (Gaston et al., 2009). Thus, if current protected area systems are assessed for their vulnerability to climate change, the survival of many species and habitats are threatened (Hannah et al., 2007). Increasing the resilience of protected area systems and maintaining their essential ecosystem services must be a part of any national strategy for adaptation.

Broadly speaking, there are five options available for increasing the effectiveness of protected area systems in contributing to climate change response strategies:

1   Increasing the total area within national protected area systems, with a focus on the ecosystems most valuable to mitigation and adaptation strategies, such as: mature natural forests particularly tropical cloud forests; mangroves and coastal wetland; peat; intact coral reefs; and forests or shrublands on steep slopes.
2   Extending existing protected areas through landscape approaches, using sustainable management systems involving natural or semi-natural vegetation types outside protected areas. These can include buffer zones, biological corridors and ecological stepping stones. They are important to build resilience within the protected area system; to facilitate connectivity for adaptation to climate change (for example, through dispersal of species along with changing climate and maintenance of essential refuges where species can persist); and to increase the total amount of natural and semi-natural vegetation under some form of protection. Expansion of protected area systems using all forms of governance, including indigenous and local community-conserved areas as well as private and co-managed protected areas, also offers an opportunity to involve a wider range of actors in mitigation and adaptation responses.
3   Increasing the level of protection within existing protected area systems, for example, by shifting management models from those that include some removal of trees (e.g. some IUCN category V approaches) to stricter forms of protection that build up biomass and carbon (e.g. IUCN categories I and II).
4   Improving management within existing protected areas, to address problems of illegal logging and conversion, other forms of poaching and detrimental impacts from invasive species, poor fire management, etc. Involving local communities in understanding the impacts of climate change on their own livelihoods is also important, including how working with protected area managers (e.g. through the establishment of grass banks or wetland restoration) will assist them to avoid the most serious effects of climate change without resorting to increased exploitation of intact ecosystems.
5   Focusing some management specifically on mitigation and sequestration needs, thus expanding management and work plans to address climate issues alongside those related to biodiversity conservation, natural resource management, recreation and social values.

Box 11.1 *The use of protected areas as tools to apply REDD carbon offset schemes*

Forests (and possibly other habitats in the future) that are contained within protected areas offer important potential in terms of meeting the criteria for a 'reduced emissions from deforestation and forest degradation' (REDD) mechanism, currently being developed under the UNFCCC.

Under the UNFCCC Kyoto Process Clean Development Mechanism (CDM) only afforestation and reforestation projects currently are eligible to be used as offsets, meaning that protection of existing forests fall outside the mechanism. However, this could change. Agreement was reached at the 13th UNFCCC Conference of Parties (COP), in Bali Indonesia in 2007, to develop a mechanism to compensate reduced emissions from avoided deforestation and degradation in the replacement to the Kyoto Protocol. This would fall under a suite of actions called 'Land Use, Land-Use Change and Forestry' (LULUCF). The details of what REDD will mean in practice are still to be worked out. To date other natural carbon stores, such as peat, some freshwater and marine ecosystems such as seagrass beds, will not fall under REDD, although in theory they might do so in the future.

Many institutions already assume that protected areas will be a part of REDD and the need for a global network of forest protected areas has been identified under the CBD, which is also now explicitly investigating the potential synergies between protected areas and carbon sequestration and storage.

The amount of money being discussed under REDD could increase conservation funding by an order of magnitude: figures of up to US$55 billion a year have been suggested although there are major differences in predictions about both the potential for storing carbon and the likely money available. The Stern report (Stern, 2006) suggests that US$10 billion a year would be needed to implement REDD mechanisms. REDD has the potential to address several critical issues within a single mechanism: mitigation of global warming, reduced land degradation, improved biodiversity conservation, increased human well-being and poverty alleviation. Institutions such as the World Bank are investing in REDD projects, which will require capacity-building and continuous, predictable and long-term funding.

However, there will be challenges in implementing REDD in forest schemes. When REDD mechanisms were rejected at the time of the Kyoto Protocol, several reasons were given, including perceived problems with baseline setting and additionality, leakage, non-permanence, scale, illegal logging, ownership of land and definition of degradation. Protected areas offer substantial additional advantages over most other land-management systems in terms of baseline, additionality, leakage, land-ownership and non-permanence, in that by their nature they have been set aside for the long-term maintenance of natural habitats (Dudley et al., 2009).

Management Options for Protected Areas

If the opportunities to use protected areas as tools for climate mitigation and adaptation are maximized, then managing protected areas under conditions of climate change will require something of a paradigm shift in the way in which protected area agencies do business.

Currently, most protected area managers seek to understand their site's biological values and, increasingly, also to measure social and economic values for local communities and other stakeholders. Extending the role of protected areas into climate stabilization implies that a number of additional values will need to be taken into account, requiring the following:

- An understanding of the amount of carbon stored within the protected area; the potential for further carbon sequestration; and the management implications of increasing stocks carbon (e.g. potential for restoration of vegetation, risks of fire, ecological implications).
- The potential for carbon release through human activities (e.g. timber poaching) and periodic disturbance factors, particularly fire, along with proposals for ways to mitigate such losses.
- Goods and services offered by the protected area that could help to mitigate climate change impacts, such as amelioration of natural disasters, supply of valuable genetic material, provision of food and water, etc.

To achieve this, a number of new tools need to be identified or refined:

- Rapid methods for calculating current and potential carbon sequestration from different vegetation types and ages within a protected area.
- Quick assessment methods to identify and measure the value (social and economic) of wider protected area benefits.
- Additional methodologies to be integrated into national protected area gap analysis to factor in potential for climate change mitigation and adaptation within protected area networks (such refinements may also be needed with some reserve selection software such as MARXAN).
- Modifications to protected area management effectiveness assessment systems to include additionality of stored carbon (the net increase in carbon stored in response, in this case, to either forming a protected area or increasing management effectiveness of an existing protected area) as well as effectiveness of climate adaptation measures – this may involve taking into account responses at a national or even a global level.
- Methods for calculating carbon trade-offs between different management strategies, for example, carbon impacts from use of prescribed burning as compared to occasional larger, hotter fires.
- Guidelines for adapting protected area management practices to ensure continuation of their ecological, economic and social functions in light of climate change.
- Guidelines and best practices for accessing funding options for protected areas including climate-related market and fund mechanisms.

- Possibly modifications to existing certification schemes, such as the Forest Stewardship Council, to address issues of climate change within certification.

One implication of placing greater emphasis on carbon sequestration is that management approaches will need to move towards models that retain standing vegetation. For example, some category V and VI protected areas, which currently permit a certain amount of timber removal or other vegetation management, might consider shifting towards management equivalent to stricter categories, such as Ia, Ib or II, or introducing different management approaches, such as replacing conventional farming with organic farming in protected landscapes to build up higher levels of soil carbon. These changes clearly have social and political consequences and imply the need for careful consultation, prior informed consent and fair compensation mechanisms; all these policy and management instruments will need to be developed.

Conclusions

The evidence presented here suggests that protected areas and the services they provide will be severely affected by the impacts of climate change. It also suggests that the well-established governance and management measures that are involved in protected area systems management can be part of the solution: protected area systems can in many cases be among the most practical, economic and effective means of addressing the challenges of climate change, and should be factored into national and particularly local strategies and investments for both climate change mitigation and adaptation.

Protected areas provide a powerful tool to address climate change, both through ecosystem-based adaptation and as a means of maximizing mitigation through reducing losses of stored carbon, inclusion of carbon-rich habitats under expanded protection schemes and through ongoing carbon sequestration. Their role has until now been noted by the international political processes addressing climate change, but generally undervalued and inadequately explored. It is time to redress the balance.

Case Study 11.1:
Protected Areas Helping to
Reduce Carbon Emissions in Brazil

Britaldo Silveira Soares Filho, Laura Dietzsch, Paulo Moutinho,
Alerson Falieri, Hermann Rodrigues, Erika Pinto, Cláudio C. Maretti,
Karen Suassuna, Carlos Alberto de Mattos Scaramuzza
and Fernando Vasconcelos de Araújo

What is left of the Brazilian Amazon forests stretches over 3.3 million km^2 and holds a large carbon stock. However, continued deforestation is resulting in substantial emissions of carbon dioxide – in addition to loss of biological diversity and reduced ecosystem services (Malhi et al., 2008). The total deforested area in the Amazon already amounts to 750,000 km^2 (18 per cent of the Brazilian Amazon biome) – an area twice the size of Germany. In the 1990s, annual deforestation rates were around 17,000km^2; corresponding to an average annual emission of 200 million tonnes of carbon (considering that 1 hectare holds an average of 120 tonnes of carbon) (Nepstad et al., 2007). Over the past few years, and after a period of intense deforestation rates in the early 2000, the rates declined to approximately 7,000 km^2 in 2009 (INPE, 2009).

Rapid deforestation

In the worst-case scenario, assuming that past trends of agricultural expansion and road development persist, 40 per cent of the remaining Amazon forests could be eliminated by 2050. The quantity of carbon to be released into the atmosphere during this period could reach 32±8 billion tons; which is almost equivalent to five years of global carbon dioxide (CO_2) emissions at 2000 levels. In addition to biodiversity losses, deforestation in the Amazon could lead to major changes in the regional climate regime, such as a substantial decrease in rainfall (Sampaio et al., 2007) and the consequent increase in forest-fire frequency, which in turn contributes to larger emissions of greenhouse gas (Nepstad et al., 1999; 2008).

More encouragingly, the decline of the Brazilian Amazon deforestation rates over the past five years demonstrates that governance in the Amazon frontier has been increasing. Brazil has demonstrated greater capacity to enforce and implement conservation policies in the Amazon forests and 148 new protected areas, equalling a total of 640,000 km², have been created between 2003 and 2008. Currently 51 per cent of the remaining forests in the Brazilian Amazon are protected.

Figure 11.4 *Rio Tapajós Amazonas, Brazil*

Source: © Michel Roggo/WWF-Canon

ARPA – protecting the Amazon

The most ambitious conservation programme related to this expansion of protected areas is the Amazon Region Protected Areas (ARPA) programme, which was created by the Brazilian government in 2003. Over a ten-year period (2003–2013), ARPA intends to protect 500,000km^2 of natural ecosystems. This expansion of the protected areas system has played an important role in biodiversity and cultural conservation in the Amazon. But what role has it played in terms of protecting carbon stocks?

To understand the role of protected areas in the reduction of greenhouse gas, especially CO_2 resulting from Amazon deforestation, WWF-Brazil, IPAM (Instituto de Pesquisa Ambiental da Amazônia), the Woods Hole Research Centre and UFMG (Universidade Federal de Minas Gerais) undertook an assessment of the protected area system's contribution to the reduction of emissions through analyses of historical deforestation rates between 1997 and 2007 and of estimated future rates obtained from modelling deforestation scenarios for 2050 (Soares-Filho et al., 2009). Until 1997, most protected areas were strictly protected for nature conservation. However, since 1998 the government has recognized many indigenous people's lands and created over 300,000km^2 of sustainable use areas. The carbon study thus addressed protected areas in their widest sense, looking at all protected areas (for nature conservation), indigenous people's lands and military areas.

The study was undertaken by overlaying protected area maps with annual deforestation maps from 2002 to 2007 (INPE, 2008), making it possible to assess deforestation both within and around protected areas. For the analysis of the region surrounding the protected areas, buffer zones of 10, 20 and 50 kilometres were defined to establish the inhibitory effects of protected areas.

Effective protection and carbon storage

The results show that protected areas inhibit deforestation. Accumulated deforestation within the areas analysed was relatively low (0.54 per cent of the total protected area of the Brazilian Amazon). Overall the effectiveness in reducing deforestation is greatest in strict conservation areas, followed by indigenous people's lands, and sustainable use areas, and, while military areas have lowest values. Protected areas also show an inhibitory effect on reducing deforestation in their surroundings. Notably, this inhibitory effect has been augmenting over time, especially in the case of sustainable use areas supported by the ARPA Programme.

The model then calculated the carbon stocks within each protected area supported by the ARPA programme and their respective emission potential if these protected areas did not exist. The figures were calculated by superimposing the map of level of deforestation threat by 2050, which is an output of a deforestation simulation model (Soares-Filho et al., 2006) on a map of the forest's biomass (Saatchi et al., 2007) and assumed that 85 per cent of forest carbon is released into the atmosphere during and after deforestation (Houghton et al., 2000).

The results showed that the 61 protected areas supported by ARPA are preserving a forest carbon stock of about 4.6 billion tonnes of carbon (18 per cent of the total stock protected in the Amazon), which is almost twice the level of emissions reduction called for in the first commitment period of the Kyoto Protocol's if fully implemented. With respect to potential emission from deforestation, the analysis on the level of deforestation threat shows that these areas have a direct potential in reducing emissions of 1.1 billion tonnes of carbon; i.e. the total released from deforestation by 2050 if they did not exist.

References

Araújo, M. B., Cabeza, M., Thuiller, W., Hannah, L. and Williams, P. H. (2004) 'Would climate change drive species out of reserves? An assessment of existing reserve-selection methods', *Global Change Biology*, vol 10, no 9, pp1618–26.

Baker, T. R., Phillips, O. L., Malhi, Y., Almeida, S., Arroyo, L., Di Fiore, A., Erwin, T., Higuchi, N., Killeen, T. J., Laurance, S. G., Laurance, W. F., Lewis, S. L., Monteagudo, A., Neill, D. A., Núnez Vargas, P., Pitman, N. C. A., Silva, J. N. M. and Martínez, R. V. (2004) 'Increasing biomass in Amazon forest plots', *Philosophical Transactions of the Royal Society B*, vol 359, pp353–65.

Bond-Lamberty, B., Peckham, S. D., Ahl, D. E. and Gower, S. T. (2007) 'Fire as the dominant driver of central Canadian boreal forest carbon balance', *Nature*, vol 450, pp89–93.

Connor, R., Chmura, G. L. and Beecher, C. B. (2001) 'Carbon accumulation in Bay of Fundy salt marshes: Implications for restoration of reclaimed marshes', *Global Biogeochemical Cycles*, vol 15, pp943–54.

Dudley, N. (1987) *Cause for Concern: An Analysis of Air Pollution Damage and Natural Habitats*, Friends of the Earth, London.

Dudley, N., Stolton, S., Belokurov, A., Krueger, L., Lopoukhine, N., MacKinnon, K., Sand-with, T. and Sekhran, N. (eds) (2009) *Natural Solutions: Protected Areas Helping People Cope with Climate Change*, IUCN-WCPA, TNC, UNDP, WCS, The World Bank and WWF, Gland, Switzerland, Washington DC and New York.

Easterling, W. E., Aggarwal, P. K., Batima, P., Brander, K. M., Erda, L., Howden, S. M., Kirilenko, A., Morton, J., Soussana, J.- F., Schmidhuber, J. and Tubiello, F. N. (2007) 'Food, fibre and forest products', *Climate Change 2007: Impacts, Adaptation and Vulner-ability. Contribution of Working Group II to the Fourth Assessment Report of the Intergovern-mental Panel on Climate Change*, Cambridge University Press, Cambridge, pp273–313.

Gambino, R. (ed.) (2008) *Parchi d'Europa: Verso una Politica Europea per le Aree Protette*, ETS Edizioni, Pisa.

Gaston, K. J., Jackson, S. F., Cantú-Salazar, L. and Cruz-Piñón, G. (2009) 'The ecological performance of protected areas', *Annual Review of Ecology, Evolution, and Systematics*, vol 39, no 1, pp93–113.

Hannah, L., Midgley, G., Andelman, S., Araújo, M., Hughes, G., Martinez-Meyer, E., Pearson, R. and Williams, P. (2007) 'Protected area needs in a changing climate', *Frontiers in Ecology and the Environment*, vol 5, no 3, pp131–8.

Hole, D. G., Willis, S. G., Pain, D. J., Fishpool, L. D., Butchart, S. M. H., Collingham, Y. C., Rahbek, C. and Huntley, B. (2009) 'Projected impacts of climate change on a continent wide protected area network', *Ecology Letters*, vol 12, pp420–31.

Houghton, R. A., Skole, D. L., Nobre, C. A., Hackler, J. L., Lawrence, K. T. and Chomen-towski, W. H. (2000) 'Annual fluxes of carbon from deforestation and regrowth in the Brazilian Amazon', *Nature*, vol 403, pp301–304.

INPE (Instituto Nacional de Pesquisas Espaciais) (2009) 'Monitoramento da floresta amazônica brasileira por satélite: projeto Prodes', www.obt.inpe.br/prodes/, accessed 12 March 2009.

IPCC (2007) 'Summary for policymakers', in *Climate Change 2007: Mitigation. Contribution of Working Group III to the Fourth Assessment Report of the Intergovernmental Panel on Climate Change*, Cambridge University Press, Cambridge and New York, NY.

Janssens, I. A., Freibauer, A., Ciais, P., Smith, P., Nabuurs, G., Folberth, G., Schlamadinger, B., Hutjes, R. W. A., Ceulemans, R., Schulze, E. D., Valentini, R. and Dolman, A. J. (2003) 'Europe's terrestrial biosphere absorbs 7 to 12% of European anthropogenic CO_2 emissions', *Science*, vol 300, pp1538–42.

Lal, R. (2004) 'Soil carbon sequestration impacts on global climate change and food security', *Science*, vol 304, pp1623–7.

Lewis, S. L., Lopez-Gonzalez, G., Sonke, B., Affum-Baffoe, K., Baker, T. R., Oja, L. O., Phillios, O. L., Reitsma, J. M., White, L., Comiskey, J. A., Djuikouo, M. N., Ewango, C. E. N., Feldpausch, T. R., Hamilton, A. C., Gloor, M., Hart, T., Hladik, A., Lloyd, J., Lovett, J. C., Makana, J.- R., Malhi, Y., Mbago, M., Ndangalasi, H. J., Peacock, J., Peh, K. S.- H., Sheil, D., Sunderland, T., Swaine, M. D., Taplin, J., Taylor, D., Thomas, S. C., Votere, R. and Wöll, H. (2009) 'Increasing carbon storage in intact tropical forests', *Nature*, vol 457, pp1003–1007.

Luyssaert, S. E., Schulze, D., Börner, A., Knohl, A., Hessenmöller, D., Law, B. E., Ciais, P. and Grace, J. (2008) 'Old-growth forests as global carbon sinks', *Nature*, vol 455, pp213–15.

Malhi, Y. J., Roberts, T., Betts, R. A., Killeen, T. J., Li, W. and Nobre, C. A. (2008) 'Climate change, deforestation, and the fate of the Amazon', *Science*, vol 319, pp169–72.

Nabuurs, G. J., Masera, O., Andrasko, K., Benitez-Ponce, P., Boer, R., Dutschke, M., El-siddig, E., Ford-Robertson, J., Frumhoff, P., Karjalainen, T., Krankina, O., Kurz, W. A., Matsumoto, M., Oyhantcabal, W., Ravindranath, N. H., Sanz Sanchez, M. J. and

Zhang, X. (2007) 'Forestry', in *Climate Change 2007: Mitigation. Contribution of Working Group III to the Fourth Assessment Report of the Intergovernmental Panel on Climate Change*, Cambridge University Press, Cambridge and New York, NY.

Nepstad, D., Soares-Filho, B. S., Merry, F., Moutinho, P., Rodrigues, H. O., Bowman, M., Schwartzman, S., Almeida, O. and Rivero, S. (2007) *The Costs and Benefits of Reducing Carbon Emissions from Deforestation and Forest Degradation in the Brazilian Amazon*, report launched in the United Nations Framework Convention on Climate Change (UNFCCC), Conference of the Parties (COP), 13th session, Bali.

Nepstad, D., Stickler, C., Soares-Filho, B. S. and Merry, F. (2008) 'Interactions among Amazon land use, forests, and climate: prospects for a near-term forest tipping point', *Philosophical Transactions of the Royal Society B*, vol 363, pp1737–46.

Nepstad, D., Verissimo, A., Alencar, A., Nobre, C., Lima, E., Lefebrve, P., Schlesinger. P., Potter, C., Moutinho, P., Mendoza, E., Cochrane, M. and Brooks, V. (1999) 'Large-scale impoverishment of Amazonian forests by logging and fire', *Nature*, vol 398, pp505–508.

Noss, R. F. (2001) 'Beyond Kyoto: Forest management in a time of rapid climate change', *Conservation Biology*, vol 15, pp578–91.

Pachauri, R. K. and Reisinger, A. (eds) (2007) *Climate Change 2007: Synthesis Report*, IPCC, Geneva, p104.

Parish, F., Sirin, A., Charman, D., Jooster, H., Minayeva, T. and Silvius, M. (eds) (2007) *Assessment on Peatlands, Biodiversity and Climate Change*, Global Environment Centre, Kuala Lumpur and Wetlands International, Wageningen.

Ramsar (2007) *Water, Wetlands, Biodiversity and Climate Change: Report on Outcomes of an Expert Meeting, 23–24 March 2007*, Ramsar, Gland.

Ramsar Secretariat (2002) *Climate Change and Wetlands: Impacts, Adaptation and Mitigation*, COP8 Information Paper DOC 11, Ramsar, Gland.

Rodrigues, A. S. L., Andelman, S. J., Bakarr, M. I., Boitani, L., Brookes, T. M., Cowling, R. M., Fishpool, L. D. C., da Fonseca, G. A. B., Gaston, K. J., Hoffmann, M., Long, J. S., Marquet, P. A., Pilgrim, J. D., Pressey, R. L., Schipper, J., Sechrest, W., Stuart, S. N., Underhill, L. G., Waller, R. W., Watts, M. E. J. and Yan, X. (2004) 'Effectiveness of the global protected area network in representing species diversity', *Nature*, vol 428, pp640–43.

Saatchi, S. S., Houghton, R. A., Dos Santos Alvalá, R. C., Soares, Z. J. V. and Yu, Y. (2007) 'Distribution of aboveground live biomass in the Amazon basin', *Global Change Biology*, vol 13, pp816–37.

Sampaio, G., Nobre, C., Costa, M. H., Satyamurty, P., Soares-Filho, B. S. and Cardoso, M. (2007) 'Regional climate change over eastern Amazonia caused by pasture and soybean cropland expansion', *Geophysical Research Letters*, vol 34, p17.

Scherr, S. J. and Sthapit, S. (2009) *Mitigating Climate Change Through Food and Land Use*, World Watch Report 179, World Watch Institute, Washington, DC.

Schuman, G. E., Janzen, H. H. and Herrick, J. E. (2002) 'Soil carbon dynamics and potential carbon sequestration by rangelands', *Environmental Pollution*, vol 116, pp391–6.

Soares-Filho, B. S.; Dietzch, L.; Moutinho, P.; Suarez, A. F.; Rodrigues, H.; Pinto, E.; Maretti, C.; Suassuna, K.; Scaramuzza, C. A.; Vasconcelos, F. Redução das emissões de carbono do desmatamento no Brasil: o papel do Programa Áreas Protegidas da Amazônia (Arpa): IPAM, 2009. 21 p. www.climaedesmatamento.org.br/biblioteca.

Stern, N. (2006) *The Stern Review on the Economics of Climate Change*, HM Treasury, London.

Stocks, B. J., Fosberg, M. A., Lynham, T., Mearns, J. L., Wotton, B. M., Yang, Q., Jin, J.- Z., Lawrence, K., Hartley, G. R., Mason, J. A. and McKenney, D. W. (1998) 'Climate change and forest fire potential in Russian and Canadian boreal forests', *Climatic Change*, vol 38, pp1–13.

Stolton, S., Dudley, N. and Randall, J. (2008) *Natural Security: Protected Areas and Hazard Mitigation*, WWF, Gland.

Trumper, K., Bertzky, M., Dickson, B., van der Heijden, G., Jenkins, M. and Manning, P. (2009) *The Natural Fix? The Role of Ecosystems in Climate Mitigation*, A UNEP rapid response assessment, United Nations Environment Programme, UNEP WCMC, Cambridge.

12

Making Peace: Protected Areas Contributing to Conflict Resolution

Trevor Sandwith and Charles Besançon

After a hard morning's horse-ride from the valleys of KwaZulu-Natal in South Africa far below, the field rangers of the Ukhahlamba-Drakensberg Park, a World Heritage site, emerge on the high plateau of the Drakensberg escarpment and head for the headquarters of Sehlabathebe National Park, the Kingdom of Lesotho's only national park. On the way up through the bands of sandstone and the towering basalt cliffs that are evidence of the ancient Gondwana landscape, they have noted the recovery of the grasslands following the spring fire-management season, the status of the alien plant-clearing operations and the condition of the footpaths and bridle paths used by hikers and travellers between the two countries. The fire-management season is always a challenge in this environment dominated by fire-prone grasslands and high winds and this year has been no different, although the firebreaks put in earlier in the year allowed the management teams from both authorities to work together to counter a number of fire incidents caused by cattle-herders wanting to promote early growth and careless hikers who had not anticipated the danger in making open campfires in this environment.

This meeting between the two parks' authorities and security personnel from both South Africa and Lesotho has a more important purpose, though, as plans and contingency operations must be put in place for the upcoming holiday period over Christmas and New Year. The area has had a conflictual past when the two countries were at a standoff over the apartheid government of South Africa's policies and this border area was a route for armed insurgence masked by cattle-rustling and other illegal activities. However, since the democratic transition of South Africa in 1994, the adjacent protected areas have been one of the means by which the two countries have sought to find common ground, learn from one another's experiences in the years of isolation and discuss ways to deal with the difficulties of managing protected areas and communities' interactions with these areas in this remote mountain highland. In particular, they are discussing this season's operational plan in terms of the 1998 transboundary agreement and strategy for the Maloti-Drakenseberg

Conservation and Development area that will address a variety of priorities including visitor management through the holiday period and the ongoing problems of illegal cattle movement across the border and how this has sometimes affected visitor-safety. A far cry from the past when most interaction was confrontational, the authorities have now settled down to discuss the most pressing issues that face them and to begin to realize the vision of a cooperative programme of management and development of this region for the benefit of both countries.

Trevor Sandwith

The Argument

The value

Many conflicts between nation states around the world focus on the borders between countries. Borders are political constructs that function as mechanisms of inclusion and exclusion. While political borders can, for a number of reasons, include some of the world's most biologically intact ecosystems, in particular those straddling watersheds or river basins, they are also places where conflicts erupt. In many parts of the developing world, current international borders were drawn arbitrarily by colonial powers that paid little attention to the ensuing division of indigenous communities and cultural heritage. This has in some cases, particularly in Africa, resulted in ambiguities about citizenship and national loyalty among border communities, fostering suspicion and political marginalization of border areas by centralized authorities, and resulting in sometimes stark disparities in rights and opportunities among people related by culture, language and tradition. Such conditions can help to promote antinational or criminal activities, including the smuggling of goods and people across borders, which can in turn contribute to the creation or escalation of tension and conflict in those same border areas (Hammill and Besançon, 2003).

Political tensions between countries or regions have led to many border areas being controlled by security forces or set aside from normal use, thus sometimes contributing an improvement in ecological integrity. The most classic example of this phenomenon is the border area between North Korea and the Republic of South Korea known as the Demilitarized Zone or DMZ. In some areas where prior land-use conditions led to habitat change, e.g. industrial forestry or intensive agriculture, the exclusion of these areas from these uses has resulted in the conservation and restoration of biodiversity. In other places, though, a lack of coordinated and collaborative management of the border zone can lead to the marginalization of these areas far from the national capitals and lost opportunities to benefit from the extraordinary environments found there.

Species and ecosystems, like human communities, do not usually fall neatly within artificial political boundaries. Borders created along lines of political influence often cut through habitats or the territories of species. Although those in the natural world do not need passports to move between countries; border demarcations such as fences or cleared vegetation can have an impact on animal movement or migration.

More importantly, different governance regimes and levels of economic and political stability can have a major impact of the policies and management of biodiversity in adjacent countries – with the same ecosystem or group of species being subject to markedly different management regimes. Increasing the level of cooperation between authorities and protected area agencies on either side of a political border therefore can clearly have important conservation benefits, but experience has shown that it can have political and social benefits as well.

The benefit

The first transboundary conservation initiative in the modern sense of the term is attributed to the Waterton-Glacier International Peace Park, which was declared in 1932. This first international peace park commemorates the peace and goodwill that exists along the world's longest undefended border (8892km) between Canada and the United States. In this case, although there is no current or even recent conflict in this border area, the two countries found it important and necessary to work together on resource management, search and rescue operations and in dealing with other emergencies.

There are, however, numerous examples of long-standing cooperative resource management arrangements in river basins, lakes, marine areas and mountains throughout the world, involving local communities and other authorities in tra-

Figure 12.1 *La trinationale de la Sangha is a unique collaboration between the countries of Cameroon, Central African Republic and Republic of Congo, conserving forests and helping to maintain traditional lifestyles*

Source: © WWF-Canon/Martin Harvey

ditional heritage territories (Singh, 1999). Whereas many of these arrangements regulate competitive resource-use and therefore support peaceful cooperation among communities, there is often also an underlying conservation purpose (i.e. to secure both sustainable use and long-term equity in access to natural resources). It has been through the understanding and development of these traditions of cooperation and conservation that the modern concept and practice of transboundary conservation initiatives have been developed over the last 80 years.

Today, the possibilities offered by transboundary conservation initiatives have captured many people's imagination. Transboundary conservation represents an ideal whereby conservation can deliver more than simply biodiversity, species and habitat protection, but also sustainable development and the promotion of a culture of peace and cooperation. In some cases, where countries have been actively in conflict over borders, jointly established transboundary protected areas have been used to forge a peaceful outcome and to foster improved relationships, thereby focusing on the area as an inclusion zone of cooperation rather than a symbol of separation.

Current Contribution of Protected Areas

Worldwide, an impressive number of transboundary conservation initiatives are being implemented in virtually all continents. When last surveyed there were at least 227 transboundary conservation areas, spanning the borders of 122 countries incorporating 3043 individual protected areas and covering 4,626,601.85km^2 (UNEP-WCMC, 2007).

To understand the complex world of transboundary conservation more easily, a typology has been developed that identifies four main types of transboundary conservation and development initiatives (Sandwith et al., 2006):

1 Transboundary protected areas.
2 Transboundary conservation and development areas.
3 Parks for Peace.
4 Transboundary migratory corridors.

Although these four types are not mutually exclusive, and may not be inclusive of all situations prevailing worldwide, they do accommodate the majority of currently known situations. Each type is considered below in more detail.

Transboundary protected areas

Protected areas that adjoin across an international boundary and involve cooperative management are the most easily defined transboundary conservation initiatives. Sandwith et al. (2001) defined a transboundary protected area (TBPA) as: an area of land and/or sea that straddles one or more borders between states, sub-national units such as provinces and regions, autonomous areas, and/or areas beyond the limit of national sovereignty or jurisdiction, whose constituent parts are especially dedicated to the protection and maintenance of biological diversity, and of natural and associated cultural resources, and managed cooperatively through legal or other effective means.

Examples of TBPAs include the Kgalagadi Transfrontier Park, which encompasses the Kalahari Gemsbok National Park in South Africa and Gemsbok National Park in Botswana. The area has been managed as a single ecological unit since 1999 and the boundary between the two parks has no physical barriers, despite being the international border between the two countries, so animals can move freely around the 38,000km² area. In Europe, the Neusiedler See/Seewinkel–Fertö Hansag Transfrontier Park ensures that the Fertö/Neusiedler Lake, which on a map has been divided artificially by the state frontier between Austria and Hungary since 1918, is managed as a bilateral national park and biosphere reserve. This joint management approach also had a historical significance when in the spring of 1989 the area was the first place where the Iron Curtain physically fell, as the fence dividing the two nations was removed (Wascher and Pérez-Soba, 2004).

Transboundary conservation and development areas

There are many examples of transboundary conservation initiatives where protected areas may be, but are not necessarily, a feature of the regional landscape, but where conservation and sustainable development goals have been asserted within a framework of cooperative management. These areas have been collectively defined as transboundary conservation and development areas, i.e. areas of land and/or sea that straddle one or more borders between states, sub-national units such as provinces and regions, autonomous areas and/or areas beyond the limit of national sovereignty or jurisdiction, whose constituent parts form a matrix that contributes to the protection and maintenance of biological diversity, and of natural and associated cultural resources, as well as the promotion of social and economic development, and which are managed cooperatively through legal or other effective means (Sandwith et al., 2006).

An example is the Maloti Drakensberg Transfrontier Conservation and Development Area, discussed at the beginning of this chapter, which is addressing conservation and community development issues in the Maloti-Drakensberg Mountains; a 300km long alpine and montane zone along the southern, eastern and northern borders of the landlocked mountain Kingdom of Lesotho and the Republic of South Africa. This aims not only to develop understanding of the area's biodiversity, and put in place effective management, but also to ensure the involvement of local communities in the conservation and development of the region, such as in the establishment of range-management areas and grazing associations (Zunckel et al., 2007).

Parks for Peace

While many transboundary conservation initiatives can contribute to stable and cooperative relationships between neighbouring nations, some have the explicit objectives of securing or maintaining peace during and after armed conflict, or of commemorating a history of peace or of past conflict. The term 'peace park' has been used to describe these situations, but this is rather loosely applied to all sorts of situations, such as memorials in city parks and battlefields. To ensure a more consistent application of terms to situations where both conservation and peaceful cooperation are goals, Sandwith et al (2001) defined 'Parks for Peace' as: transboundary protected areas that are formally dedicated to the protection and maintenance of biological diversity, and of natural and associated cultural resources, and to the promotion of peace and cooperation.

Transboundary protected areas have been particularly effective in helping resolve boundary disputes between countries. One of the first examples of this type of initiative was the establishment of protected areas in the Carpathian Mountains between 1949 and 1967, which helped settle boundary disputes and begin the process of reconciliation. A more recent example of using Parks for Peace comes from Ecuador and Peru along a portion of their common border. Here the Cordillera del Cóndor Transboundary Protected Area was declared as part of the resolution of a boundary dispute between the two countries. The boundary conflicts, which went back to Spanish colonial times, flared up in the 1990s and some 80 people lost their lives in a 19-day conflict in 1995. The mountainous Cordillera del Cóndor region between Peru and Ecuador has been an area in dispute for decades. The concept of using a peace park to help reduce conflict and build cooperation had been discussed since the 1980s and was the first driver for the initiative. Interest in conservation and a strong desire for peace among local inhabitants led to the signing of a Presidential Act in October of 1998, where both countries reached an agreement that ended hostilities and opened new avenues for bilateral cooperation on conservation issues. The consolidation of the peace process has been cemented by both the establishment and management of protected areas and the promotion of sustainable development projects for local communities. The result was several jointly managed transboundary protected areas which were to be free of any sign of national demarcation. Although local communities were lobbying for a park for peace for some years, the key factor for success in the development of the transboundary initiative was that momentum increased once funding was available to carry out research and to draw up comprehensive proposals. The fact that the area contains important biodiversity was a key factor which has helped leverage additional support for impoverished human communities living in the same area (Mittermeier et al., 2005).

By making conservation a major focus for areas such as these, former territorial disputes can be dissipated and replaced by cooperation towards the 'new' aim of conservation, as in effect neither side 'owns' the area. Parks for Peace have also sometimes provided a valuable physical buffer zone between communities in conflict, to allow a cooling off period and a rebuilding of trust.

Transboundary migratory corridors

The final group of transboundary conservation initiatives covers those situations where the habitat requirements of species include areas in several countries, such as a migratory route. These migration routes could involve two or more adjacent countries for the seasonal movement of elephants, for example, or might constitute the widely separated feeding, resting or breeding areas of migratory birds, sea turtles or whales. Such areas are defined as: areas of land and/or sea in two or more countries that are not necessarily contiguous, but are required to sustain a biological migratory pathway, and where cooperative management has been secured through legal or other effective means (Sandwith et al., 2006). Examples of transboundary migratory corridors include the Palearctic Flyway (Siberia to Senegal), Western Hemisphere Shorebird Reserve Network, European Green Belt and the Meso-American Biological Corridor.

The Potential for Transboundary Conservation to Contribute Towards Peace

Interest in the potential for transboundary conservation to contribute towards a culture of peace and political cooperation has grown considerably over the past few decades. Politicians, conservation organizations and governments have recognized that conservation can contribute to the achievement of multiple goals simultaneously. As illustrated above, Parks for Peace have been established in many parts of the world already and are being proposed in many other contentious areas, including the demilitarized zones between North and South Korea, between Kuwait and Iraq (Alsdirawi and Faraj, 2004) and in the Kashmiri region at the border of India and Pakistan at the Siachen Glacier – the longest glacier in the world and the site of the highest battlefield where troops are stationed at 6700m (Mittermeier et al., 2005).

International discussion of Parks for Peace can be traced back to the 1980s (Hamilton, 2004), with a major impetus in recognizing, defining, promoting and supporting their establishment coming after the 1997 International Conference on Transboundary Protected Areas as a Vehicle for International Co-operation organized by IUCN and the Peace Parks Foundation. The conference culminated in a declaration from the 72 expert participants from 32 countries, which concluded that a 'major contribution can be made to international co-operation, regional peace and stability by the creation of transfrontier conservation areas which promote biodiversity conservation, sustainable development and management of natural and cultural resources, noting that such areas can encompass the full range of IUCN protected area management categories' (UNEP-WCMC, 1997).

Although different situations are likely to require different solutions when Parks for Peace are developed as a contribution to peace and reconciliation, from a conservation perspective a mutual starting place remains important, whether it be a shared value or a shared problem. Thus, having some unifying theme that promotes common values and a mutual vision can help in promoting common understanding, the development of relationships and finally joint management. Such values can be seen as the river itself in the case of international efforts for conservation of the Danube basin in Europe or a common animal such as the endangered Andean bear for abutting parks in Venezuela and Colombia. This in turn can produce a culturally identifiable icon that binds together not only staff but local people on both sides of the border through pride in the designation (Hamilton, 1997). In other cases, the supporting rationale behind transboundary conservation may be that countries need to work together to solve mutual problems (Brock, 1991). Here, rather than environmental problems creating negative interactions between countries, the concept of 'environmental peacemaking' allows these interactions to be viewed as the building blocks for future cooperation (Conca and Dabelko, 2002). Thus being able to assess the favourable conditions under which countries are likely to engage with one another over environmental issues for mutual benefit may help the development of institutional structures and processes capable of facilitating progress in the development of Parks for Peace.

Of course, the fact should not be overlooked that, in some cases, conservation itself can be an instrument of conflict, especially when the implementation of conservation strategies impinges on the rights of local people or limits their options to pursue livelihood strategies in times of stress. In transboundary situations, these impacts can extend across national boundaries, engendering conflict at a number of different levels, from national to local. It is also possible that efforts to promote peace at a political level may inadvertently promote conflict locally, or vice versa (Hammill and Besançon, 2003).

Future Needs:
Recognizing the Role of Protected Areas

If designed and managed effectively, transboundary conservation may help to address some of the underlying causes of conflict such as poverty, environmental degradation, livelihood insecurity and institutional capacity, as well as inter- and intra-state relations. However, although the role of transboundary conservation initiatives and Parks for Peace is often extolled for its peace-building potential this outcome is in practice rarely thoroughly documented or evaluated. Cooperation and peace-building is an assumed outcome of bringing together different – and sometimes, previously opposing – stakeholders for the common purpose of managing biodiversity and protecting livelihoods (Hammill and Besançon, 2003). The need to assess the impacts of transboundary initiatives and learn lessons from the role of protected areas in conflict resolution and peace-building is therefore an area which continues to require more attention.

Issues of governance and community relationships need more consideration. The establishment of transboundary protected areas is primarily driven by high-level, non-local forces such as government departments or national or international non-governmental conservation organizations, although a few notable exceptions do exist like the Kgalagadi Transfrontier Park between South Africa and Botswana, which began as an informal agreement between protected area authorities. The heightened role of the state in these developments makes sense, given that transboundary arrangements involve issues of sovereignty and national security. However, as the centre of control for planning projects moves further away from the physical location of the protected area to capital cities or even to foreign countries, the potential to exclude local communities in decision-making and benefit-sharing increases and may further marginalize and isolate border communities, creating tensions and instability.

Management Options

Cross-border coordination can raise the profile of a particular site or sites and can help to increase management capacity and expertise in these areas. However, the complexity of managing sites across borders should not be overlooked. The need for consensus and approval of management decisions from two or more governing bodies can slow decision-making. Also, if the two or more partnering protected areas or other conservation areas have different management objectives, for instance, a category II national park promoting education and recreation next to a category Ib wilderness area aiming to be undisturbed by significant human activity, differing mandates can complicate cooperation and management. Differences in language across borders can also be a limiting factor, and major differences in resources between protected areas in different countries can create management difficulties and tensions.

Border areas can also create significant problems of their own which have little direct relation to protected area management but can cause major impacts. Borders are often associated with refugees, smuggling, militarization and armed conflict. The string of protected areas on the border between the US and Mexico suffer major problems in this regard. However, it is often because of these problems, which makes areas less attractive for settlement and development, that they remain areas with high biodiversity and conservation potential (Mittermeier et al., 2005). The establishment of cooperation on one type of objective, for example, nature conservation, can and will generate opportunities and implications for other objectives, for example, promoting peace, regional integration or economic development, involving a complex array of actors including communities and institutions on both sides of the border in the cooperative arrangement. This national to local scale of governance and interests can result in extremely complex diplomatic and institutional arrangements and involve agencies that do not regularly interact with one another, for example, nature conservation, immigration, customs, traditional authorities and security forces.

Conclusions

Whereas the protected area estate has performed relatively well in securing representative samples of biodiversity patterns (distribution of species, communities and ecosystems), it remains inadequate for conserving the ecosystem processes that will secure either the protected areas or biodiversity in the wider landscape. Multiple-agency, landscape-level approaches that involve a range of sectoral interests and objectives (the ecosystem approach) can help resolve this problem. At the same time such approaches, when taking place across boundaries of different countries which do not have a harmonious relationship, can result in the additional benefit of helping secure cooperation or at least ease boundary area dispute and conflict.

Of course, not all transboundary conservation efforts achieve what can sometimes be portrayed as quite idealist objectives in terms of conflict resolution, but there are enough examples in existence to illustrate that this is a real benefit which, in the right place and at the right time, protected areas can offer. It is therefore possible that transboundary conservation areas will increasingly be seen as a mechanism to resolve political disputes, especially boundary disputes, and, more importantly, create the conditions for peaceful cooperation among nations. This will require a more sophisticated analysis of situations and the development of appropriate tools and processes that link national to local processes and engender cooperation across sectors. While transboundary conservation areas may not be the first resort in situations of active conflict, processes that lead to their establishment can be used to engender reconciliation after conflict, both symbolically between nations and practically, at the local level between communities and authorities who depend on and are charged with securing sustainable natural resource management.

Case Study 12.1:
La Amistad Binational Biosphere Reserve
in Costa Rica and Panama

Manuel Rámirez

La Amistad Biosphere Reserve and binational World Heritage site is located in the Talamanca–Tabasara Mountain Range. La Amistad, which means 'friendship' in Spanish, was officially declared on the Costa Rican side in 1982 and on the Panamanian side in 1998 as a symbol of binational cooperation. Stretching from southern Costa Rica to western Panama, it is a conservation and multiple-use area acting as a backbone and linking these two countries. The reserve protects one of the largest and richest ecosystems in Central America. Its system of protected natural and cultural areas includes approximately 633,000ha in Costa Rica (12 per cent of the country) and 655,000ha in Panama (8.7 per cent of the country).

Biodiversity and flagship species

La Amistad sits on the narrow land bridge between North and South America, where two distinct biotas and extreme ranges of temperatures, rainfall, altitude, slopes and exposure converge to make it one of the most biologically diverse protected regions in the Western Hemisphere.

The reserve contains a great expanse of pristine forest, including the largest portion of cloud forest in Central America, and provides a unique refuge for native wildlife species whose populations depend upon large tracts of land. This diversity is evident not only in the high levels of endemism (between 20–50 per cent for all groups), but also in the numbers of species present within the biosphere reserve; for example, La Amistad has the second most diverse butterfly fauna in the world (DeVries, 1987). Populations of large mammals thrive within this complex of protected areas, including the tapir (*Tapirus bairdii*), the giant anteater (*Myrmecophaga tridactyla*) and six species of cats, most notably the jaguar (*Panthera onca*). Nearly 70 per cent of Costa Rica and Panama's bird species inhabit the core areas of the biosphere reserve. The national bird of Panama, the harpy eagle (*Harpia harpyja*), a magnificent predator whose highly restricted distribution is a direct consequence of extensive deforestation, is found here. The reserve is also the convergence point for 75 per cent of all migratory birds in the Western Hemisphere.

Political-economic-social significance

In 1979 Costa Rica and Panama established their first transboundary cooperation agreement for the purpose of jointly developing investment and assistance projects. Presidential declarations issued both in 1979 and 1982 with reference to the establishment of La Amistad International Park emphasized two important arguments: the need to conserve the countries' joint natural and cultural heritage; and the importance of having a model for peace and friendship between neighbouring countries.

Over the years, governmental and non-governmental agencies in these two countries have engaged in coordinated efforts to foster joint plans and binational cooperation under the transboundary agreement signed 30 years ago.

The region is of great cultural importance, as shown by the numerous archaeological sites discovered within the biosphere reserve, silent testimony to more than 12,000 years of human history that spans occupation of the first settlers, who were hunter-gatherers, to the complex, agriculturally based tribal societies encountered by Europeans in the 16th century. Today, the area includes the ancestral lands of the two largest indigenous groups in Costa Rica: the Bribri and the Cabecar. Their combined population of 26,000 (Guevara, 2000) represents nearly two-thirds of the country's total number of indigenous people. Three ethnic groups live in and around the Panamanian side of the biosphere reserve: the Guaymi or Ngobe, the Naso and the Bribri. Their population numbers about 75,000. Through traditional practices of shifting agriculture (corn, beans, plantain and rice), hunting, fishing and utilization

Figure 12.2 *Naso children performing a dance in La Amistad, Panama*

Source: © Manuel Rámirez

of forest products, these groups have maintained a relatively sound relationship with their natural environment.

Benefits and threats

La Amistad is important biologically and economically to these two countries. The high annual rainfall of 2000–7000mm, combined with the short and steep watersheds common to the region, creates both serious flood hazards and a potential for hydroelectric energy production. Half of Costa Rica's freshwater flow originates from catchments in La Amistad. In Panama, the land surrounding La Amistad is vital to the country's economy, producing 80 per cent of the country's fruits and vegetables. Currently, both Costa Rica and Panama have major hydroelectric projects inside or adjacent to La Amistad, e.g. the Fortuna dam that produces a significant portion of Panama's energy, and the Cachi dam that produces energy for the Costa Rican economy. Additional hydro projects are in the planning phase in both countries, all of them within the buffer zones of the parks and some in indigenous territories.

The Talamanca region has undergone little development compared with the rest of Costa Rica and Panama. While the majority of land within the core of the Talamanca remains relatively pristine and legally protected, adjacent areas have suffered major land-use change. Two decades after its declaration, land tenure within La Amistad is still a source of conflict. For example, indigenous territories are progressively losing land to non-indigenous settlers, particularly on the Pacific side of the reserve and encroachment is severe in the Panama sector of the reserve.

Outlook for the future

The geographic, cultural and biotic complexity of the Talamanca region requires a broad range of institutional involvement. The full support of national entities, governmental agencies and international organizations is needed to ensure the success of La Amistad as a transboundary conservation area. Only coordinated action between these entities will generate the required level of integrated management and development fundamental to the long-term survival of the biosphere reserve. Finding common ground between these and the local landscape-users remains a difficult task. However, local and regional civil society groups and international agencies recognize that working together is the only way to achieve desired outcomes.

The recognition that conservation of biodiversity and its entire ecosystems is of economic benefit to both countries has created a renewed interest in the coordinated management of La Amistad ecoregional complex. There is a growing awareness of binational and regional ecosystem services that the area provides, particularly in terms of the role of conserving forest cover in the upper watersheds of rivers originating in the La Amistad complex to ensure continued water supplies to population centres, hydropower and other economic activities. Clean air, biodiversity and scenic beauty values for ecotourism are also beginning to be appreciated, as are the carbon stocks of the forests which will certainly add value to climate change mitigation and adaptation.

References

Alsdirawi, F. and Faraj, M. (2004) 'Establishing a transboundary peace park in the demilita-rized zone (DMZ) on the Kuwaiti/Iraqi borders', *Parks*, vol 14, no 1 pp48–55.

Brock, L. (1991) 'Peace through parks: The environment on the Peace Research Agenda', *Journal of Peace Research*, vol 28, no 4, pp407–23.

Conca, J. and Dabelko, G. D. (eds) (2002) *Environmental peacemaking*, Woodrow Wilson Center Press and Johns Hopkins University Press, Washington, D.C. and Baltimore

DeVries, P. (1987) *The Butterflies of Costa Rica and Their Natural History*, Princeton University Press, Princeton, NJ.

Guevara, M. (2000) *Perfil de los Pueblos Indígenas de Costa Rica*, RUTA-Banco Mundial, Costa Rica.

Hamilton, L. (1997) 'Guidelines for effective transboundary cooperation: Philosophy and best practices', in the *Proceedings of Parks for Peace International Conference on Trans-boundary Protected Areas as a Vehicle for International Co-operation*, www.unep-wcmc. org/protected_areas/transboundary/somersetwest/somersetwest.pdf, accessed 4 Septem-ber 2009.

Hamilton, L. (2004) 'Review of transboundary protected areas: The viability of regional con-servation strategies', *Mountain Research and Development*, vol 24, no 2, p187.

Hammill, A., and Besancon C. (2003) *Peace and conflict impact assessment – An emerging tool for TBPA planning and monitoring*, paper prepared for the workshop on Transboundary Protected Areas in the Governance Stream of the 5th World Parks Congress, Durban, South Africa, 12–13 September 2003

Hammill, A. and Besançon, C. (2007) 'Measuring Peace Park performance: Transboundary mountain gorilla conservation in central Africa', in S. H. Ali (ed.) *Peace Parks: Conserva-tion and Conflict Resolution*, MIT Press, Cambridge, MA.

Mittermeier, R. A., Kormos, C. F. Mittermeier, C. G., Gil, P. R., Sandwith, T. and Besançon, C. (2005) *Transboundary Conservation*, Cemex, Monterrey.

Sandwith, T., Lockwood, M. and Gurung, C. (2006) 'Linking the landscape', in M. Lock-wood, A. Kothari and G. L. Worboys, *Managing Protected Areas: A Global Guide*, Earth-scan, London.

Sandwith, T. S., Shine, C., Hamilton, L. S. and Sheppard, D. A. (2001) *Transboundary Pro-tected Areas for Peace and Co-operation*, IUCN, Gland and Cambridge.

Singh, J. (1999) *Global Review: Lessons Learned, Study on the Development of Transboundary Natural Resource Management Areas in Southern Africa*, Biodiversity Support Program, Washington, DC.

UNEP-WCMC (1997) 'Parks for Peace International Conference on Transboundary Pro-tected Areas as a Vehicle for International Co-operation', www.unep-wcmc.org/protect-ed_areas/transboundary/somersetwest/, accessed 4 September 2009.

UNEP-WCMC (2007) 'UNEP-WCMC Transboundary Protected Areas Inventory 2007', www.tbpa.net/tpa_inventory.html, accessed 4 September 2009.

Wascher, D. M. and Pérez-Soba, M. (eds) (2004) *Learning from Transfrontier Landscapes – Project in Support of the European Landscape Convention*, Alterra report 964, Wageningen.

Zunckel, K., Mokuku, C. and Stewart, G. (2007) *Case Study – Maloti Drakensberg Transfron-tier Project*, www.tbpa.net/case_08.htm, accessed 4 September 2009.

13

Nature Conservation:
Leaving Space for Biodiversity

Nigel Dudley

We're sitting in the park office of a protected area in southern Vietnam. We have driven down yesterday from Ho Chi Minh and just had lunch with the warden and his staff who are, as always, charming. My colleague and I are here to get feedback on the results of a monitoring programme the park has introduced and they have just finished the first systematic field survey. I don't speak Vietnamese so things go a little haltingly. However, everyone is very excited about the research. The monitoring officer starts to tell me what they found: Elephas maximus! I turn to my colleague from Hanoi and try to get it straight in my head – you mean they really just found elephants in the park for the first time? Well, yes they did. And this is a good park I think; keen young staff, good people working with them from the university in the capital, support from the government; it is just that they are quite a new protected area, with very few resources available and enormously tricky terrain to operate in. Someone told me in the Congo Basin a few years back that he estimated there was an area the size of France and Germany combined where scientists had no idea about the distribution of even large animals like elephant. Conservation under these circumstances cannot be as precise as the planners in central offices would like us to suppose, but it is often critically important in the face of rapid change and huge pressures on wildlife. Even in the places – especially in the places – where we still know so little about the variety of plant and animal species, protected areas play a key role in keeping them in existence.

Nigel Dudley

The Argument

The value

The underlying message of this book is that the tenth or more of the world's land surface set aside for protection, coupled with the growing amount of coastal zones and oceans, provide a far wider range of goods and services than has generally been recognized. Far from being a net drain on human resources, protection of natural capital leaves us well in pocket.

However, for most people protected areas are, and will remain, primarily tools for conserving wildlife, particularly endangered plant and animal species. The more technical term 'biodiversity', encompassing the full range of biological variation at ecosystem, species and genetic level, is increasingly recognized. Biodiversity has a wide range of use values – for food, medicines and other materials – but also has intrinsic value. Most people instinctively agree that we should not be causing or increasing the rate of extinction of species, whether or not they are of direct value to us, and this philosophy has been confirmed by all the world's major religious systems (Palmer and Findlay, 2003).

Efforts to conserve biodiversity use three major approaches:

1 Taking species away from their natural habitat and maintaining them in artificial conditions, known as *ex situ* conservation and including zoos, artificial breeding centres and seed or gene banks. Such approaches may be essential in emergency situations, as an insurance policy and if the natural habitat has entirely disappeared (which may become more common under climate change).
2 Conserving species in semi-natural habitat, including, for example, agricultural areas, commercial forestry, waste ground and in urban settings. Careful management and usually some trade-offs between production and conservation can hugely increase the number of species supported in semi-natural habitats and at an extreme diversity can come close to fully natural conditions, but in most cases a proportion of species will be unable to survive or will be unwelcome. This may be because they are too specialized to adapt to changing conditions such as is the case with some shy primate or bird species. Alternatively, it could be because they are associated with habitats that are unlikely to survive in managed habitats, like the many species associated with dead wood, which tends to be removed in managed forests to maintain tree health. Finally, some species compete directly with humans, a category including many large carnivores or species such as elephants that carry out crop-raiding.
3 Conserving species in a natural or near-natural habitat (protected areas), where because of an area's remoteness or through deliberate management policies habitat is managed directly for nature, including management decisions to leave it entirely alone.

The distinction between the second and third of these approaches inevitably remains slightly blurred. Most conservation biologists agree that effective biodiversity conservation is in almost all cases built around a framework of protected areas.

The benefit

Nowadays, protected areas are usually established primarily as a means of biodiversity conservation. Whereas in the past national parks were established either because of their scenic value or with an eye to protecting one or two key species, new tools and approaches are increasing the precision with which protected areas are selected (Margules and Pressey, 2000; Eken et al., 2004; Dudley and Parrish, 2006) and managed (Hockings et al., 2004), and the key role they play in biodiversity conservation is acknowledged in national and global policies, including those of the Convention on Biological Diversity. Climate change is creating additional challenges in this respect both in terms of the design and management of protected areas. An understanding of the various ways in which protected areas function as tools for biodiversity conservation helps to lay the ground for developing response strategies.

Protected areas offer a number of unique benefits for species and ecological processes that cannot survive in managed landscapes and seascapes. They provide space for evolution and a benchmark for future restoration (Sinclair et al., 2002), which is especially important in a time of rapid ecological change. Protected areas are often the only remaining natural or semi-natural areas in countries or regions, and significant numbers of species are found nowhere else (Ricketts et al., 2005).

Current Contributions of Protected Areas

Protected areas play multiple roles in biodiversity conservation; nine different contributions can be distinguished depending on the species, ecological situation and types of pressures and opportunities present:

1   Conservation of natural ecosystems without human interference.
2   Conservation of large, intact ecosystems for the protection of known and unknown species.
3   Conservation of particular endangered fragments of ecosystems.
4   Conservation of particular habitats or species by management tailored to their specialized needs.
5   Conservation of species adapted to culturally influenced ecosystems by maintaining traditional management.
6   Providing high levels of protection for very limited, range-restricted and endemic species.
7   Conservation of particular aspects of species' life-cycles through time-limited interventions.
8   Conservation of habitat fragments of importance for migratory species.
9   Providing places to experiment with sustainable natural resource management.

Each of these will be examined in greater detail below.

Conservation of natural ecosystems without human interference

Some species and habitats are highly susceptible to human interference and are likely to decline in managed landscapes or seascapes and in extreme cases even where there are a relatively few human visitors. This could be, for example: plant species that are damaged by light trampling (Cole, 1995); animals with social structures that are easily disturbed (e.g. Kirika et al., 2008); species susceptible to introduced diseases or invasive species (e.g. Daszak et al., 2000); or species subject to over-collection or hunting (e.g. Walsh et al., 2003). Here the most strictly protected areas provide a partial or complete buffer from interference. Such sites can range from very small to extremely large, depending on the type of habitat and species under consideration.

'Classic' strict reserves include seabird colonies, which can be devastated by human interference (and particularly by the introduction of pest species such as the brown rat), and some areas set aside for sensitive primate species or for very fragile vegetation types. In some cases, this sensitivity may be caused by the isolation of a site. Cors Fochno National Nature Reserve is, at 65ha, the largest remaining lowland raised bog in Wales, UK, and part of the core of the Dyfi UNESCO Biosphere Reserve. Because of its small size, sensitive vegetation types and risks of fire, it is now kept off-limits to visitors, except for occasional access on boardwalks accompanied by the warden. The wilderness concept has developed in part out of such concerns, although here there are also social and cultural issues involved regarding perceptions of space and untamed nature.

Conservation of large, intact ecosystems

These are areas at a scale that allows natural ecosystem processes to continue without interference, with populations of species large enough so that they are likely to remain genetically viable and able to withstand environmental pressures over time (Sanderson et al., 2002). Areas on this scale ensure protection both of known species and, particularly important in biologically rich areas, species that have not yet been described by science (Peres, 2005). In reality, costs and human pressures often mean that there is a trade-off between ideal size and possible size. Wardens at Bwindi Impenetrable Forest National Park in Uganda worry whether the area is large enough to sustain the 300 pairs of mountain gorillas that live there, but farming takes place right up to the borders and there is local resentment about the area being set aside at all.

Ecological processes may be as important as individual species or habitats. Serengeti National Park in Tanzania and the neighbouring Masai Mara National Park in Kenya protect not only the savannah ecosystem of the region but also the unique migration patterns of large herbivores such as the zebra and wildebeest (Sinclair and Norton-Griffiths, 1984). Massive tropical rainforest reserves, such as the Tumuacumaque National Park in Brazil which at 3.9 million hectares is around the same size as Switzerland, have the capacity to accommodate viable populations of top predators, migration routes and natural disturbance patterns, and to protect unknown species that have not as yet been described within scientific literature. Protected areas as insurance policies are particularly important in places where knowledge remains fragmentary. We still know far less about the wildlife of the planet than

Figure 13.1 *The migration spectacle in Serengeti National Park, Tanzania*

Source: © Sue Stolton

might be assumed. Halfway through the period of writing this chapter researchers have discovered 40 new species from a volcano in Papua New Guinea, including new mammals and amphibians and as the vignette that starts this chapter shows the same kinds of things are happening in Indochina. When we start considering plants or invertebrates our level of ignorance rises exponentially.

Conservation of endangered fragments of ecosystems

This strategy is used in places where degradation and replacement of natural ecosystems have already been widespread, and also where key features are at risk within otherwise managed landscapes or seascapes. It is a trade-off between conserving entire ecosystems and carrying out conservation in altered or highly pressured areas. This use of protected areas is increasingly integrated into wider conservation strategies, so that conservation within protected areas is one element in a suite of responses (Groves et al., 2002). In theory, these fragments allow the survival of species (for example, by providing breeding places) that can also utilize part of the wider landscape or seascape for feeding and dispersal. These fragments also help to preserve plant species that would not find suitable habitat in managed landscapes. They are predicated, in the long-term, on the assumption that species will be able to disperse and thus mix genetic material, to avoid inbreeding, because most are too small for populations to remain viable if completely isolated.

Small reserves have proved particularly important in aquatic environments to create secure spawning and breeding spaces for fish and other commercially valuable species (see Chapter 5). They are also used in terrestrial areas that are otherwise managed and are a key feature in conservation strategies in most west European countries. For example, a system of mini-protected areas protect natural mires in Finland, thus maintaining an important habitat type and associated biodiversity in areas of forest that are otherwise managed for timber or recreation (Gilligan et al., 2004). Small reserves are also increasingly being used in marine environments beyond the immediate need to secure fisheries. The Bowie Seamount, Canada's seventh marine protected area, protects a complex of three seamounts 180km west of Haida Gwaii (Queen Charlotte Island); these are unusual in rising to within 24m of the surface and are biologically rich but also highly fragile and susceptible to damage from unregulated fishing and boating activities (Canessa et al., 2003).

Conservation of species or habitats through management tailored to their specialized needs

In places where ecosystem change has been profound, or where disturbance factors (e.g. invasive species) can upset the local ecology, protected areas may be places where management actions can be tailored explicitly to maintain a particular species or way of ecosystem functioning. Of necessity, such areas may be highly managed but here management decisions are driven primarily by conservation needs. Management interventions might include, for example, artificial removal of invasive species (increasingly important in many protected areas); restoration of native vegetation; re-introduction of native species; or simpler measures like mimicking natural grazing pressures (which might mean reduction of livestock in some cases or reintroduction of artificial grazing in others).

In Jirisan National Park, Korea, some plantations are being restored to native forests and the Asiatic black bear (*Ursus thibetanus*), whose population had fallen to an estimated five individuals, is being restored through captive breeding and reintroductions. In Lüneberger Heide Nature Reserve in Germany, the immediate threat to ecological stability is from forest encroachment due to loss of natural herbivores and here the heath habitat is looked after by controlled grazing, chemicals and scything to maintain a seral vegetative community, including important populations of black grouse (Mertens et al., 2007). Conversely in Dana Nature Reserve in Jordan (308 km², IUCN category IV), a key aspect of management is a reduction in domestic goat numbers to allow vegetation to regenerate (Schneider and Burnett, 2000).

Conservation of species adapted to culturally influenced ecosystems

In situations where long-term management has produced changes in ecology, protected areas can be based on the maintenance of traditional practices. Implicit in this is that such practices are themselves under threat, often from changing technologies or social conditions, so that protected areas frequently support traditional management through financial or other means. Here the objective is to maintain the mix of species currently present within the cultural landscape. It is frequently said that without management in these situations biodiversity will 'decline'. In fact, protection without management intervention in these situations would certainly cause biodiversity to change but in many cases the absence of research means that it is not possible to tell if the overall richness will rise or fall, or to put it another way how the degree of threat faced by different species will alter. There are many examples of such approaches in the European Mediterranean, such as maintenance of culturally defined grassland habitats in the Minorca Biosphere Reserve in Spain, which helps to protect plant and animal species adapted to grassland, in an island where human influences have created the vegetation mosaic over centuries (Chust et al., 1999; Borrini-Feyerabend et al., 2004).

Protecting range-limited and endemic species

Some species are so rare or have such restricted distribution that protected areas conserve all or a significant proportion of the population to buffer them from current pressures or as an insurance against future threats. Many islands fall into this category, because their isolation means that they have evolved unique species types. Examples of protected areas conserving island populations include Teide and Garajonay National Parks on the Canary Islands of Spain with unique plant and bird species and the Galápagos National Park in Ecuador, protecting a large but still unquantified number of species endemic to the islands (Willerslev et al., 2002). As natural habitat becomes increasingly isolated, ecological 'islands' also occur on the mainland and in

Figure 13.2 *Waved albatross (*Phoebastria irrorata*) on the Galápagos Islands*
Source: © Sue Stolton

marine areas. Kaziranga National Park in Assam, India, supports the world's largest population of Asian rhinoceros (see Case Study 13.1). Many other protected areas have been created to conserve less iconic endemic species, which occur throughout the world. In Scotland, a country not usually noted for high biodiversity levels, Keen of Hamar National Nature Reserve in the Shetland Islands protects the only known population of Edmondston's chickweed (*Cerastium nigrescens*).

Conservation of particular aspects of species' life-cycles

Protected areas are sometimes established specifically to conserve particular periods of the life-cycle of a species or group, in ways that include a temporal aspect in protection or some kind of flexible zoning. The most common cases are temporary zoning to protect the breeding grounds of marine or freshwater fish (which are described in Chapter 5), or to allow recovery of plant species with high economic or social value such as medicinal herbs (Chapter 2). However, such focused protection can also be aimed at species without economic value, for example, through the preservation of veteran trees to maintain nesting sites for birds of prey in managed forestry in Sweden, or the protection of ponds during the spawning season of frogs and toads.

Conservation of habitat fragments for migratory species

Migratory species face particular challenges in needing suitable habitat along routes of hundreds or even thousands of miles. Protected areas that maintain flyways, 'swimways' or mammal routes have specialized management approaches. These may include, for example, provision of food for migratory birds, as for several crane species including the white-necked crane; fishing restrictions on rivers with spawning salmon; or protection of 'stepping stones' for migratory birds, like the Western Hemisphere Shorebird Reserve Network in the Americas. Birds or flying insects are relatively easier to develop strategies for because they can pass easily over inhospitable habitat, although hunting pressure in between sites can undermine protection, as is currently the case in Malta and was the cause of the disappearance of the western Siberian crane population, despite protection at both ends of the migration route. Mammals that migrate face immediate problems if there is a single break in their route, which can be caused by something as simple as a road or by management changes that make then unwelcome. The planting of oil palm right up to the banks of the Kinabatangan River in Sabah, Borneo, (which is illegal) has broken the migration route for Borneo forest elephants, which now literally have to swim around areas to avoid being shot at during their twice-yearly journey along the river. Other examples of the use of protected areas for migratory species include the Monarch Butterfly Biosphere Reserve in Mexico (Alonso-Mejía et al., 1997) and maintaining biological connectivity along heavily modified stretches of the River Danube in Austria (Chovanec et al., 2002). Because they are often needed in crowded or modified landscapes and seascapes, many such sites are protected under governance forms other than direct management by governments.

Test sites for sustainable management

Less well recognized, but of considerable importance, is the role that protected areas in the less 'strict' categories play in providing test sites for combining sustainable management and biodiversity conservation that can be expanded more generally into the wider landscape (Phillips, 2002). This is a very different use to the ones described above, with its implicit trade-offs between conservation and other uses. It can create tensions between conservation and other social or economic drivers, which has led to criticism of protected landscapes and extractive reserves, and some governments have used these designations as easy options to meet conservation targets. The debate about the precise role of IUCN categories V and VI remains unresolved. However, increasing attention on these protected-area designations has built pressure to deliver and the best examples of IUCN categories V and VI demonstrate a variety of ingenious ways in which conservation and development can be integrated successfully. Examples include some extractive reserves in the Amazon, where rubber tappers and other users extract economic value from otherwise protected forests, and some of the protected landscapes in Europe, where large mammals such as the bear and wolf survive alongside farming and recreational interests.

Future Needs

Most wild nature exists outside protected areas and many species (Rodrigues et al., 2004) and habitats (Hoekstra et al., 2005) remain unprotected or underprotected by the global protected areas network. Protected areas also remain severely under pressure from illegal use, conflict, social tensions and climate change. Protected areas on their own cannot maintain all species, but most people still recognize them as an essential element – perhaps the most essential element – in conservation strategies. While much of this book has focused on wider values of these areas, their underlying importance in biodiversity conservation should never be underestimated.

Case Study 13.1:
A Hundred Years of Conservation Success
at Kaziranga National Park, India

Vinod Mathur and Sue Stolton

The valley of the Brahmaputra River covers some 60 per cent of the state of Assam in northeastern India. The immense river is fed by the southwest summer monsoon, when over 80 per cent of India's total precipitation occurs, making the valley one of the most fertile stretches of land in India. Over 73 per cent of the Brahmaputra watershed's original forest has been lost, much of it to tea plantations, and currently only 4 per cent of the land area is protected (Mathur et al., 2007).

The grasslands, floodplains and floodplain lakes of Assam provide ideal habitat for a wide variety of species. Many of these are endangered and have had their habitat limited to small areas within the state – most notably Kaziranga National Park. The park has the largest grassland area left in the region, stretched along some 50km of

Figure 13.3 *Park staff survey the great Brahmaputra River*

Source: © Sue Stolton

the Brahmaputra's south bank. The annual river floods replenish the wetlands and allow the grassland areas to flourish (Choudhury, 2004). Preliminary notification of the area as a forest reserve was given in 1905, making it one of the oldest protected areas in the world. The park was designated as a natural World Heritage site in 1985.

The park is home to about 60 per cent of the world population of the Indian one-horned rhinoceros (*Rhinoceros unicornis*), about 50 per cent of the endangered Asiatic wild water buffalo (*Bubalus arnee*) and has the only viable population of eastern swamp deer (*Cervus duvaucelii*) in the northeastern region. Its major conservation success has been the increase in rhino numbers. A mere handful were recorded when the park was first established, with population counts recovering to 366 at the time of the first survey in 1966 and 1552 in 1999, and numbers are still increasing (Vasu, 2003).

An 'island' in a sea of development

Kaziranga is a relatively small park (430km^2) and the nature of the ecosystem means that land is being lost to the floods. While there have been attempts to add more land to the park, only one addition of just over 40km^2 has so far been gazetted as well as a new 96km^2 sanctuary in Karbi Anglong (Choudhury, 2004). While efforts to expand the park will continue, it is clear that the park management needs to adopt an approach which looks beyond the boundaries of the protected area and works with regional government and private interests to agree a landscape mosaic that will provide a supportive environment in which Kaziranga can continue to flourish.

Some key landscape-scale issues include: changes to hydrology in the Brahmaputra system due to dam construction; road development, especially widening the current highway and its impact on the periodic animal migration that takes place to avoid flooding; expected impacts of climate change; and more general land-use change due to population pressure and agricultural development.

The 54km length of the National Highway (NH) 37 running parallel to the southern boundary of the park is a case in point. During the rainy season flooding forces many animals to move southwards to elevated grounds, but some are killed by vehicles while crossing the road. The park managers have identified crucial animal-crossing corridors on the NH-37 and have implemented several measures to reduce animal mortality. However, plans are underway to convert the existing NH-37 to a six-lane expressway, which would in effect cut the park off from the higher ground (Bonal and Chowdhury, 2004).

The Karbi Plateau to the south of park is another important area of high ground. Large-scale habitat changes in the plateau include conversion to tea gardens, settlement, logging and *jhum* (shifting agriculture). One impact is that the gap between the park and the plateau is increasing, as suitable habitat is destroyed. This has serious implications for the ability of Kaziranga to maintain healthy animal populations. For example, the 2000 census recorded 86 tigers in the park, which is a growing and healthy population. A global study identified the Kaziranga-Meghalaya region as one of the priority tiger conservation habitats in the Indian subcontinent (Wikramanayake et al., 1998). However, as land-use changes increase around the park the

resident population of tigers and other animal species risk becoming genetically isolated and over time no longer viable.

Although Kaziranga has seen major conservation successes, there are still many
endangered species within or passing though the park. There are, for example, nearly
200 species of aquatic vertebrates in the Brahmaputra River System; including the
endangered river dolphin, (*Platanista gangetica*), which is in steady decline. The conservation of this species is urgent, but will require strategies which go far beyond
the boundaries of Kaziranga, in particular, the better implementation of the Indian
Fisheries Act (Boruah and Biswas, 2002).

Conclusions

Over the last 100 years Kaziranga National Park has been able to secure the habitat of
several endangered species including rhino, elephant, tiger, wild buffalo and swamp
deer. The park managers, frontline staff, local communities and civil society have, under the guidance of the administrative as well as political leadership in Assam, played
a vital role in achieving this success. Over the next century, Kaziranga, in common
with many other protected areas, will likely find management within its boundaries threatened by changes in the wider landscape. Future success will depend on the
Assam government's commitment to adopting a landscape approach to conservation
throughout the state, and ensuring that changes that take place outside the park do
not create pressures so large that Kaziranga can no longer function effectively.

References

Alonso-Mejía, A., Rendon-Salinas, E., Montesinos-Patiño, E. and Brower, L. P. (1997) 'Use
    of lipid reserves by Monarch butterflies overwintering in Mexico: Implications for con-
    servation', *Ecological Applications*, vol 7, pp934–47.
Bonal, B. S. and Chowdhury, S. (2004) *Evaluation of Barrier Effect of National Highway 37 on
    the Wildlife of Kaziranga National Park and Suggested Strategies and Planning for Providing
    Passage: A Feasibility Report to the Ministry of Environment & Forests,* Ministry of Environ-
    ment & Forests, Government of India, New Delhi.
Borrini-Feyerabend, G., Rita Larrucea, J. and Synge, H. (2004) 'Participatory management in
    the Minorca Biosphere Reserve, Spain', in H. Synge (ed.) *European Models of Good Prac-
    tice in Protected Areas*, IUCN and the Austrian Federal Ministry of Agriculture, Forestry,
    Environment and Water Management, IUCN, Cambridge, pp16–24.
Boruah, S. and Biswas, S. P. (2002) 'Ecohydrology and fisheries of the upper Brahmaputra
    basin', *Environmentalist*, vol 22, no 2, pp119–31.
Canessa, R., Conley, K. and Smiley, B. (2003) *Bowie Seamount Pilot Marine Protected Area: An
    Ecosystem Overview Report*, Canadian Technical Report of Fisheries and Aquatic Science
    no 2461, Fisheries and Oceans Canada, Sidney, British Columbia, p96.
Choudhury, A. (2004) *Kaziranga: Wildlife in Assam*, Rupa & Co, New Delhi.

Chovanec, A., Schiemer, F., Waidbacher, H. and Spolwind, R. (2002) 'Rehabilitation of a heavily modified river section of the Danube in Vienna (Austria): Biological assessment of landscape linkages on different scales', *International Review of Hydrology*, vol 87, pp183–95.

Chust, G., Ducrot, D., Riera, J. L. and Pretus, J. L. (1999) 'Characterising human-modelled landscapes at a stationary scale: a case study of Minorca, Spain', *Environmental Conservation*, vol 26, pp322–31.

Cole, D. N. (1995) 'Experimental trampling of vegetation 1: Relationship between trampling intensity and vegetation response', *Journal of Applied Ecology*, vol 32, pp203–14.

Daszak, P., Cunningham, A. A. and Hyatt, A. D. (2000) 'Emerging infectious diseases of wildlife: Threats to biodiversity and human health', *Science*, vol 287, pp443–9.

Dudley, N. and Parrish, J. (2006) *Closing the Gap. Creating Ecologically Representative Protected Area Systems*, Technical Series no 24, Secretariat of the Convention on Biological Diversity, Montreal.

Eken, G., Bennun, L., Brooks, T. M., Darwall, W., Fishpool, L. D. C., Foster, M., Knox, D., Langhammer, P., Matiku, P., Radford, E., Salaman, P., Sechrest, W., Smith, M. L., Spector, S. and Tordoff, A. (2004) 'Key biodiversity areas as site conservation targets', *BioScience*, vol 54, pp1110–18.

Gilligan, B., Dudley, N., Fernandez de Tejada, A. and Toivonen, H. (2004) *Management Effectiveness Evaluation of Finland's Protected Areas,* Metsähallitus Natural Heritage Services, Helsinki.

Groves, C. R., Jensen, D. B., Valutis, L. L., Redford, K. H., Shaffer, M. L., Scott, J. M., Baumgartner, J. V., Higgins, J. V., Beck, M. W. and Anderson, M. G. (2002) 'Planning for biodiversity conservation: Putting conservation science into practice', *Bioscience*, vol 52, pp499–512.

Hockings, M., Stolton, S., and Dudley, N. (2004) 'Management effectiveness: Assessing management of protected areas?', *Journal of Environmental Policy and Planning*, vol 6, pp157–74.

Hoekstra, J. M., Boucher, T. M., Ricketts, T. H. and Roberts, C. (2005) 'Confronting a biome crisis: Global disparities in habitat loss and protection', *Ecology Letters*, vol 8, pp23–9.

Kirika, J. M., Farwig, N. and Böhning-Gaese, K. (2008) 'Effects of local disturbance of tropical forests on frugivores and seed removal of a small-seeded afrotropical tree', *Conservation Biology*, vol 32, pp318–28.

Margules, C. R. and Pressey, R. L. (2000) 'Systematic conservation planning', *Nature*, vol 405, pp243–53.

Mathur, V., Verma, A., Dudley, N., Stolton, S., Hockings, M. and James, R. (2007) 'Kaziranga National Park and World Heritage Site India: Taking the long view', in *World Heritage Forests: Leveraging Conservation at the Landscape Scale. Proceedings of the 2nd World Heritage Forests Meeting, March 9–11 2005, Nancy, France*, World Heritage Papers no 21, UNESCO, Paris.

Mertens, D., Meyer, T., Wormanns, S. and Zimmermann, M. (2007) *14 Jahre Nuturchutzgroßprojekt Lüneberger Heide*, VNP-Schiften 1, Niederhaverbeck.

Palmer, M. and Findlay, V. (2003) *Faith in Conservation*, World Bank, Washington, DC.

Peres, C. A. (2005) 'Why we need megareserves in Amazonia', *Conservation Biology*, vol 19, pp728–33.

Phillips, A. (2002) *Management Guidelines for IUCN category V Protected Areas, Protected Landscapes/Seascapes*, WCPA Best Practice Protected Areas Guidelines Series no 9, Cardiff University and IUCN, Gland and Cambridge.

Ricketts, T. H., Dinerstein, E., Boucher, T., Brooks, T. M., Butchart, S. H. M., Hoffmann, M., Lamoreux, J. F., Morrison, J., Parr, M., Pilgrim, J. D., Rodrigues, A. S. L., Sechrest, W., Wallace, G. E., Berlin, K., Bielby, J., Burgess, N. D., Church, D. R., Cox, N., Knox,

D., Loucks, C., Luck, G. W., Master, L.L., Moore, R., Naidoo, R., Ridgely, R., Schatz, G. E., Shire, G., Strand, H., Wettengel, W. and Wikramanayake, E. (2005) 'Pinpointing and preventing imminent extinctions', *Proceedings of the National Academy of Sciences*, vol 102, pp18497–501.

Rodrigues, A. S. L., Andelman, S. J., Bakarr, M. I., Boitani, L., Brooks, T. M., Cowling, R. M., Fishpool, L. D. C., da Fonseca, G. A. B., Gaston, K. J., Hoffmann, M. Long, J. S., Marquet, P. A., Pilgrim, J. D., Pressey, R. L., Schipper, J., Sechrest, W., Stuart, S. N., Underhill, L. G., Waller, R. W., Watts, M. E. J. and Yan, X. (2004) 'Effectiveness of the global protected area network in representing species diversity', *Nature*, vol 428, pp640–43.

Sanderson, E. W., Redford, K. H., Vedder, A., Coppolillo, P. B. and Ward, S. E. (2002) 'A conceptual model for conservation planning based on landscape species requirements', *Landscape and Urban Planning*, vol 58, pp41–56.

Schneider, I. E. and Burnett, G. W. (2000) 'Protected area management in Jordan', *Environmental Management*, vol 25, pp241–6.

Sinclair, A., Mduma, S. and Arcese, P. (2002) 'Protected areas as biodiversity benchmarks for human impact: Agriculture and the Serengeti avifauna', *Proceedings of the Royal Society of London Series B-Biological Sciences*, vol 269, pp2401–2405.

Sinclair, A. R. E. and Norton-Griffiths, M. (eds) (1984) *Serengeti: Dynamics of an Ecosystem*, University of Chicago Press, Chicago.

Vasu, N. K. (2003) *Management Plan of Kaziranga National Park (2003–2013)*, Forest Department, Assam.

Walsh, P. D., Abernethy, K. A., Bermejo, M., Beyers, R., De Wachter, P., Akou, M. E., Huijbregts, B., Mambounga, D. I., Toham, A. K., Kilbourn, A. M., Lahm, S. A., Latour, S., Maisels, F., Mbina, C., Mihindou, Y., Obiang, S. N., Effa, E. N., Starkey, M. P., Telfer, P., Thibault, M., Tutin, C. E. G., White, L. J. T. and Wilkie, D. S. (2003) 'Catastrophic ape decline in western equatorial Africa', *Nature*, vol 422, pp611–14.

Wikramanayake, E. D., Dinerstein, E., Robinson, J. G., Karanth, U., Rabinowitz, A., Olson, D., Mathew, T., Hedao, P., Conner, M., Hemley, G. and Bolze, D. (1998) 'An ecology-based method for defining priorities for large mammal conservation: The tiger as case study', *Conservation Biology*, vol 12, no 4, pp865–78.

Willerslev, E., Hansen, A. J., Nielsen, K. K. and Adsersen, H. (2002) 'Number of endemic and native plant species in the Galápagos Archipelago in relation to geographical parameters', *Ecography*, vol 25, pp109–19.

14

Precious Places: Getting the Arguments Right

Nigel Dudley, Marc Hockings and Sue Stolton

Getting to the top of the mountain in Girraween National Park in Queensland, Australia, is quite a scramble, but the reward is the chance to stand beside a magnificent 10m-high boulder, perfectly balanced in equilibrium on a tiny point of rock. The three of us went there about the time that the long process of research, which has culminated in this book, began. We walked through the forests and among the scattering of gigantic boulders arranged higgledy-piggledy across the landscape, camped out and ate a memorable meal in one of the local vineyards. And maybe it is stretching the point a little, but the balanced rock could also stand as a metaphor for some of the things that underlie this book. The world's protected area system is itself a massive effort to maintain equilibrium: of ecosystems, of people, even of climate and, in another way, of keeping a balance between the various demands and pressures that continue to assail natural ecosystems. The project that we imagined was going to be a short and rather simple collection of good news stories about protected areas has developed into something altogether more difficult and complex. In many ways we found more benefits – more arguments for protection – than we had expected but at the same time we came to realize that the challenges of management for multiple values is often greater than we had first thought.

Nigel Dudley

Figure 14.1 *Girraween National Park, Australia*

Source: © Nigel Dudley

Effective Tools for Conservation

Protected areas – including those controlled by the state but also indigenous and community conserved areas, private reserves and protected areas managed by companies or trusts – provide the most effective tools yet developed to maintain natural habitats in the face of development pressures. Worldwide there are certainly differences in their delivery of conservation outcomes, distribution of social benefits or in their management effectiveness, but they are currently the strongest approach to *in situ* conservation that we have. The preeminent examples serve as a set of inspirational models for the maintenance and management of natural ecosystems in the 21st century.

A number of factors help to make protected areas flexible and effective tools for conservation. Recognition of the importance of a particular site at local, national and international level often itself provides significant protection for the site's values. The existence of legal or other effective frameworks for conservation means that protected areas provide a ready-made tool for maintaining ecosystems. Many already have agreed management plans (or at least tried and tested methodologies for drawing these up), clear governance structures and are backed up by staff with management skills, expertise and capacity.

A Portfolio of Benefits

We hope that this book has shown that protected areas also contain an abundance of different values, some of which accrue or could accrue significant financial benefits, some of which are vital for subsistence and others that are more intangible but no less important to recognize and maintain. Many of these benefits are a long way from traditional perceptions of national parks and nature reserves. They are summarized in Box 14.1.

Box 14.1 *Values of protected areas*

Biodiversity
1   Ecosystems.
2   Species.
3   Intra-specific genetic variation.

Protected Area Management
4   Permanent and temporary jobs in management, tourism services, administration, maintenance, etc.

Food
5   Wild game.
6   Wild food plants.
7   Fisheries (permissible fishing and maintaining fish stocks by protecting spawning area).
8   Genetic material (e.g. crop wild relatives, tree species).
9   Traditional agriculture (i.e. use of locally adapted crops [landraces] and/or practices).
10 Livestock grazing and fodder collection.

Water
11 Non-commercial water use (e.g. subsistence agriculture, drinking, cooking).
12 Commercial water use (e.g. for large-scale irrigation, waterways, bottling plants, hydro-electric power or municipal drinking-water source).

Cultural and Spiritual
13 Cultural and historical values (e.g. archaeology, historic buildings, land-use patterns).
14 Sacred natural sites or landscapes, pilgrimage routes.
15 Wilderness values or other similar iconic values.

Health and Recreation
16 Local medicinal resources (e.g. herbs).
17 Genetic material for the pharmaceuticals industry.
18 Recreation and tourism.

---

19 Physical exercise.
20 Mental health values.

Knowledge
21 Resource for building knowledge.
22 Contribution to education (formal and informal dissemination of information).

Environmental Services
23 Climate amelioration (carbon storage and sequestration and ecosystem-based adaptation).
24 Soil stabilization (e.g. avalanche prevention, landslide and erosion).
25 Coastal protection (e.g. mangroves, sand dunes, coral reefs).
26 Flood prevention (e.g. mitigation in small watersheds, floodplains and wetlands).
27 Water quality and quantity (e.g. filtration, groundwater renewal, natural flows).
28 Pollination of nearby crops or pollination products such as honey.

Materials
29 Timber, including for fuelwood.
30 Other materials (e.g. coral, shells, resin, rubber, grass, rattan, minerals, etc.).

Note: whether or not some of these values are permitted in protected areas will depend on measures such as customary laws and management plans. This is therefore an indicative list of possible values from protected areas.

Protected areas can support these benefits in a number of different ways, by providing the following:

- *Protection of unique values*: benefits that rely on a particular ecosystem or a landscape/seascape and therefore cannot be replaced (e.g. some aspects of biodiversity; sacredness related to particular features or traditions; appreciation of landscape).
- *Cost-effective solutions*: benefits supplied most cost-effectively, easily or efficiently by retaining natural ecosystems (e.g. clean water from forests; carbon storage in peat and other habitats; coastal protection through retention and restoration of mangroves).
- *Protection as an insurance policy*: benefits that are important for the subsistence of poorer members of society and that can be maintained in protected areas and extracted in a sustainable manner (e.g. medicinal herbs; game; fish; some building materials and fuel).
- *Conservation of genetic potential*: there are some species of animals and plants that are now only found surviving and continuing to adapt to changing conditions in protected areas; this *in situ* protection remains a vital strategy for genetic

conservation. However, much of our world remains unknown or unassessed by science, including species that may have high value in the future, (e.g. genetic material for crop-breeding and medical research).

- *Convenient solutions*: benefits that are not uniquely associated with protected areas and can be replaced in other environments but are an easy option given the existence of a protected area (e.g. use for exercise; crop pollination).

Virtually all protected areas support multiple values; even the strictest nature reserves will usually on closer inspection provide a wider range of benefits than is obvious at first glance. Many of these protected area benefits are currently often ignored, misunderstood and under-valued, or to be more accurate, most managers are only aware of some of the benefits that their protected areas provide. We have sat many times with managers and local communities in different countries around the world and seen at first hand that the people writing the management plans are unaware of many of the values that local people hold dear. We have run assessments of protected areas where local communities, protected area staff and attendant NGOs have all identified radically different suites of values. By bringing the 'other' benefits more centrally into management and by making sure other stakeholders simultaneously recognize their worth, perceptions about the relative value of protected areas can be altered dramatically.

Figure 14.2 *The role of protected areas in providing pollen for bees is often overlooked*

Source: © R. Isotti, A. Cambone – Homo ambiens/WWF-Canon

Figure 14.3 *Rubber tapping from the bark of a wild rubber tree,*
Alto Juruá Extractive Reserve, Brazil

Source: © Edward Parker/WWF-Canon

The Costs and Benefits of Looking at Broader Protected Area Values

Such an approach involves a certain level of trade-off. Spreading management to address multiple needs also often means spreading available resources unless some of the benefits can be used directly to generate income. In addition, many benefits may not remain constant over time. Some may become redundant (for example, some subsistence values will decline in importance with economic development) or new values can be recognized (for example, the increasing interest in protected areas as part of climate-change response strategies). Some of these changes will strengthen protection regimes, others tend to undermine them. Inclusion of wider values must not ignore or underplay core values.

A problem in all walks of life is that in economic terms it is often more cost-effective for an individual to exploit resources unsustainably even if the net value to the community from conservation of the resources would be greater. For example, it may make perfect economic sense for the owner of a cloud forest to fell the trees and sell the timber even if the costs to the downstream community in terms of lost water far exceed the value of the timber. This is one of the key justifications for protected areas as communities are often not strong enough to maintain useful natural ecosystems against the wishes of a powerful minority, but it also still leaves many protected areas open to both legal and illegal challenges from those with a different vision for how the resources should be used. As we write this chapter, the New Zealand government has announced its intention of opening its protected areas for mineral exploration and we can expect such challenges to increase rapidly as resources become increasingly in short supply.

Generally, recognition that protected areas are supplying more than simply 'nature conservation' or recreation increases the comfort felt by many local and national governments and makes it easier for them to justify management costs to taxpayers.

Managing for Multiple Benefits

The basic premise laid out in this book is that if protected areas are to survive as a principal conservation tool, they will need to demonstrate a far wider range of benefits than has been appreciated until now; this also implies that aspects of management will have to change quite radically. In meeting these fresh challenges, managers are faced with a two-step process:

1   Developing ways of assessing all the values of the protected area, and their associated costs and benefits, and building partnerships in order to ensure that management reflects the full range of benefits.
2   Ensuring that the benefits from protected areas accrue more equitably than is often the case today, particularly with respect to ensuring that benefits reach the poorest members of society and those local communities whose livelihoods are most intimately bound up with a particular protected area.

These tasks need to be located within a wider framework of policy, legislation and good governance. It is not always easy to ensure that protected areas are both effective at conserving biodiversity and successful at maintaining the wider range of values and associated benefits, as discussed in the previous chapters. Such changes take time and resources in terms of research, development of skills and sometimes investment in infrastructure or equipment, although there should also be potential economic returns. Some initial thoughts on a strategy for realizing the full suite of protected area values are outlined below.

International policy instruments

Most governments have, in one way or another, already committed to many of the ideas outlined in this book, even if they do not always recognize this. A number of important global commitments and reviews such as the Millennium Ecosystem Assessment already note the importance of ecosystem services and, actually or implicitly, the role played by protected areas in supplying these services. Similarly, governments have made a number of substantial commitments to protected areas through conventions such as World Heritage, Man and the Biosphere, Ramsar (for wetlands) and, most important of all, the CBD's Programme of Work on Protected Areas (PoWPA). The last, a wonderfully ambitious multi-year programme, encourages governments to complete ecologically representative protected area networks and includes a wide array of important social safeguards regarding local communities and indigenous peoples.

Virtually all these instruments stress wider uses of protected areas; for example, Ramsar is based around the philosophy of 'wise use' and biosphere reserves focus on sustainable management in a 'transition zone' around the core protected area. The CBD PoWPA also includes important reference to wider benefits from protected areas and this component is likely to increase in importance in the future. Many associated institutions, such as the World Health Organization, International Strategy for Disaster Reduction and the Food and Agricultural Organization of the UN increasingly recognize the importance of protecting and maintaining natural ecosystems as a major policy response. In addition, and significantly, the UN Framework Convention on Climate Change could use protected areas as a major strategy for carbon storage, sequestration and ecosystem-based adaptation, as outlined in Chapter 11 on climate change. The CBD PoWPA could, in this scenario, become deployed as a major mitigation and adaptation tool by the UNFCCC.

Benefit-sharing

The equitable distribution of benefits among different sectors of society is a critical factor in widespread recognition of protected area values. Often benefits fail to reach some of the very poorest within societies, such as ethnic or religious minorities, women or the elderly. On the other hand, the cost of establishing protected areas has often fallen squarely on the shoulders of poor people (Marrie, 2004). These inequalities appear between countries, within countries and within households. Unfortunately, research suggests that the majority of benefits accrue to the most wealthy, whether at the scale of a foreign-owned ecotourism company reaping healthy profits and paying local workers very little, or the better-off members of a community next to a protected area getting the lion's share of compensation packages, trust funds or start-up projects (Dudley et al., 2008). While for those people, the benefits of a protected area really may outweigh the costs, for the poorest people impacts such as crop damage and loss of resources can mean that setting up a protected area means that they are worse off than before. These inequalities are often rooted in larger inequities in society, including poor governance that provides little support for the politically, socially or physically weakest people.

The CBD PoWPA rather optimistically defined a target to: 'Establish by 2008 mechanisms for the equitable sharing of both costs and benefits arising from the establishment and management of protected areas' (CBD, 2004). While the date has already passed, the intentions remain clear and benefit-sharing mechanisms are developing, albeit sometimes falteringly. Some potential responses that could help better distribute protected area benefits were described in Chapter 7.

Understanding and identifying benefits

As noted above, many protected area managers do not recognize anything like the full range of benefits supplied by the land or water under their control. To an even greater extent, there can be few directors of protected area agencies who could list with confidence all the values of their system. The pressure to produce these kinds of data is growing all the time. Unfortunately, although we have referred to many individual studies of costs and benefits throughout this volume there is currently no agreed methodology for detailed cost-benefit analyses that looks at all benefits and, critically, that compares these with alternative management options. This is currently hampering the debate, which all too often relies on claims and counter-claims without credible quantitative information to help make decisions.

In the absence of an alternative WWF has developed a questionnaire – the Protected Area Benefit Assessment Tool or PA-BAT – to help collate information on the important values of protected areas as part of the Arguments for Protection project (see Box 14.2). The PA-BAT can also be used by local communities to identify values/benefits and by protected area advocates, such as NGOs, to help promote the range of benefits a protected area can bring. However, this is a very simple, qualitative measure; it in no way replaces the need for a stronger and more exact methodology. Such an assessment system needs to look at both economic and non-economic issues; while economic benefits are important an over-emphasis on these can mean that other important subsistence, rights and cultural issues get underplayed.

Box 14.2 *The Protected Area Benefit Assessment Tool*

One of the shortcomings identified in evaluating protected area benefits is that most studies have tended to look at one particular benefit and not tried to carry out an overall cost-benefit analysis. For example, research in the Annapurna Conservation Area in Nepal found that while most people within the area recognized some benefits from conservation, such as improved infrastructure, healthcare, etc., only 14.9 per cent received direct cash income from tourism (Bajracharya et al., 2006). If the financial benefit alone is reported, as is so often the case, then it would seem that Annapurna benefits only a few people; if the wider picture of the 'compensatory benefits' is reviewed then the benefits become widely applicable to many more people.

The Protected Area Benefit Assessment Tool has been developed as part of the wider WWF Arguments for Protection project to fill some of the gaps in information about the whole range of benefits that protected areas can provide (Stolton and Dudley, 2009). It aims to help protected area managers consider all the benefits that could arise from the area they manage, both to aid understanding about the importance of an area and to help ensure management protects this wide variety of values. It has been designed to help protected area managers and others to extract more detail about a range of real or potential benefits that protected areas can provide for different stakeholders, from local communities to the global community, including industry, government, etc.

The PA-BAT has two sections, both of which should be filled in for each protected area assessed.

1 Background information datasheet: i.e. name, IUCN category, location, etc., along with an opportunity to identify key management objectives

and to make a value judgement about how much the protected area
contributes to well-being.
2   Benefits to protected area stakeholders datasheet: a set of datasheets
    that collect basic information about: the types of benefits; who they are
    important to; and qualitative information about their level of importance,
    their relationship to the protected area and the times of year in which
    they are important.

Each datasheet has introductory text which provides more specific guidance
on how each should be completed.
    The PA-BAT is thus mainly an *aide-mémoire* to help those working in
protected areas to think logically about the types of benefits that come, or
could come, from their protected area; to consider who benefits and by
how much; and to assess how much of the protected area is important for a
particular benefit and how much of the time the area supplies these goods
or services. If used to its full capacity the PA-BAT can also record economic
valuation, sustainability issues, biodiversity impacts and management responses
to particular issues that have been identified in the assessment.

Tools for using multiple benefits

Maximizing the benefits requires a range of tools, varying from codes of practice
through various techniques or equipment to assessment and monitoring systems.
Much material is available already but some notable gaps remain, which are probably
delaying progress. The need for a more thorough and equitable cost-benefit analysis
methodology has already been made but some additional issues include:

*   assessment of governance issues in protected areas, including both type of gover-
    nance and also governance quality;
*   links between different management models in protected areas and biodiversity
    conservation – in this context whether increasing emphasis on broader protected
    area benefits will undermine biodiversity conservation and if so by how much.;
*   management models for ensuring social equity and poverty reduction with espect
    to existing and proposed systems for accessing broader protected area benefits
    including, in particular, Payment for Environment Service schemes, REDD and
    other climate change amelioration schemes;
*   rapid ways of assessing carbon storage and sequestration, along with ways in
    which ecosystems can be managed to maximize carbon-capture benefits.

Capacity building

Developing wider benefits of protected areas not only relies on better knowledge
and tools but also increased capacity within protected area staff and partners. Most
protected area managers are trained as ecologists and perhaps also in traditional

management; in a wider model of protected area benefits they, or at least some of their staff, will need a new range of skills both in understanding values and in negotiating and implementing their exploitation. This needs to cover ecosystem goods and services that are already well understood, such as crop wild relatives and water quality but also benefits that have only been recognized more recently, including some of the climate change response contributions derived from well-managed protected areas.

In addition, many beneficiaries do not understand either the full suite of values that protected areas supply or the management required to maintain these benefits. We were surprised during our work on the links between water and cities, for example, that so few water companies really understood the links between forests and water, even if they were investing in forest protection for water services. There is a need for capacity-building about the role and management implications of natural ecosystems in relationship to a range of economic and socio-cultural activities.

Communicating benefits

Knowing about the range of benefits is important for protected area agencies and for local and national governments but will not in itself help to build support from other stakeholders. A wider strategy for communicating benefits is needed, focusing in particular on the following:

- Commercial beneficiaries: both local and distant, including, for example, water companies; bottling or food-processing companies needing clean water; agricultural enterprises relying on irrigation water; hydroelectric enterprises; crop-breeding companies using crop wild relatives; pharmaceutical and health insurance companies; infrastructure projects susceptible to flooding, etc.
- Local communities: that may be benefiting from services from protected areas, including, for example, recreational groups; faith groups; people legally using non-timber forest products from protected areas; communities benefiting from water resources or flood mitigation services from protected areas.
- National and local government: to understand better the potential benefits from protected areas either under their management or within territory under their influence, focusing particularly on wider tourism values; ecosystem values; and issues relating to cultural and spiritual heritage.

Such understanding can also help to grow the protected area network, including the wider use of different governance types and management approaches.

In Closing

Protected areas offer a rare fusion of ethical and utilitarian values. At their best, they represent the high moral purpose of protecting the rest of nature from the impacts of human mismanagement, while at the same time they offer us some immediate and tangible rewards.

It has become almost a truism in the US that the National Park system is 'America's best idea'. We would argue that protected areas – in their modern incarnation – almost certainly were one of the best and most revolutionary ideas of the 20th century; they have so far survived better than the far more famous revolutionary political creeds of that period, most of which have already been consigned to the museum. It is easy to forget just how radical an idea setting aside land and water from development appeared when it was first proposed. However, anyone who has witnessed the genuine fury and bafflement shown by some opponents of protected areas, for example, to the concept that there would be anywhere on the planet that was not open to mineral exploitation, will be left in no doubt that the ideal really is radical and still far from universally accepted.

We believe that protected areas are an essential and irreplaceable management option, the benefits of which are still only just being properly recognized. Better understanding of their values, coupled with a conscious building of new partnerships among stakeholders that have something to gain from the protection of land and water, can ensure that the ideas and practice of protected areas continue to grow into the future. We hope that this book has made some small contribution to this understanding.

References

Bajracharya, S. B., Furley, P. and Newton, A. C. (2006) 'Impacts of community-based conservation on local communities in the Annapurna Conservation Area, Nepal', *Biodiversity and Conservation*, vol 15, no 8, pp2765–86.

CBD (2004) *Programme of Work on Protected Areas*, CBD, Montreal.

Dudley, N., Mansourian, S., Stolton, S. and Suksuwan, S. (2008) *Safety Net: Protected Areas and Poverty Reduction*, WWF, Gland.

Marrie, H. (2004) 'Protected areas and indigenous and local communities', in CBD (2004) *Biodiversity Issues for Consideration in the Planning, Establishment and Management of Protected Area Sites and Networks*, CBD Technical Series no 15, Montreal.

Stolton, S. and Dudley, N. (2009) 'The Protected Areas Benefits Assessment Tool', WWF, Gland.

www.panda.org/what_we_do/how_we_work/protected_areas/arguments_for_protection/, accessed 29 September 2009.

Index